'SURFACING' THE POLITICS OF DESIRE:
LITERATURE, FEMINISM, AND MYTH

RAJESHWARI S. VALLURY

'Surfacing' the Politics of Desire

Literature, Feminism, and Myth

UNIVERSITY OF TORONTO PRESS
Toronto Buffalo London

© University of Toronto Press Incorporated 2008
Toronto Buffalo London
www.utppublishing.com
Printed in Canada

ISBN 978-0-8020-9038-6

Printed on acid-free paper

Library and Archives Canada Cataloguing in Publication

Vallury, Rajeshwari S. (Rajeshwari Suryamohan)
Surfacing the politics of desire : literature, feminism and myth / Rajeshwari S. Vallury.

(University of Toronto romanace series)
Includes bibliographical references and index.
ISBN 978-0-8020-9038-6

1. French fiction – 19th century – History and criticism.   2. Women in literature.   I. Title.   II. Series.

PQ295.W6V35 2008   843′.7093522   C2007-906669-0

Parts of chapter 1 appeared in my '*Pierre et Jean* or the Erring of Oedipus,' *Dalhousie French Studies* 71 (summer 2005): 39–51.

University of Toronto Press acknowledges the financial assistance to its publishing program of the Canada Council for the Arts and the Ontario Arts Council.

For Raymond, best friend and fellow tortoise

Contents

Acknowledgments

First of all, I would like to thank my editor, Jill McConkey, for her tireless patience, help, and support during the preparation of this manuscript. Sylvie Coulibaly, for suggesting that the ideas contained in this book would find a receptive ear at the University of Toronto Press. Susan Andrade, for her gentle, but unyielding push to make a more thoughtful feminist out of me. Yves Citton and Philip Watts, under whose caring and dedicated guidance my book first took shape. Giuseppina Mecchia, for introducing me to Deleuze, an intellectual gift of a lifetime. I reserve my deepest gratitude for my husband, Raymond, for his seemingly silent and invisible, but unswerving companionship along the long intellectual road that led to this book.

'SURFACING' THE POLITICS OF DESIRE:
LITERATURE, FEMINISM, AND MYTH

Introduction

Literature is a health.

Gilles Deleuze[1]

What if, wonders Marguerite Duras, when we have a male in front of us, we asked whether he had some female in him? What if we reversed all analysis and criticism?[2] This book may be considered as an attempt to respond to Duras's questions by studying the representation of women in four male-authored literary texts of the nineteenth century: Maupassant's *Pierre et Jean*, Balzac's *Le chef-d'oeuvre inconnu* and *Sarrasine*, and Gautier's *Mademoiselle de Maupin*. In many respects, this study is something of an anomaly within the context of current feminist literary scholarship which even over the past few years has focused almost exclusively on writing by women, and especially on the works of women who have been ignored by the dominant literary canon. My study perversely goes back to the writings of the 'great' nineteenth-century realists, Balzac and Maupassant, and to the most famous work of one of the most prominent of French Romantics. It is a throwback to the 'images of women' criticism with which feminist literary criticism began three decades earlier,[3] a tradition that can trace its roots as far back as Simone de Beauvoir's *The Second Sex*, published for the first time in France in 1949. What then is the justification for such an outmoded topic of research for a feminist scholar, given that feminism has for the most part distanced itself from the 'great' works of the past? And especially in light of the rather clear gender divide that seems to have been established in the field of feminist literary studies over the last few years?

Before this justification can be articulated in a clearer fashion, it must be noted that 'images of women' criticism was far from dead and buried in the 1980s. If anything, psychoanalysis, post-structuralism, and deconstruction made for some very sophisticated feminist theory regarding the representational systems at work in art, cinema, and literature – analyses that proposed ways of rereading that would challenge the 'great' texts of established literary canons by exploring their biases with respect to race, class, sex, and gender. Foucault and Derrida brought important insights that helped either to understand or undermine the signifying systems that produced the categories with which bodies were read, including that of the body itself. They also permitted a feminist questioning of literature's ability to extend representation and visibility to the disenfranchised and the marginalized despite its claims to an objective and universal point of view.[4] In fact, it was literature's claim to the universal that itself instituted the marginalization it claimed to rectify. If no literary movement bore the brunt of the attack on its pretensions to representation more than nineteenth-century realism, nonetheless, almost all of Western European literature came under suspicion for its unique privileging of the point of view of the 'white upper-class male subject.'[5] With specific regard to feminist literary criticism, the works of Luce Irigaray and Hélène Cixous have been extremely influential, both in formulating a feminist critique of the phallogocentric biases of a male-dominated literature, and in articulating an alternative to it through the specificity of feminine writing (*parler-femme* in the case of Irigaray, and *écriture féminine* with respect to Cixous). They have also been vital to a project that seeks to render visible the repression of feminine materiality and alterity within a masculinist economy of desire.

Although Irigaray and Cixous are classified under the rubric of French psychoanalytical feminism, they work out of a set of concerns that they share with other schools of feminist thought that may not necessarily be heavily invested in psychoanalysis. To the extent that they wish to account for female oppression and repression, and insofar as they are engaged with the issue of feminine difference and subjectivity, they are involved in a political struggle that brings together such diverse feminist theorists as Simone de Beauvoir, Gayatri Spivak, Elaine Showalter, Monique Wittig, Julia Kristeva, and Judith Butler, to name a sketchy few. Furthermore, their common engagement with the categories of the Hegelian dialectic that they critique place Cixous and Irigaray much closer to de Beauvoir than one might suspect. Admittedly, what distinguishes their thought from that of Simone de Beauvoir is their attention to the moments of the failure of the dialectic, moments when the feminine escapes the binary logic of the latter.

It seems to me that many of the assumptions that have subtended feminist literary theory and criticism (as applied to male-authored texts) over the past three decades have remained true to the spirit of *The Second Sex*, whether they have done so from a Marxist, socialist, phenomenological, humanist, post-structuralist, or psychoanalytical point of view. The feminist analyses of male-authored texts have proceeded according to the general assumption that within the representational economy of literature, the figure of the Woman in a male text functions as an idealized Other, as a space for the projection of male fantasies, and as a site of androcentric self-valorization. Irigaray continues this critique by providing a brilliantly argued account of the narcissism of philosophical (and scientific) thought in *Speculum de l'autre femme*. Together with Cixous's *The Newly Born Woman*, *Speculum de l'autre femme* has been crucial to the feminist understanding of how the figure of the woman serves as a lynchpin or guarantee of masculine self-representation, while being simultaneously excluded from its economy. Simone de Beauvoir's analysis of how the male subject must necessarily configure woman as both Other and other, denying the slave enough subjectivity in order to assert itself as master, while simultaneously conferring enough subjectivity upon the slave in order to be recognized as a master by another conscious subject, is a problem that both Cixous and Irigaray continue to grapple with in their thought. When applied to literature, such analyses have proceeded from and resulted in an understanding of literature as a repressive system of representation that is either despotic or doomed to lack and failure, a victim of its illusions and dupe to its falsehoods.[6] It is the very simple conviction that such is not always the case that provides the impetus for the present work.

The purpose of this study, then, is to work through some of the above assumptions and to question the conclusions that a certain politics of reading and interpretation might generate about the desire at work in literature. To do this, it will argue that the representation at work in literature does not always correspond to the paradigms of feminist critique, and will propose a different reason for the failure of these paradigms. At the risk of oversimplification, I have isolated four mythic paradigms that have been consistently used to understand and critique the relationship between male authors and their female characters or creations: the myths of Oedipus, Narcissus, Pygmalion, and androgyny. The myths of Oedipus and Narcissus form the inter-texts of the psychoanalytical formulations of desire and subjectivity (as well as the feminist critique thereof), while the myth of Pygmalion has been used to structure the dialectics of desire between a male artist and his female creation. The myth of androgyny has

figured in explorations of bisexuality and the blurring of gender categories, and has also been understood as an important myth in the effacement of feminine difference. In each instance, I have chosen to analyse
a male-authored literary text that is (sometimes overtly and sometimes
subtly) structured according to one of the myths mentioned above, but
which nevertheless troubles the sexual politics imputed to these myths,
thereby asking for a reevaluation of their pertinence for feminism. In
other words, it is through a more extensive inquiry into the 'exceptional'
moments of the appearance of feminine difference in texts written by
men that I wish to challenge the presuppositions that have thus far
guided feminist conceptualizations of 'masculine' desire and of the 'sex-
ual/textual politics' of literature. Such a confrontation of the limits of its
thought paradigms (however aleatory, contingent, or sporadic they may
appear to be) can alone, I believe, allow feminist thought to renew and
sustain itself for the future.

My book seeks to explore the encounter between philosophy, politics,
and literature by studying the spaces where the textual productions of literature exceed or challenge certain paradigms of feminist reading. In
order to do so, it proceeds on the basis of two assumptions: first (a very
Mallarméan one), that something like literature exists; and second (perhaps a very un-Mallarméan one), that literature is political. However, it
will argue that the politics practised by literature cannot be understood
as a function of the fixed identities of sex or gender.[7] The visibility or
perceptibility that literature makes possible cannot be reduced to the
hierarchies and stable categories of a representational politics. Politics,
in other words, cannot always be understood in terms of representation
and signification. Literature extends visibility in ways that differ from the
expectations of a political sphere committed to distinct divisions and
separations of identity. The politics of literature does not perhaps correspond to or coincide with the claims articulated by groups that constitute
themselves as an entity on the basis of a specificity (be it sex, gender,
race, class, nationality, or even a historical lived). But this study proceeds
according to the suspicion that perhaps literature makes politics possible
only to the extent that neither literature nor politics can be reduced to
the fixed categories of the political.[8] Finally, this study hopes to open up
the debate between aesthetics and politics to the question of ethics by
calling for a politics of reading that would be most faithful to the ethics
of literature.

In chapter 1, '*Pierre et Jean*, or the Erring of Oedipus,' I look at how
Maupassant's novel undermines the status of the Oedipal as a normative

model of masculine subjectivity, making room for feminine difference and desire. In chapter 2, 'The Error of Narcissus,' I question the narcissistic model of masculine desire elaborated by Irigaray. Through a rereading of the myths of Narcissus and Pygmalion, and using the spirit/matter dualism as a principal point of analysis in Balzac's *Le chef-d'oeuvre inconnu*, I challenge the assumption that masculine desire works to repress feminine materiality. This will allow us to rethink the feminist critique of realism as a claim to representation founded upon a domination and/or erasure of female corporeality. In chapter 3, 'The Three Virtues of Imperceptibility, Indiscernibility, and Impersonality,' I use the spaces where desire escapes its narcissistic model to articulate the need to understand desire in terms other than those of the Oedipal and the narcissistic. Blanchot and Deleuze and Guattari will help us move towards a different conception of the subjectivity and desire engaged in writing. In chapter 4, 'Becoming-flower, Becoming-imperceptible: Oedipus, Narcissus, and Their Lines of Flight in *Sarrasine* and *Le chef-d'oeuvre inconnu*,' I show how Balzac preempts accusations of narcissism by affirming a multiplicity of sexuality and desire that cannot be contained within systems of representation and signification. *Le chef-d'oeuvre inconnu* will be revisited in light of the deliberations of the preceding chapter. In chapter 5, 'Beyond the Dialectic of Self and Other: Towards a Thought of the Surface,' I argue for an alternative (feminist) critique of affirmation and difference. Deleuze's *Logic of Sense* will provide the bases for such a critique. In chapter 6, '"Une jouissance d'épiderme": From Platonic Height and Depth to the Deleuzian Surface in Gautier's *Mademoiselle de Maupin*,' I show how Gautier makes possible an aesthetics (and ethics) of difference through the figure of the androgyne. In conclusion, through a reading of Virginia Woolf's *A Room of One's Own*, I will argue for a feminist ethics and politics that would be capable of affirming the ethics of literature.

What I hope will emerge from this book is not so much the idea that feminism makes for a poor reading of literature as an urgent need to reconfigure the relationship between (feminist) politics, literature, and thought. What will emerge, I hope, is an engagement that will allow feminist thought to articulate itself as both a politics and an ethics, and that will allow us to affirm literature as an aesthetics and ethics of the possible.

1 *Pierre et Jean,* or the Erring of Oedipus

The riddle of the Sphinx? An expression to be taken in two senses: the riddle that the Sphinx proposes, and the one that the Sphinx herself constitutes. Oedipus thought he had resolved the first and Freud the second. But what if neither had found the answer?[1]

Jean-Joseph Goux

This chapter pursues two strands of inquiry that the myth of Oedipus lays out for the feminist challenge to psychoanalytical formulations of desire and subjectivity. Among the first is Barthes's thesis (following Freud's intuition) that the myth of Oedipus is emblematic of all narrative, while the second concerns the status of the Oedipal as a normative model of subjectivity and desire. This chapter thus follows the dual movement of feminist thought as it grapples with the complex conceptual nexus constructed by (and through) the myth of Oedipus, namely, the notions of Oedipal vision, desire, knowledge, and subjectivity. I first look at how Barthes defines narrative in *Le plaisir du texte* before examining alternative narratives of feminine desire proposed by feminist critics such as Teresa De Lauretis, Laura Mulvey, and Naomi Schor. For the most part, the feminist challenge to the phallogocentrism of psychoanalytical discourse has consisted in an unworking of 'Oedipal vision.' Freud's question 'What Does Woman Want' continues the gesture of Oedipus with regard to the Sphinx: psychoanalysis endows itself with the power to resolve and vanquish the mystery of woman. As Luce Irigaray notes, the project that seeks to explain and understand female desire effectively preempts the response to the question it sets out to answer, thereby effacing feminine difference.[2]

This chapter explores and questions some of the above assumptions. Using *Pierre et Jean*, a 'family romance' that goes to the heart of the Freudian question, I show that the novel problematizes Oedipal vision and the Oedipal quest for truth, posing a challenge to Freudian and Lacanian readings of the myth of Oedipus. Borrowing the theoretical formulations of Jean-Joseph Goux, I argue that the myth is coded as a violation and an aberrance, rather than as a normative model of (masculine) subjectivity. Ostensibly structured according to the Barthesian model of narrative, *Pierre et Jean* demonstrates the very feminist narrative strategies articulated by De Lauretis, Mulvey, and Schor, thereby allowing for the emergence of an alternative economy of desire that multiplies differences to the Name of the Father. The chapter will conclude with a call for a rethinking of the 'narcissism' of masculine desire.

Of Oedipal Narrative

Although it is in his 'Introduction à l'analyse structurale des récits' that Roland Barthes first posits a link between desire and narrative, the relationship between the two is made more explicit in his subsequent work *Le plaisir du texte*, where the myth of Oedipus is seen as exemplary of all narrative: 'Tout récit ne se ramène-t-il pas à l'Oedipe? Raconter, n'est-ce pas toujours chercher son origine, dire ses démêlés avec la Loi, entrer dans la dialectique de l'attendrissement et de la haine?'[3] Narration deploys an inexorable Oedipal movement towards a final truth and the assumption of a subjectivity that the uncovering and naming of the truth make possible. Every narrative act is propelled forward by the pleasure that meaningful closure promises. Knowledge, desire, and voyeuristic pleasure are tied together in a 'dévoilement progressif [où] toute l'excitation se réfugie dans l'*espoir* de voir le sexe (rêve de collégien) ou de connaître la fin de l'histoire (satisfaction romanesque).'[4] Narration thus seems to be defined in terms of a desire and knowledge that are uniquely masculine: 'plaisir oedipéen (dénuder, savoir, connaître l'origine et la fin), s'il est vrai que tout récit (tout dévoilement de la vérité) est une mise-en-scène du Père (absent, caché ou hypostasié).'[5]

This view of the myth of Oedipus as a paradigm for all narrative and the insight into the complicity between narration and masculine knowledge has led feminist critics to challenge the Barthesian model of narrative and what they perceive as its foreclosure of the female subject and reader. For instance, denouncing the patriarchal bias in Barthes's hermeneutic code (with its emphasis on closure and climax), Naomi Schor calls for an 'hieratic' one that, by stressing 'deferral' and 'interminability,' would specifically address the female reader's pleasure.[6]

Teresa De Lauretis provides a more nuanced critique (and alternative) to Barthes's formulation. Referring to the work on myth and folktales carried out by the Russian formalists, she notes that narrative is predicated on the active passage or transformation of the mythical male subject. In this movement, the figure of the woman is a boundary to be crossed, an obstacle that must be overcome if the subject is to complete his journey and recount his story. The woman represents a figure of narrative closure, or the final point of narrativization that confirms the male hero in his status as mythical subject. Narrative speaks a desire, and the desire is that of Oedipus. Narrative, however, is not merely a medium through which male ideology and desire are reproduced; it is an apparatus that itself produces desire and its representations. Narrative maps sexual desire, difference, and meaning onto its plot space and by so doing encodes its reader or spectator into specific positions. 'Therefore, to say that narrative is the production of Oedipus is to say that each reader – male or female – is constrained and defined within two positions of sexual difference thus conceived: male-hero-human, on the side of the subject; and female-obstacle-boundary-space, on the other.'[7] This conception of narrative as both a product and a producer of cultural codes allows De Lauretis to theorize the access of women to the means of social production and to lay out the bases of an alternative feminist narrative practice.

Rejecting the avant-garde program of antinarrative as a viable feminist strategy, De Lauretis argues for one that would be 'narrative and Oedipal with a vengeance.' Narrativity, in its movement towards meaning and mastery, engages the scopic drive. According to Freud, scopophilia is linked to a desire for mastery (i.e., the drive to occupy a position of activity instead of passivity), and the desire for knowledge (epistemophilia).[8] Traditionally, the woman is coded as the passive object of the active gaze of the male hero. Spectators (both male and female) are drawn into a complicitous relationship with the look of the male protagonist. Female spectators are thus forced to identify with either the voyeuristic masculine gaze or the passive, exhibitionist, feminine image.[9] De Lauretis proposes a different model of identification whereby the female spectator would identify with both the figure of narrative movement and the figure of narrative closure (the narrative image). The feminist project would then be to 'enact the contradictions of female desire in terms of narrative, to perform it in the figures of movement and closure, image and gaze.'[10] In other words, a feminist narrative would problematize the question of the female subject caught in the logic of a 'duplicitous' Oedipal scenario. Instead of producing the protagonist/spectator as Oedipus, it would create another measure of desire and another social subject – one caught in the tenuous position between the look and the image. In short, what De Lauretis advocates for a feminist agenda is 'an interruption of the triple track by which narrative, meaning and pleasure are constructed from his [Oedipus's] point of view.'[11]

While De Lauretis's work essentially deals with the semiotic practice of cinema, I would like to read Maupassant's *Pierre et Jean* in the light of her elaborations. They are especially pertinent to an author associated with the realist/naturalist tradition, and whose aesthetics strongly privilege the primacy of vision. 'Je suis avant tout un regardeur,' declares Maupassant, 'chez le romancier, la vision en général domine.'[12] 'Voir, tout est là, et voir juste.' And in his theoretical treatise 'Le Roman' that precedes *Pierre et Jean*, Maupassant institutes the act of looking as that which empowers and distinguishes an artist: 'Il s'agit de regarder tout ce qu'on veut exprimer assez longtemps et avec assez d'attention pour en découvrir un aspect qui n'ait été vu et dit par personne.'[13]

A theory exploring the links between visual pleasure and narrative is equally germane to a novel dominated by a scopophiliac protagonist. The action in *Pierre et Jean* is driven by the hero's desire to elucidate a mystery that revolves around the figure of a woman. In this respect, the novel sets up the familiar dichotomy between an active male gaze and its passive female object. The protagonist is impelled towards the acquisition of a knowledge (the solution to the mystery) while the female figure is set up as that which must offer itself to appropriation by his gaze. For the male hero and reader, knowledge and meaning are constructed through his look, his perceptions, his subjectivity. But, as I hope to show, this projection of the narrative towards its telos is, in a manner very similar to that outlined by De Lauretis, not without its deflections and its derailments.

Maupassant and Feminism?

Feminist scholarship on Maupassant ranges from a condemnation of his overt misogyny to a more tempered look at the social roles accorded to women in his fiction. Thus, Uwe Dethloff argues that Maupassant's misogynistic conception of women must not blind one to the often emancipatory role they play in his novels, where they are allowed to express themselves in ways not sanctioned by nineteenth-century French society.[14] Chantal Jennings points out a similar ambivalence in Maupassant's attitudes towards women: his derogatory statements about their biological, intellectual, and artistic inferiority on the one hand, and what appears to be a genuine sympathy for their social and legal oppression on the other.[15] For both Jennings and Ðethloff, Maupassant's ardent defence of the woman's right to free love constitutes his most radical subversion of bourgeois ideology. Usually condemned to loveless marriages, women suffered even more under a Napoleonic Code that required them to surrender all rights, properties, and privileges to their husbands. Female adultery is a recurrent theme in Maupassant's work, and almost always condoned.

Mary Donaldson-Evans concurs with Jennings that Maupassant shows a surprising lucidity towards the misogynistic discourses of his time, particularly those of the religious and medical communities. Having attended Charcot's lectures on hysteria at the Salpêtrière between 1884 and 1886, Maupassant expresses his doubts about a scientific discourse that was regularly used to 'pathologize' and confine troublesome women. He is equally suspicious of a knowledge that so unmistakeably speaks masculine desire in a scenario that offers a passive, exhibitionist female hysteric to the voyeuristic gaze of a male audience. Maupassant's writings often deride or negate the medical community's attempts to understand and explain 'woman.'[16]

At this point, Donaldson-Evans makes an abrupt turnaround in her argument, and the following comment by Maupassant constitutes the basis for this shift:

> L'homme, en jugeant la femme, n'est jamais juste; il la considère toujours comme une sorte de propriété réservée au mâle, qui conserve le droit absolu de la gouverner, moraliser, séquestrer à sa guise; et une femme indépendante l'exaspère comme un socialiste peut exaspérer un roi.[17]

Reiterating Maupassant's preference for the ancien régime, Donaldson-Evans argues that the above quotation betrays his fear of the social equality associated with the liberation of women. Much like the medical discourse he criticized, Maupassant's own discourse serves to imprison the woman more firmly within a masculinist one. To the doctor's straitjacket corresponds the writer's prose – Maupassant's prison is his narrative framework. Despite the predominance of woman as theme, narrative competence in Maupassant is almost always masculine. Woman is what is narrated, discoursed about, recounted. Maupassant in this light is a sadist: 'il serre l'instrument de torture – le conte – dans lequel il comprime, déforme l'être jusqu'à en faire un monstre.'[18] 'Comme montreur de phénomènes, Maupassant se spécialise en femmes, question de "contenir", de "neutraliser", d'enfermer celle qui reste, malgré tous les efforts de son talent, enfermée en elle-même, irréparablement, définitivement Autre.'[19]

From a sceptic wary of the dominant medical and religious discourses on women to their sadistic torturer and oppressor, the transformation is effected within the space of a four-line citation, and the ambivalence in Maupassant's literary work foreclosed in an abrupt, totalizing gesture that discounts the ironic dissonance that works to undermine the authority of the master voice of narrative in Maupassant's fiction.[20]

Donaldson-Evans's linking of sadism and narrative brings to mind a similar connection made by Laura Mulvey: 'Sadism demands a story, depends on making something happen, forcing a change in another person, a battle of will and strength, victory/defeat, all occurring in a linear time with a beginning and an end.'[21] Voyeurism and sadism are jointly implicated in the construction of a pleasure which 'lies in ascertaining guilt (immediately associated with castration), asserting control and subjecting the guilty person through punishment or forgiveness.'[22] Donaldson-Evans's assimilation of sadism and narrative is thus strangely reminiscent of the operations at work in a detective story, where the energies of the detective are directed towards determining guilt in order to enable the law to exact its punishment. To solve the mystery, the detective needs to wrestle the hidden story of the crime from the criminal and to obtain a confession that would complete his appropriation and possession of it. *Pierre et Jean* is constructed very much like a detective story insofar as the action of the novel consists of the investigation undertaken by its main protagonist. What sadistic impulses function to generate the hero's narrative that must also be that of woman as object? How and whose desire is engaged, and how are meaning and knowledge constructed both in and by the narrative? These are some questions I would like to address by taking a detour through the operations at work in detective fiction. I suspect that if, as Donaldson-Evans suggests, the greater part of Maupassant's fiction only collaborates to suppress the alterity of the woman's voice, *Pierre et Jean* is a novel in which the authorial voice not only recognizes the otherness of the feminine in its opposition to itself, but sees its narrative as inhabited and radically decentred by it.[23]

Pierre et Jean and the Detective Story

The Russian Formalists identify two elements of narrative: the *fabula* and the *sjŭzet*. While the *fabula* is composed of events that take place in their 'natural' and 'real' order, the *sjŭzet* corresponds to the order in which they are presented in the narrative. Within the *fabula*, the order of events follows the linear course of time, whereas in the *sjŭzet*, their chronology can be completely reversed. What is peculiar to the detective novel, as Tzvetan Todorov observes, is that it articulates both aspects of narrative at the same time.[24]

There are two stories in a detective novel: the story of the crime and that of its discovery. The first recounts 'what really happened' while the second explains how the detective learns about or becomes aware of it.[25] Hence, the detective novel contains two narratives, that of the crime and that of the investigation. The latter takes as its starting point the culmination of the former (the crime) in order to retrace or reconstruct the events that constitute it. The story of the investigation is manifest while that of the crime is absent; the former imposing itself to the extent that the latter is absent. The duality of narrative in detective fiction is that of 'l'absence face à la présence.'[26] Every detective novel is constructed on a 'narrative gap.' Before the investigation, something takes place, a secret that everybody (with the exception of the criminal) is unaware of. The narrative of the investigation projects itself towards this 'blind spot' in order to bring it to light. What the investigator seeks is the absent story of the crime and once it appears, the novel ends.[27]

If we accept the above characteristics of the detective novel, *Pierre et Jean* displays several features which assimilate it to the genre. A family's relatively placid existence is disrupted when the younger of two brothers, Jean, inherits a sizable fortune bequeathed solely to him by an old friend of the family. The legacy sets off the action of the novel in that the older brother Pierre is now faced with an enigma: 'Puisqu'il [Maréchal] m'a connu le premier, qu'il fut si dévoué pour moi, puisqu'il m'aimait et m'embrassait tant, puisque je suis la cause de sa grande liaison avec mes parents, pourquoi a-t-il laissé toute sa fortune à mon frère et rien à moi?' (120–1). The novel thus sets up a mystery (why is Jean Maréchal's unique legatee), and moves towards its solution. There is a secret (adultery) unknown to everybody except the guilty person (Mme Roland), and the greater part of the novel is devoted to the hero's uncovering of the secret (the investigation led by Pierre). The confession of the guilty person ends the novel's narrative.

Hence, what could have been a novel à la Madame Bovary on adultery and its consequences on a family inscribes itself, due to its narrative structure, in the genre of the detective story. Maupassant could have meticulously traced the history of the Roland family by starting with the husband and wife, building up their respective psychological profiles, establishing the reasons and circumstances which led Mme Roland to commit adultery, and so on. But instead of using a narration that would follow the chronological order of events, he employs a reverse narrative structure that unfolds through his principal protagonist. Mme Roland's story is one she cannot (must not) narrate; it is what must be appropriated by Pierre in order to be told. She cannot be the subject of her own story; she and her story must be the object of a male narration. Pierre Roland starts from an event that constitutes the end point of her tale (the inheritance) and from this fact, reconstructs the entire drama of adultery. Pierre's investigation is a retracing of the itinerary from origin to end, cause to effect. To explain the events of the present, he reaches back into the past, in search of the 'primal event' that marked the present with its configuration. In the answer to his question lies the truth, not only to Pierre's identity, but to that of his family members. For the first time in his life he looks at them, questions them, and tries to 'see' them. His painstaking search for the solution to the mystery is mimetic of Oedipus's quest in that it is propelled by a movement from ignorance to knowledge, darkness to light, secret to truth: 'Et tout seul, en errant par la nuit, il allait faire, dans ses souvenirs, dans sa raison, l'enquête minutieuse d'où résulterait l'éclatante vérité. Après cela ce serait fini, il n'y penserait plus, plus jamais. Il irait dormir' (123). Like Oedipus, what distinguishes him from the others is his desire to know, and his inability to bear the anguish of incertitude: 'il fallait que ce soupçon si léger, si invraisemblable, fût rejeté de lui, complètement, pour toujours. Il lui fallait la lumière, la certitude, il fallait dans son coeur la sécurité complète ...' (122). 'Il faut savoir. Mon Dieu, il faut savoir' (125). Pierre's investigation could thus be read as an Oedipal journey that would lead its protagonist to his true place within the patriarchal order and mark his rite of passage from the imaginary into the symbolic. But it is one, as we shall see, that is fraught with much peril for its Oedipal subject.[28]

Narrative Power and Oedipal Knowledge

As mentioned earlier, a detective novel is built around a narrative gap, which is the absence of the story of the crime. Because the guilty person is the only one who knows the truth about the crime, s/he is the only one capable of narrating it. But s/he is unable to do so. As for the detective, s/he does his/her best to acquire the story of the crime in order to narrate it. The conflict in a detective novel is thus articulated around the question of narrative power – the investigator seeks to obtain it, the guilty person to suppress it.[29]

Once he has recognized his mother's duplicity and betrayal, Pierre chafes at his powerlessness to denounce her: 'il ne pouvait rien dire, rien faire, rien montrer, rien révéler' (145). His fear of scandal and his desire to preserve social appearances are responsible for his mutism. To keep their reputation intact in front of Mme Rosémilly, Pierre will hide the portrait of Maréchal from her eyes in order to prevent her from guessing the truth. In doing so, he yields to 'une peur brusque et horrible que cette honte fût dévoilée' (148). The detective who wanted to 'faire éclater la vérité' now collaborates with the criminal to suppress it.

Because Pierre cannot openly exercise his narrative power, he takes an inordinate pleasure in wielding it in a covert fashion. Henceforth begins a game of cat and mouse in which Pierre brings to bear his 'ruses de tortionnaire,' where his veiled allusions, gestures, and looks are aimed at making Mme Roland aware of his knowledge without the others knowing. Each reaction of Mme Roland serves to reinforce his power over her and affirms the veracity of his convictions. But the power of the veiled word cannot satisfy Pierre for long; he will finally give in to the imperious urge to narrate:

Mais il fallait qu'il vidât son coeur! et il dit tout, ses soupçons, ses raisonnements, ses luttes, sa certitude, et l'histoire du portrait encore une fois disparu.

Il parlait par phrases courtes, hâchées, presque sans suite, des phrases d'halluciné.

Il semblait maintenant avoir oublié Jean et sa mère dans la pièce voisine. Il parlait comme si personne ne l'écoutait, parce qu'il devait parler, parce qu'il avait trop souffert, trop comprimé et refermé sa plaie. Elle avait grossi comme une tumeur, et cette tumeur venait de crever, éclaboussant tout le monde. Il s'était mis à marcher comme il faisait presque toujours; et les yeux fixés devant lui, gesticulant, dans une frénésie de désespoir, avec des sanglots dans la gorge, des retours de haine contre lui-même, il parlait comme s'il eût confessé sa misère et la misère des siens, comme s'il eût jeté sa peine à l'air invisible où s'envolaient ses paroles. (175)

Pierre assumes the narrative act in an extremely powerful emotional state, 'en proie à une de ses folies de rage qui font commettre des crimes' (174). His advent as the final narrator is placed not under the sign of a denunciation of crime, but under that of crime itself. The passage quoted above reverses the hierarchical opposition between justice and guilt: Pierre's narrative is now relegated to the status of a sinful confession ('il parlait comme s'il eût confessé sa misère'). His attempt to retrieve or recapture the absent story of the crime is thus likened to a misappropriation, an infringement. Far from 'l'éclatante vérité,' his search brings about an insalubrious tainting ('cette tumeur venait de crever, éclaboussant tout le monde'). Oedipus's search cannot disclose the salutary truth but only bring about a fetid plague. Or rather, Oedipal knowledge *is* the plague. His delirious account of his investigation is less an appropriation of his mother's story than his expropriation from it.[30] Pierre cannot control or master his discourse; it bursts forth inspite of him ('il *fallait* qu'il vidât son coeur'; 'il *devait* parler') and against him ('des retours de haine contre lui-même'). It is a story with no narratee ('Il semblait maintenant avoir oublié Jean et sa mère dans la pièce voisine'; 'Il parlait comme si personne ne l'écoutait') and no narrator – Pierre's utterances are disjointed both from each other ('Il parlait par phrases courtes, hâchées, presque sans suite, des phrases d'halluciné') and from their locatory origin in a speaker ('il parlait ... comme s'il eût jeté sa peine à l'air invisible où s'envolaient ses paroles'). Pierre's narration is thus transformed into a non-narration. The quest for a tale that was to be a quest for the seeker's meaning and origin is divested of both its object and its ultimate destination. What we have here is not the display of narrative power through the possession of a story, but rather, the dispossession of the story from its owner.[31] Pierre is ousted from his mother's story as well as from his own.

Pierre's eviction from the narrative equally constitutes a displacement from its knowledge. Jean will be privy to his mother's confession while Pierre will be denied it. All of Pierre's efforts to seek out the truth are deconstructed and rendered ineffective by the text. His quest does not bring him the peace and knowledge he wanted; rather, it precipitates him into greater suffering and an almost psychotic state of self-fragmentation: 'Tu ne vois donc point que j'en crève de chagrin depuis un mois, que je passe mes nuits sans dormir et mes jours à me cacher comme une bête, que je ne sais plus ce que je dis ni ce que je fais, ni ce que je deviendrai tant je souffre, tant je suis affolé de honte et de douleur, car j'ai deviné d'abord et je sais maintenant' (174–5). His knowledge of the truth is undermined by an epistemic gap: Pierre will never know if what he knows is true. Barely acquired, his knowledge is immediately transformed into a non-knowledge:

> Il se demandait: 'Que se sont-ils dit après mon départ?'
> Jean répétait avec tendresse 'mère' et 'chère maman', prenait soin d'elle, la servait et lui versait à boire. Pierre alors comprit qu'ils avaient pleuré ensemble, mais il ne put pénétrer leur pensée! Jean croyait-il sa mère coupable ou son frère un misérable? (191)

> Toujours il se demandait: 'Qu'a-t-elle pu dire à Jean? A-t-elle avoué ou a-t-elle nié? Que croit mon frère? Que pense-t-il d'elle, que pense-t-il de moi?' Il ne devinait pas et s'en exaspérait. (203)

In an ironic twist to the detective story, only the criminal and her accomplice dispose of the answer to the mystery. Pierre is thus realigned with his father into the domain of ignorance.

At the end of Pierre's Oedipal journey lies not knowledge and self-discovery, but ignorance and self-alienation. His access to the symbolic is marked not by the birth of a speaking subject, by its entry into the order of language, but by its silencing: Pierre is henceforth denied the power to speak. He is unable to display the knowledge of his mother's adultery through speech: unlike the classic detective, Pierre cannot restore the absent story of the crime in a plenitude of meaning. In fact, after his outburst in front of his brother, Pierre is practically effaced from the text's narrative. The Law of the Father cannot guarantee subjectivity for all of its sons.

In *Pierre et Jean*, Maupassant depicts an Oedipal scenario in which the Father is divested of the logos. M. Roland suspects nothing of his wife's adultery from one end of the novel to the other. But it is he who resolves the enigma even before it poses itself as such to Pierre: 'comme il [Maréchal] n'avait aucun héritier il s'est dit: "Tiens, j'ai contribué à la naissance de ce petit-là, je vais lui laisser ma fortune"' (82). It is he who alerts Pierre to Mme Roland's deception when he informs him that she had been looking at Maréchal's portrait only a few days before she tells him that she had not seen it in a while and that she was ignorant of its whereabouts. Because he does not realize the truth value of his pronouncements, his knowledge lacks self-recognition and is thereby assimilated to a non-knowledge. In *Pierre et Jean*, truth and logos are divorced from their origin in a Father.

The Vision and Blindness of Oedipus

In *Oedipus, Philosopher*, Jean-Joseph Goux studies the importance of the figure of Oedipus for the birth of modern thought. Echoing Hegel, he views Oedipus as one who heralds the birth of Western philosophy through an exodus from Egypt to Greece. Oedipus thus inaugurates the transition from Egyptian myth to Greek reason. Oedipus conquers the Sphinx by solving a riddle and triumphs over her by virtue of his intelligence and power of reflection. His victory is accomplished with no help from the gods: 'the flight of my own intelligence hit the mark.'[32] In accepting the challenge of the Sphinx, Oedipus acts alone. When Tiresias refuses to reveal the true murderer of Laius, Oedipus continues the investigation by himself and as before, seeks the truth with no help from a god or master. His dismissive stance towards Tiresias and his contempt of divine symbols[33] is the stance of fifth-century rationalism:

> Oedipus seeks complete knowledge and enlightenment. In opposition to Teiresias and Jocasta, he wants to understand everything, he wants all the details, he wants to reconstitute events in an objective narrative, leaving no traces of obscurity. Knox shows the importance of the verb *zētein* (to undertake research, to carry out an investigation) and its derivatives; their connotations are at once scientific (medicine, philosophy) and juridical (inquest). Words like *skopein* (contemplate, examine), *historein* (seek, investigate), and *tekmairesthai* (judge according to the evidence, infer) also seem specially chosen by Sophocles to evoke the style of discussion of the new *sophos*.[34]

For Goux, Oedipus announces a different mode of subjectivity; he is emblematic of the new 'anthropocentering' gesture of philosophy which consists in the recognition of gods, demons and monsters as symbolic projections of man and in their recuperation as such. The human subject withdraws the projections with which it invests the universe in order to restore them to the self. The supernatural is henceforth recognized as a product of the human imagination, and the power formerly imputed to the gods is relocated or reattributed to the human. Oedipus embodies the Greek passage from myth to reason, from a universe dominated by the gods to a culture centred on man. He represents that moment in history when the self-conscious human subject recognizes itself and institutes itself as such. Oedipus thus heralds the birth of the modern subject 'as an autonomous agent and juridical subject':

> Oedipus has only to withdraw his projective belief by reducing every enigma to man, by establishing man as the unique source and agent; this is all it takes to make the Sphinx vanish before his eyes. The simple hand gesture by which Oedipus points to himself (brings the question back to himself) brings about the monster's immediate disappearance ... Autoreflection, self-consciousness, sends the monster headlong into the abyss. (120)

According to Goux, Oedipus marks the passage from unconscious projections to the 'deprojection' of conscious self-mastery: 'Oedipus is emblematic of the movement by which the human subject, recognizing itself as the source and agent, withdraws what it had projected onto the external world, with the result that in a single two-sided operation of deprojection, the subject discovers the world as an object (rather than a sign) and situates himself as a subject' (121). The subject now situates itself as the centre of vision. In art and architecture this leads to the constitution of the perspective subject wherein the representation of the object is relativized according to the subject's point of view, and thereby brought under the mastery of its perspective: 'imitative art, contrary to the symbolist and magical art of the Egyptians, corresponds to the type of objective truth that the effort of the Greek *epistēmē* attempts to identify' (124; emphasis in original). Egyptian art presents the object as an eternal, immutable, and endlessly repeatable form undistorted by perception. The object is fixed in a canonical and invariable form independent of the changing spatial location of the viewing subject. The development of Greek perspective centres the subject as source and goal. With the passage from (Egyptian) aspective to (Greek) perspective, the human subject withdraws the unconscious projections it has imposed on the world to confer meaning upon it: 'No longer an obscure symbol overinvested with inexhaustible meanings, the perceptual landscape becomes a fact, an object' (127). The Oedipus myth epitomizes the transition from aspective to perspective in that, by solving the riddle that the Sphinx poses with the answer 'man,' Oedipus places himself at the centre of vision and refuses to acknowledge her symbolic truth:

> The victory over the Sphinx is thus tantamount to the emergence of the

perspective view of the world ... It is, in every sense of the word, a victory of perspective – or the rational viewpoint of man – over aspective. By situating himself as a viewpoint on the world, as the central and unique measure of all things, man simultaneously acquires the objective view that solves all riddles, calms all terrors, hurls all Sphinxes into the abyss. (128–9)

Oedipus thus defines a new mode of vision and subjectivity, one that does away with symbolist profundity and enigmatic alterity.[35] Man becomes the agent capable of shedding light on what was previously considered to be the obscure signs of the gods. Enigmatic alterity is conquered through a denial of symbolist profundity.[36]

In *Pierre et Jean*, it is with 'Oedipal vision' that Pierre is endowed. As doctor and judge, Pierre will deploy during his investigation 'un regard aigu à qui rien ne devait échapper' (123). Pierre's ruminations take place at night during his walks along the quay, in the presence of two electric lighthouses that, 'semblables à deux cyclopes monstrueux et jumeaux, jetaient sur la mer leur longs et puissants regards' (87–8). The play on the words *mer/mère* announces the investigation he will carry out, likens his vision to that of the Cyclops and reinforces the idea of a unique, centred source of vision that will penetrate his mother's mystery. Pierre's privileged point of view is attributable to both an acute vision and an intelligence capable of going beyond appearances, lifting veils, interpreting words, gestures, and looks in order to pierce enigmas. Pierre does not take signs at their face value but reconfigures the relationship of signifiers to their signifieds. If signs are capable of signifying more than they appear to, their polysemy is far from unbridled. For Pierre, signs do not overflow with meaning and plenitude because he is able to reduce their enigmatic density to a single and coherent narrative.

As the constant objects of Pierre's look, the women in the novel seem to be visually impaired. Their short-sightedness stems from an innate deficiency as well as an inability to manipulate the instruments of culture. During the first fishing expedition, Mme Rosémilly is unable to fix her sight onto a boat at sea, even with the help of binoculars:

Elle prit l'objet qu'elle dirigea vers le transatlantique lointain, sans parvenir sans doute à le mettre en face de lui car elle ne distinguait rien, rien que du bleu, avec un cercle de couleur, un arc-en-ciel tout rond, et puis des choses bizarres, des espèces d'éclipses, qui lui faisaient tourner le coeur.

Elle dit en rendant la longue-vue:

– D'ailleurs, je n'ai jamais su me servir de cet instrument-là. Ça mettait

même en colère mon mari qui restait des heures à la fenêtre à regarder passer les navires.
    Le père Roland, vexé, reprit:
    – Ça doit tenir à un défaut de votre oeil, car ma lunette est excellente. (68)

As for Mme Roland, she declines the offer of the binoculars, knowing in advance that she would be incapable of using them to her advantage.
    The novel codes Mme Roland's vision as aspective, that of Pierre as perspective. During the second fishing trip, both Pierre and his mother are witness to the seduction scene being played out between Jean and Mme Rosémilly. Mme Roland's perception of it provides a striking contrast with that of Pierre:

> Puis son regard indécis, qui errait devant elle, aperçut, au milieu des varechs, son fils Jean qui pêchait avec Mme Rosémilly. Alors elle les suivit, épiant leurs mouvements, comprenant confusément, avec son instinct de mère, qu'ils ne causaient point comme tous les jours. Elle les vit se pencher côte à côte dans l'eau, demeurer debout face à face quand ils interrogeaient leurs coeurs, puis grimper et s'asseoir sur le rocher pour s'engager l'un envers l'autre.
>   Leurs silhouettes se détachaient bien nettes, semblaient seules au milieu de l'horizon, prenaient dans ce large espace de ciel, de mer, de falaises, quelque chose de grand et de symbolique.
>   Pierre aussi les regardait, et un rire sec sortit brusquement de ses lèvres.
>   Sans se tourner vers lui, Mme Roland lui dit:
>   – Qu'est-ce que tu as donc?
>   Il ricanait toujours:
>   – Je m'instruis. J'apprends comment on se prépare à être cocu. (164–5)

For Mme Roland, the perceptual landscape is pregnant with a signification that surpasses her ability to limit it within the confines of an epistemological framework: her understanding of it is confused and instinctual. The images impose and erect themselves in a plenitude of meaning that extends beyond her cognitive grasp: 'leurs silhouettes se détachaient bien nettes ... prenaient dans ce large espace ... quelque chose de grand et de symbolique.' Where she reverently sees symbols overloaded with an impenetrable mystery, Pierre is the heretic capable of translating them into immediate knowledge ('Je m'instruis,' 'j'apprends') in an act of self-conscious mastery. With Mme Roland, erratic projection prevails; with Pierre, it is deprojection or self-conscious reflection.

But the novel is equally inscribed with signs of Pierre's myopia. His reconstruction of the crime will take place in a dark fog, and two monstrous Cyclopic eyes can only result in a skewed and lopsided view of things. Pierre has a formidable adversary in Mme Rosémilly, since her faulty sense of vision could very well be a mere dissimulation: 'Mme Rosémilly semblait ne pas voir, ne pas comprendre, ne pas entendre' (71). At one point in the narrative, Pierre encounters a look as discomfiting as his own in its ability to fathom secrets:

> Pierre, soudain, rencontra l'oeil de Mme Rosémilly; il était fixé sur lui, limpide et bleu, clairvoyant et dur. Et il sentit, il pénétra, il devina la pensée nette qui animait ce regard, la pensée irritée de cette petite femme à l'esprit simple et droit, car ce regard disait:
> 'Tu es jaloux, toi. C'est honteux, cela.'
> Il baissa la tête en se remettant à manger. (110)

Pierre's hiding of the portrait is a tacit recognition of her capacity for divining the truth. But until that moment in the narrative, any power imputed to Mme Rosémilly is only recuperated as a basis for constructing his arguments and affirming the validity of his hypotheses. Pierre's reasonings are for the most part founded on his faith in his ability to read and understand women. Thus, it is Mme Rosémilly's reaction (or lack thereof) that will constitute the 'proof' that will lead him to discard his supposition: 'Mme Rosémilly, bien que son intelligence fût limitée, avait le tact, le flair et le sens subtil des femmes. Or cette idée ne lui était pas venue puisqu'elle avait bu, avec une simplicité parfaite à la mémoire bénie du feu Maréchal. Elle n'aurait point fait cela, elle, si le moindre soupçon l'eût effleurée. Maintenant il ne doutait plus ...' (115). If later, Pierre seeks concrete visual proof for his now reinstated belief that Maréchal is Jean's father, all it takes is his mother's gestures to convince him absolutely of the fact: 'Or, ce qui fut pour Pierre plus décisif encore que cette allure des visages, c'est que sa mère s'était levée, avait tourné le dos et feignait d'enfermer, avec trop de lenteur, le sucre et le cassis dans le placard. Elle avait compris qu'il savait ou du moins qu'il soupçonnait!' (146).

Pierre's hypothetico-deductive method largely applies itself to the reading of looks, gestures, and expressions. But Pierre's perceptions and his subsequent interpretations of behavioural clues are constantly problematized with the text's consistent use of the verbs 'paraître,' 'sembler,' and 'croire,' and with its use of the conditional tense.[37] Pierre's setting up of chance remarks as 'clues' and the precipitous conclusions he draws from them become equally suspicious. The barmaid's comment provokes an immediate reaction and 'solution' to the mystery of the inheritance:

> Maintenant il se répétait cette phrase: 'Ça n'est pas étonnant qu'il te ressemble si peu.'
> Qu'avait-elle pensé, qu'avait-elle sous-entendu dans ces mots? Certes, il y avait là une malice, une méchanceté, une infamie. Oui, cette fille avait dû croire que Jean était le fils de Maréchal. (104)

Later on in the narrative, Marowsko's resentment towards the preference shown to Jean taken in conjunction with his initial reaction to the news of Jean's inheritance ('Cela ne fera pas un bon effet' [93]) will cause Pierre to attribute a similar belief to the old pharmacist:

> Et Pierre croyait l'entendre penser, devinait, comprenait, lisait dans ses yeux détournés, dans le ton hésitant de sa voix, les phrases qui lui venaient aux lèvres et qu'il ne disait pas, qu'il ne dirait point, lui si timide, si prudent, si cauteleux.
> Maintenant il ne doutait plus, le vieux pensait: 'Vous n'auriez pas dû lui laisser accepter cet héritage qui fera mal parler de votre mère.' Peut-être même croyait-il que Jean était le fils de Maréchal. Certes il le croyait! Comment ne le croirait-il pas, tant la chose devait paraître vraisemblable, probable, évidente? Mais lui-même, lui Pierre, le fils, depuis trois jours ne luttait-il pas de toute sa force, avec toutes les subtilités de son coeur, pour tromper sa raison, ne luttait-il pas contre ce soupçon terrible? (122)

Pierre's investigation begins to appear not so much as the discovery of an already past and distinct prior event, as the gradual creation of one through the force of a desire:

> Quel étrange besoin le poussa tout à coup à raconter à cette servante de brasserie l'héritage de Jean? Pourquoi cette idée, qu'il rejetait de lui lorsqu'il se trouvait seul, qu'il repoussait par crainte du trouble apporté dans son âme, lui vint-elle aux lèvres en cet instant, et pourquoi la laissa-t-il couler, comme s'il eût eu besoin de vider de nouveau devant quelqu'un son coeur gonflé d'amertume? (103)

What appears to be an objective appraisal of facts turns out to be an outward projection of unconscious fears and desires, or rather, the production of meaning generated by a desiring unconscious. Pierre's deprojective stance, that is, his claims to an impartial and objective account of an untainted truth, conceals an overinvestment of words, expressions, and events. If he is aware of the unconscious mechanisms at work in his investigation, this awareness is rapidly suppressed with the discovery of a new 'clue.'[38]

Pierre's piecing together of the solution to the mystery of the inheritance disturbs the traditional hierarchy set up by narrative, wherein the *fabula* as a set of events is postulated as prior to and independent of its representation in discourse (*the sjŭzet*). That is to say, the *fabula* is construed as a preexisting series of events uncontaminated by a narrative investment that would order its discursive representation. In this light, events are 'givens,' not 'products of discursive forces or requirements.'[39]

In *Pierre et Jean*, meaning is not determined by a prior event (adultery), but rather, it is the act of adultery that seems to be engendered by a desire for meaning. Once again, Pierre's investigation is not so much an uncovering of a truth as the production of an event. Pierre's narrative is generated by an Oedipal desire that leads him to posit the deed of adultery. Pierre succumbs to the demands of narrative coherence generated by an Oedipal unconscious, and it is these demands that 'produce' the 'primal event.' His mother's crime becomes the result of Pierre's desire for signification, not one that leads him to it. His investigation is less the revelation of the truth of the crime than a creation of one, less the piercing of an enigma than the fabrication of one. In *Pierre et Jean*, the narrative validity of the *sjŭzet* cannot be measured against the objective truth of the *fabula*, since each is inhabited or implicated by the other. The narrative of the investigation cannot disclose an unproblematical narrative of the crime of adultery, but reveals itself as adulterated by the investigator's desire in the first place. There is no means of preserving the purity of the event as an originary cause; it is rather a configuration produced by a specific movement of desire. And the narrative of *Pierre et Jean* does not proceed towards the establishing of an undisputed equivalence between the *sjŭzet* and *fabula*. Instead, the two are suspended in a movement of unresolved tension and conflict.

Pierre's reconstruction of his mother's adultery constitutes a writing of Mme Roland and Maréchal's love story, and his analysis of her sentiments a writing of her desire. Mme Roland's confession to Jean presents a different version of the story. By initiating the reader into a confession of which he deprives Pierre, Maupassant operates a subtle split in the identification of the reader with the protagonist. S/he is henceforth dislocated from Pierre's point of view and realigned with that of Mme Roland. The former object of the masculine gaze is now set up as the subject of her own story. As a consequence, the reader's point of view is displaced and reinscribed onto a different axis of desire. S/he enters into a relationship of connivance with the female figure where pleasure no longer derives from the affirmation of the male protagonist as an Oedipal subject, but comes from seeing him foiled in his attempts to assume that position.

The novel reveals that Pierre, like Oedipus, can completely miss the mark. During one sleepless night, Pierre hears his father and Jean snoring and is struck by the gulf that separates the two:

> Un bruit léger lui parvint à travers le mur.
>
> Jean dormait tranquille et ronflait doucement. Il dormait lui! Il n'avait rien pressenti, rien deviné! ... Puis il entendit de nouveau un ronflement, un ronflement de vieux, court, pénible et dur, celui de son père sans aucun doute; et il fut crispé par cette idée, comme si elle venait seulement de jaillir en lui, que ces deux hommes qui ronflaient dans ce même logis, le père et le fils, n'étaient rien l'un à l'autre! Aucun lien, même le plus léger, ne les unissait, et ils ne le savaient pas! ... C'était un mensonge qui faisait cet amour paternel et cet amour filial, un mensonge impossible à dévoiler et que personne ne connaîtrait jamais que lui, le vrai fils. (133–4)

What Pierre fails to realize is that the snoring strengthens the bonds between Jean and M. Roland in more pernicious ways than he can see: it signals his future expulsion from the family. In the end, Pierre will be eclipsed from the circuit of desire: where he was once the controlling subject of the gaze, he is now severed from its circuit. 'Jamais il ne rencontrait plus le regard de sa mère ou le regard de son frère. Leurs yeux pour lui avaient pris une mobilité surprenante et des ruses d'ennemis qui se redoutent de croiser' (203).

In *Pierre et Jean*, the figure of Mme Roland is not established as the figure of narrative closure that ensures the coming together of the male hero, but is one that dislodges him from this position. Pierre's attempts to pierce the secret of his mother's identity are doomed to failure: she remains an enigmatic figure who escapes her son's attempts to either idealize or denigrate her. Pierre wishes to cast her in the mould of either Virgin Mother or Whore: she is neither. Pierre's misogynistic statements about women[40] are continually belied by the narrative's refusal to pin Mme Roland into any fixed position. In fact, by constantly drawing attention to M. Roland's vulgarity, the text is complicitous with Mme Roland's adultery. Where Oedipus was able to solve the riddle of the Sphinx, Pierre cannot, and is chastized for even trying. His questioning of her desire will be punished – Pierre will be cast out of the family unit.

Pierre's *roman familial*

Like Oedipus and Hamlet, Pierre is dually a detective and an incestuous son. Where he, like Hamlet, differs from Oedipus is that he exhibits the classic 'symptoms' of the Oedipus complex in its Freudian formulation.[41] Pierre's desire for other women is always mediated by the image of his mother, and marked by the same tendency to idealize: 'Il devait exister cependant des créatures très bonnes, très douces et très consolantes. Sa mère n'avait-elle pas été la raison et le charme du foyer paternel ? Comme il aurait voulu connaître une femme, une vraie femme!' (101).[42] Pierre's discovery of his mother's desire is also a discovery of her alterity: 'Pierre, en allant vers elle, regardait sa mère ; et il lui sembla tout à coup qu'il ne l'avait jamais vue ... Il comprenait à présent que, l'aimant, il ne l'avait jamais regardée' (137–8). In lieu of an idealized object, he is confronted with a desiring subject.

With the recognition of his mother's adultery comes the articulation of his own desire for her:

> Pierre regardait sa mère qui avait menti. Il la regardait avec une colère exas-pérée de fils trompé, volé dans son affection sacrée, et avec une jalousie d'homme longtemps aveugle qui découvre enfin une trahison honteuse ... Et il ne pouvait rien dire, rien faire, rien montrer, rien révéler ... Si la fureur dont il était soulevé arrivait presque à de la haine, c'est qu'il la sentait plus criminelle envers lui qu'envers son père lui-même. (145)

Pierre's desire to supplant the father and displace his mother's transgression from his father towards himself once again corresponds to the symptoms of an unresolved Oedipal complex and sets the stage for his 'family romance.' He feels increasingly estranged from his father, 'ce gros homme flasque, content et niais ... qu'il n'aimait pas, malgré lui' (143–4). Pierre's disavowal of the father could thus be viewed as an unconscious desire to be the bastard son.[43] His first reaction to the news of the inheritance is a vague malaise whose cause he cannot articulate and which he quickly attributes to a jealousy of his brother. But as his inquiry proceeds, Pierre is troubled by 'un nouveau mal' and confronted with the question that was mentioned earlier in this chapter: 'Puisqu'il m'a connu le premier, qu'il fut si dévoué pour moi, puisqu'il m'aimait et m'embrassait tant, puisque je suis la cause de sa grande liaison avec mes parents, pourquoi a-t-il laissé toute sa fortune à mon frère et rien à moi?' (120–1). The problem at stake for Pierre is not just his jealousy of his brother's fortune nor the possible infidelity of his mother (the thought crosses his mind a little earlier), but the preference shown to Jean. In other words, the lack of a mark of recognition from Maréchal: 'Il a vu naître Jean? – Oui, mais il me connaissait auparavant. – S'il avait aimé ma mère d'un amour muet et réservé, c'est moi qu'il aurait préféré puisque c'est grâce à moi, grâce à ma fièvre scarlatine, qu'il est devenu l'ami intime de mes parents. Donc, logiquement, il devait me choisir, avoir pour moi une tendresse plus vive' (123). Pierre cannot come to terms with an exclusion that did not seem to have existed before: 'Il appelait Pierre et Jean "mes chers enfants," n'avait jamais paru préférer l'un ou l'autre, et les recevait ensemble à dîner ... Maréchal tendait ses deux mains aux jeunes gens, la droite à l'un, la gauche à l'autre, au hasard de leur entrée' (124). Where there was once symmetry between the two brothers, there is now an unbearable disequivalence. Recalling Maréchal's earlier generosity towards him, Pierre is haunted by the following thought:

> Donc cet homme l'aimait toujours, s'intéressait toujours à lui, puisqu'il s'inquiétait de ses besoins. Alors ... alors pourquoi laisser toute sa fortune à Jean? Non, il n'avait jamais été visiblement plus affectueux pour le cadet que pour l'aîné, plus préoccupé de l'un que de l'autre, moins tendre en apparence avec celui-ci qu'avec celui-là. Alors ... alors ... il avait donc eu une raison puissante et secrète de tout donner à Jean – tout – et rien à Pierre.
>
> Plus il y songeait, plus il revivait le passé des dernières années, plus le docteur jugeait invraisemblable, incroyable la différence établie entre eux.
>
> Et une souffrance aiguë, une inexprimable angoisse entrée dans sa poitrine, faisait aller son coeur comme une loque agitée. (125)

Pierre suffers because he cannot understand the difference that Maréchal has created between two brothers who were once so alike. Nor can he accept what he perceives as a betrayal on the part of a surrogate father figure who once saved his life. Pierre's anguish is not unlike that of Cain's before God's arbitrary preference for Abel. And the answer that would 'explain' the Father's rejection and make it bearable is that of his mother's infidelity. In other words, had Maréchal demonstrated a proportional measure of love towards the two brothers by dividing his fortune equally between them, Mme Roland's adultery might never have been an issue. It is Pierre's exclusion from a Father's affection that makes it one. Pierre's desire to make sense of his disowning by Maréchal produces adultery as the answer. Woman's desire becomes a question to the extent that it provides a key to the hero's search for his source, origin, and identity.

Maupassant's own precarious position as bastard son and the obsessive, recurrent theme of the absent father that runs through his work has been well documented.[44] *Pierre et Jean* would appear to be yet another instance of Maupassant's Oedipal torments. Everywhere in *Pierre et Jean*, the Father is contaminated (by the adulteror) or absent (as signalled by Pierre's stubborn appellation of Mme Rosémilly as 'la veuve'). Even the bastard son is only too happy about his newly discovered status:

> Il lui en coûtait moins d'être le fils d'un autre; et après la grande secousse d'émotion de la veille, s'il n'avait pas eu le contre-coup de révolte, d'indignation et de colère redouté par Mme Roland, c'est que depuis bien longtemps il souffrait inconsciemment de se sentir l'enfant de ce lourdaud bonasse. (196)

The legitimate order is consistently undermined by the illegitimate: both Maréchal and Jean can occupy le père Roland's position and Jean can displace Pierre; it is Maréchal who performs the husbandly duty of fetching the doctor while Mme Roland goes into labour and wears M. Roland's hat instead of his own while doing so, while Jean is allowed to occupy his father's seat at the dining table, a privilege that is never once accorded to Pierre.[45] And it is unquestionably the illegitimate that is privileged over the legitimate, the 'false' son over the 'true': it is Pierre who will be rejected in the end.

The favouring of the bastard son could very well be the wish fulfilment of Maupassant's own *roman familial* or a vindication of the author's own social and psychological humiliations. What is interesting is that in *Pierre et Jean*, it is the Oedipal subject who fails and who is denied subjectivity. Of all the characters in the novel, Pierre is the only one who adopts the Oedipal stance, and the one subject who is most punished by it. It is the Oedipal subject who is unable to function in the Oedipal scenario. This is why I believe that *Pierre et Jean* cannot be reduced to an unproblematical living out of Maupassant's Oedipal conflicts. What it articulates is a far more disturbing and subversive possibility: one that would challenge

the very status of the Oedipus myth as a normative model of human subjectivity and desire.

A 'Normal' and 'True' Oedipal Desire?

For Freud, the myth of Oedipus is paradigmatic of human subjectivity. In
this sense, it constitutes a prototypical narrative, or a 'master plot' as it
were.[46] The Barthesian model of narrative (and the feminist critique
thereof) take as their premise the privileged status of the myth of Oedipus among those of the male hero. In other words, the Oedipus myth is
that which best exemplifies the standard myth of the male hero and his
quest. Goux's study on Oedipus provides an interesting challenge to this
assumption. For Goux, the myth of Oedipus is a departure from what he
terms the 'monomyth' or the prototypical plot of Western myth.[47] It is
thus an aberration of fundamental plot structure. Because the monomyth is centred upon the hero's killing of the female monster,[48] it is
matricide and not patricide that constitutes the central trial of the monomyth and that opens up the hero's access to the non-maternal feminine.[49] While with the monomyth, matricide leads to an engagement
with the feminine other, with the Oedipus myth, patricide leads to incest.
It is the monomyth that provides the typical measure of fundamental
masculine desire rather than the myth of Oedipus, which 'gives a distorted, skewed version of this desire.'[50] It is not the conflict with paternal
interdiction that allows for the realization of masculine desire (in fact,
the king of the prototype myth helps the male subject realize his desire
by dispatching him on a trial); it is the confrontation with the monster-
mother. What has to be overcome is the incestuous attachment to the
mother, and what has to be confronted is female alterity.[51]

   According to Goux, to the extent that Oedipus's answer to the Sphinx
makes man the measure of all things, Oedipus obliterates monstrous
(female) alterity. In other words, Oedipus's anthropomorphic gesture is
one that is based on an avoidance of female difference. The positing of
the centrality of the category 'human' is founded upon a denial of feminine alterity.[52] For Goux, the Oedipus myth is a myth of 'failed initiation'
because unlike his mythic counterparts, Oedipus does not actually kill
the Sphinx by engaging in a battle of sheer physical courage. She com-
mits suicide after a battle of wits. Because Oedipus avoids a physical confrontation with the Sphinx and eludes the initiatory trial, he will commit
incest: 'it is the protagonist who does *not* kill the female monster in a
bloody struggle who marries his own mother' (33; emphasis in original).

The avoidance of the trial (that is, the physical battle with the monster) through an act of self-centred intelligence prevents Oedipus's access to the non-maternal feminine: 'The tragedy of Oedipus is the vengeance of the desire for the mother when this desire has not been burned away, transfigured in depth by the trial, but only set aside by the reflective response, by the monocentered consciousness ... The fate that pursues Oedipus is not vengeance for a murder accomplished, but spite for a deadly but also regenerative act that has not been carried out' (38).

For Goux, Oedipus's avoidance of the initiatory encounter with the female monster is thus an avoidance of castration: 'Rather than revealing the true nature of desire (the object of true desire is impossible and not simply forbidden) and reaching the most decisive form of castration (a confrontation with the lack of the Thing, more terrible than the paternal threat), the Oedipus complex constitutes a veil that dissimulates the overwhelming radicality of that desire and that castration' (30). In order to escape confrontation with lack,[53] and rather than accept the fact that satisfaction of desire is impossible, the Oedipal subject protects himself by believing that it is his father's threat that forbids him from doing so. The subject instates the father as the obstacle which must be surmounted if he is to realize his fantasy of pure jouissance. The Oedipal subject is one who has internalized the causal sequence whereby patricide leads to incest. It is in this sense that it is an irregular divergence from the monomyth: '[I]t is the avoidance of castration that makes the Oedipus complex a fantasy, a neurosis, a myth in the pejorative sense, with respect to the truth of masculine desire which is to confront symbolic castration as lack' (32). Or rather, '[t]he avoidance of castration is the Oedipal neurosis' (38).

Goux's rereading of the myth of Oedipus continues the Lacanian suspicion of the Oedipal as a fiction of the imaginary, a distorting mechanism that is operated upon the unconscious. For Lacan, the Oedipal subject is one who operates within a skewed conception of desire, because the real threat of lack is covered over by the imaginary threat of castration by the Father. However, what is more interesting than the explanation that Lacan and Goux offer as to the nature of the distortion of the Oedipal (which they take to be its dissimulation of true lack), is their intuition of Oedipal desire as an aberrant or perverted one. The Oedipal is a skewed mechanism that comes to function as a normalized structure of subjectivity. 'The madness of Oedipus has become Western reason.'[54]

Pierre et Jean, it seems to me, articulates this intuition quite clearly. One could read Pierre's failed Oedipal quest as a result of his failure to successfully resolve his Oedipal complex: Pierre cannot accede to a normalized subjectivity because he is unable to accept the paternal metaphor or make the mother's desire (the phallus) his own. But by hiding the portrait from Mme Rosémilly and sanctioning his mother's violation of paternal law, Pierre does accept her desire and circumscribe himself within it. By not denouncing his mother publicly (or to the legitimate father), Pierre places himself under Maréchal's law. But where Jean (who does the same by keeping his mother's adultery a secret) is retained within the symbolic order, Pierre is expelled from it. What cannot go uncondoned is less his acceptance of her (illegitimate) desire than his questioning of it. Pierre's failure appears to stem not so much from his inability to resolve his Oedipal complex as from his having one in the first place.

Herein lies, perhaps, the key to Pierre's failed Oedipal quest. Oedipal desire is an aberrant, perverted desire that cannot possibly lead to 'normalized' subjectivity through the magical internalization of a paternal metaphor. The Oedipal subject is always, already neurotic; always, already deviant. To the extent that it is based on a non-recognition of female otherness, the Oedipal scenario cannot but provide a dysfunctional model of human subjectivity.

Subversion of Patriarchy in *Pierre et Jean*

'La différence qui oppose la société féodale à la société bourgeoise, l'indice au signe,' writes Barthes, 'est celle-ci: l'indice a une origine, le signe n'en a pas; passer de l'indice au signe, c'est abolir la dernière (ou la première) limite, l'origine, le fondement, la butée, c'est entrer dans le procès illimité des équivalences, des représentations que rien ne vient plus arrêter, orienter, fixer, consacrer. L'indifférence parisienne à l'origine de l'argent vaut symboliquement pour l'inorigine de l'argent; un argent sans odeur est un argent soustrait à l'ordre fondamental de l'indice, à la consécration de l'origine.'[55] Under bourgeois ideology, money symbolizes the effacement of origin in a Father, the erasure of his Name and a disruption of the linear, hereditary chain that ensures the continuity of the paternal metaphor. Money is that which can interrupt the perpetuation of the Name of the Father and collapse the entire patriarchal economy constructed on the status of the phallus as a master signifier. In this light, money operates as '[le] signifiant le plus annihilant qui soit de toute signification.'[56] *Pierre et Jean* articulates this very threat posed by money to the familial and kinship structures mediated by bourgeois economy. The universe of the novel is one in which the stability of the Name of the Father is under continual attack by the subversive power of money. Money becomes the medium for the instatement of an (other) order, one that would challenge the legitimacy of the existing one by setting up an (other) name within the dominant one. Money thus fractures or disseminates the Name of the Father. This reveals the paradoxical duality of money as both the articulation of the lack of a signifier and as the signifier of lack. Maréchal's bequest of his money to Jean serves as a bequest of his name. But if the inheritance confers a different origin onto Jean, it can also cover up or neutralize this difference. In other words, it can simultaneously signify and conceal his non-origin in the Name of the Father. It can both mark Jean with an alternative name and dissimulate this naming.

Mme Roland's adultery works to disperse the Name of the Father in a similar fashion. As Jane Gallop remarks: 'Any suspicion of the mother's infidelity betrays the Name-of-the-Father as the arbitrary imposition it is ... Infidelity then is a feminist practice of undermining the Name of the Father ... Infidelity is *not* outside the system of marriage, the symbolic, patriarchy, but hollows it out, ruins it, from within.'[57] By sanctioning the expression of adulterous love with impunity, *Pierre et Jean* deconstructs the integrity of the patriarchal order and the negation of the female subject upon which it is founded. The confession scene between Jean and Mme Roland is explicitly sexual: it takes place in the nuptial bedroom (which Mme Roland helps decorate) and is played out like an amorous scene, replete with sighs, caresses, and declarations of mutual love. The end of her confession finds Mme Roland 'brisée et soulagée comme après un accouchement' (185). While Bernard Pingaud regards the scene as one of incestuous love between mother and son, it could equally be viewed as a reliving of Mme Roland's love affair with Jean's father: 'Elle monta, à pas furtifs, l'escalier silencieux, entra dans sa chambre, se dévêtit bien vite, et se glissa, avec l'émotion retrouvée des adultères anciens, auprès de Roland qui ronflait' (185). In other words, the scene between Jean and Mme Roland is a means whereby her absent narrative of desire is allowed to be reperformed, and this time, with no possibility of censure. By placing the confession under the sign of an 'accouchement' Maupassant reinforces the idea of woman as producer and owner of her discourse of desire.[58]

What comes after the dismantling of patriarchy? A new structure of power, I believe, that is no longer a male prerogative – one that can be articulated by and within the matriarchal, or rather, as Jane Gallop suggests, it is a matriarchy that hollows out the patriarchal order from within. Henceforth, Mme Roland controls the manner in which this new structure of power will be perpetuated. What she demands (and obtains) from Jean is not so much his forgiveness as his complicity (non-resistance): 'Pour cela, pour que nous puissions nous voir encore, nous parler, nous rencontrer toute la journée dans la maison, car je n'ose plus ouvrir une porte dans la peur de trouver ton frère derrière elle, pour cela il faut, non pas que tu me pardonnes – rien ne fait plus de mal qu'un pardon – mais que tu ne m'en veuilles pas de ce que j'ai fait' (182). It is she who will dictate the terms and conditions of the new economical configuration: 'Si tu veux que je reste, il faut que tu acceptes d'être son fils et que nous parlions de lui quelquefois, et que tu l'aimes un peu, et que nous pensions à lui quand nous nous regarderons' (183).

The mother now has the power to substitute or exchange the Name of the Father. In this new permutation of power, she has the prerogative of replacing one term with another. Mme Rosémilly will take the place of her son: 'Elle avait perdu un fils, un grand fils, et on lui rendait à sa place une fille, une grande fille' (199). What is more remarkable than Mme Roland's power to manipulate the terms of patriarchal culture is the suggestion of the complicity of the system with her desire through the use of the indefinite pronoun *on*.

The novel brings about a change in the traditional patriarchal coding of women. The first fishing expedition clearly places women on the side of nature. They share a profound bond with the sea, but are unable to participate in its cultural exploitation – they do not fish. The second fishing trip, however, codes Mme Rosémilly as a particularly adept hunter: 'Elle était adroite et rusée, ayant la main souple et le flair de chasseur qu'il fallait. Presque à chaque coup, elle ramenait des bêtes trompées et surprises par la lenteur ingénieuse de sa poursuite' (161). Women now gain access to the means of cultural production and are established as subjects, not objects, of cultural exchange.[59] Despite the terms within which it is played out, Mme Rosémilly's acceptance of Jean's proposal of marriage becomes more a matter of mutual or consensual exchange between her and Mme Roland rather than an inscription of Mme Rosémilly as the captured object of a masculine chase: 'Quand elles se retrouvèrent face à face, sur leurs sièges, elles se prirent les mains et restèrent ainsi, se regardant et se souriant, tandis que Jean semblait presque oublié d'elles' (199). On a similar, earlier occasion when Mme Rosémilly is invited to visit Jean's newly decorated apartment for the first time, we read: 'Il [Jean] regardait Mme Rosémilly qui se mit à sourire en regardant Mme Roland; et Mme Roland, lui prenant la main, la serra' (169). To borrow Irigaray's terms, the 'hom(mo) sexuel' exchange of women (i.e., one controlled by men for men as subjects) is replaced by a 'homosexuel' exchange between women as subjects.[60] As the above passages show, it is an exchange free of the controlling gaze of the third (male) term, unmediated by the alien value of the masculine general equivalent.[61] In this respect, Mme Roland's preparation of her son's apartment is perhaps not so much an incestuous gesture as a 'homosexual' one:

> Elle [Mme Rosémilly] était gênée un peu cependant, un peu confuse dans cette chambre à coucher qui serait sa chambre nuptiale. Elle avait remarqué, en entrant, que la couche était très large, une vraie couche de ménage, choisie par Mme Roland qui avait prévu sans doute et désiré le prochain mariage de son fils; et cette précaution de mère lui faisait plaisir cependant, semblait lui dire qu'on l'attendait dans la famille. (170)

The novel thereby seems to concretize a possibility that Irigaray envisions theoretically:

> Et si les 'marchandises' refusaient d'aller au marché?
> Entretenaient entre elles un 'autre' commerce?
> Échanges sans termes identifiables, sans comptes, sans fin ... Où l'usage et l'échange se confondraient ... Où la nature se dépenserait, sans épuisement; s'échangerait, sans travail; se donnerait à l'abri des transactions masculines – pour rien: plaisirs gratuits, bien-être sans peines, jouissances sans possessions ...
> Utopie? Peut être. A moins que ce mode d'échange mine depuis toujours l'ordre du commerce.[62]

The ability of Mme Roland and Mme Rosémilly to set up and define the modalities of an alternative economy of desire and exchange can be read as an effective act of feminist resistance against the confinements of masculine homosociality.

Pierre et Jean and the Name of the Father

How can we understand the alternative order proposed by *Pierre et Jean*? Can we say that the text merely reproduces the terms and conditions of the old one? It would appear that the underlying logic of its structure is still governed by the primacy of the paternal metaphor, insofar as the progression of the novel is dictated by the readequation of Jean's lack of the Name of the Father. *Pierre et Jean* may thus be considered as a reinvestiture or reinstatement of a missing patronym. In other words, the Name of the Father, even if repressed, insists upon returning. The manner in which it functions within the 'other' order (that of the illegitimate son) remains the same – it is the mother's word that authenticates the phallus in its status and permits the Name of the Father to exercise its role. This dialectic can best be illustrated with reference to the portrait that comes to occupy the position of the paternal metaphor and be invested with its power. At first, Jean's relationship to it is one of misrecognition (or rather, non-recognition): he cannot identify the face in the portrait as his father. It is Mme Roland's confession and her naming of Maréchal as Jean's father that will lead Jean to identify with it. By accepting the gift of the portrait from his mother, Jean places himself under its law and authority.

Initially, the portrait works as a symbol of plenitude and potency: 'Et ce petit portrait, moins grand qu'une main ouverte, semblait une personne vivante, méchante, redoutable, entrée soudain dans cette maison et dans cette famille' (148). The portrait is endowed with excess or surplus meaning that derives from its inherently ambiguous status. It is capable of signifying more than it appears to, and otherwise than it appears to. It is both a denunciation of Jean's status as bastard son and an insistent reminder of the claims of a bastardized paternity. It threatens to expose Jean's 'true' status within an illicit order at the same time as it articulates that order's appeal for recognition. It threatens to undermine Jean's position within the family, but wields the power to destroy the very integrity of the family structure against which illegitimacy may be measured.

If at first the portrait is dangerous because it signifies too much,[63] later, when Mme Roland gives it to Jean, it seems to have lost its connotative power and is relegated to the status of a 'petit objet enveloppé dans un papier blanc' (200). In addition to being veiled over, it is henceforth only denoted by its frame: 'il comprit en reconnaissant la forme du cadre' (201). The ellipsis of the portrait evacuates the signified from the sign; it becomes a signifier emptied of its content. And in an interesting parallel, Mme Roland will place the portrait on the mantelpiece in Jean's apartment, thereby completing the circuit initiated by its displacement from the mantelpiece in the Roland's living room.

In many respects, the portrait plays a role similar to the one Lacan ascribes to the letter in Edgar Allen Poe's tale, *The Purloined Letter*.[64] Like the letter, the portrait is that which insists upon returning, persists in repeating itself. And like the letter, it takes the form of a stubborn, unconscious inscription that refuses to be effaced. Even though Mme Roland tries to render it insignificant by hiding it, the portrait finds a way of manifesting itself by resurging in Pierre's memory: 'Mais la lettre, pas plus que l'inconscient du névrosé, ne l'oublie.'[65] As a signifier of absence, it is its disappearance from the mantelpiece in the Roland's living room that renders it significant in Pierre's eyes.

Again, in a manner analogous to the letter, the portrait determines the position of one subject relative to another in the signifying chain: 'Notre apologue est fait pour montrer que c'est la lettre et son détour qui régit leurs [the subjects'] entrées et leurs rôles. Qu'elle soit en souffrance, c'est eux qui vont en pâtir. A passer sous son ombre, ils deviennent son reflet. A tomber en possession de la lettre, – admirable ambiguïté du langage, – c'est son sens qui les possède.'[66] The portrait confers a special status on the subject depending on whether s/he has it or not. In other words, the acquisition of the portrait places the subject in a privileged position with respect to knowledge and power. Mme Roland's secret possession of the portrait assures her unique proprietorship over the knowledge it contains. But like the position of the characters in Poe's tale (as analysed by Lacan), the possession of the signifier carries with it a blind spot: M. Roland notices her hiding it and exposes her to Pierre. Forced to yield it to Pierre, she surrenders her power and knowledge over to him. But Pierre's knowledge is also accompanied by a blind spot: by hiding the portrait in his turn, he violates the law and places himself on the side of the transgressor. His own position of power and knowledge will be subsequently undermined – he will be supplanted by Jean. When Jean finally acquires the portrait, he will protect it from future misappropriations by consigning it to a drawer 'enfermé à double tour.' Despite its detours and waylays, the portrait returns to the mother and from there to the son in order to reassume its hidden place in a drawer. It thus completes its rightful trajectory from Father to Mother to son; its itinerary obeying the principle whereby 'une lettre arrive toujours à destination.'[67]

For Derrida, the above statement by Lacan is an assertion that the letter has a truth that cannot be lost, but is always recovered and reintegrated into its proper place and destination. The letter can never be emptied of its meaning because in Lacan's analysis, the signifier's lack of a signified itself becomes the signified of the text: 'Quelque chose manque à sa place, mais le manque n'y manque jamais.'[68] For Lacan (or so Derrida alleges), the letter functions as a phallus, i.e., as a transcendental signifier that cannot be displaced from its origin and destination:

> [C]e que le Séminaire tient à montrer finalement, c'est qu'il y a un seul trajet *propre* de la lettre qui retourne vers un lieu déterminable, toujours le même et qui est *le sien*; et que si son sens (ce qui est écrit dans le billet en circulation) nous est (selon l'hypothèse dont la fragilité soutient cependant toute la logique du Séminaire) indifférent et inconnu, le sens de la lettre et le sens de son trajet sont nécessaires, uniques, déterminables en vérité, voire comme la vérité.[69]

Given the place where both Dupin (the inspector in charge of recovering the stolen letter in Poe's story) and the analyst Lacan (who doubles for him) know where it must be found, i.e., 'entre les jambes de la femme,' for Derrida, the letter brings us back to the truth of woman as lack or woman as castration: 'Cette détermination du propre, de la loi du propre, de l'*économie*, reconduit donc à la castration comme vérité, à la figure de la femme comme figure de la castration *et* de la vérité. De la castration comme vérité.'[70]

While Lacan never makes the equation between the letter and the phallus explicit in his seminar, he does clearly associate the letter with the sign of the woman: 'Car ce signe est bien celui de la femme, pour ce qu'elle y fait valoir son être, en le fondant hors de la loi, qui la contient toujours, de par l'effet des origines, en position de signifiant, voire de fétiche.'[71] The letter is a sign that places the woman outside of the symbolic order: 'l'existence de la lettre la situe dans une chaîne symbolique étrangère à celle qui constitue sa foi.'[72] In addition, the letter can only place its possessor in a position of transgression with respect to phallic law: 'Ce signe ravi, voici donc l'homme en sa possession: néfaste de ce qu'elle ne peut se soutenir que de l'honneur qu'elle défie, maudite d'appeler celui qui la soutient à la punition ou au crime, qui l'une et l'autre brisent sa vassalité à la Loi.'[73]

Similarly, in *Pierre et Jean*, the portrait of Maréchal threatens the legitimate order and Mme Roland's position in it. As pointed out earlier, it necessarily defines its holder as transgressor, as is the case first with Mme Roland and then with Pierre. But the representatives of the Law are powerless to either recognize (M. Roland) or denounce (Pierre) its illicit status. When Jean and Mme Roland regain control of it, if this repossession brings with it another blind spot or constitutes another violation of symbolic law, the system appears to turn a blind eye upon it.

What we have in *Pierre et Jean* is a symbolic order that is tolerant of the breaches inflicted upon it by an illegitimate one. The one offence it cannot seem to condone is the questioning of female desire. Interestingly enough, the text finally affirms the portrait neither in its capacity as a transcendental signifier (a role to which Derrida accuses Lacan of elevating it), nor as a general equivalent cut off from the circuit of exchange (which is the role reserved for the phallus),[74] but as a 'relique douloureuse.' In other words, it is neither an indivisible totality nor a master signifier that structures a signifying chain, distributing signification and regulating exchange while itself remaining unaffected by or unsubjected to the latter. Instead, it functions as a partial object of female desire, subject to exchange and control, but yet, one that cannot (will not) be waylaid.

Pierre et Jean articulates an ambiguity to the signifier that Lacan's analysis of Poe's tale itself brings forth. The signifier is that which both ensures and threatens the stability of the law – the letter symbolizes the Queen's desire to uphold her allegiance to the law (as manifested in her attempt to ensure that it never reaches the King), as well as her transgression of it (to which the very existence of the letter attests). Similarly, in *Pierre et Jean,* the portrait is both the upholder of the legitimate symbolic order (in its capacity as a 'portrait d'ami') and a violation of it (as a 'portrait d'amant'). It is simultaneously the innocuous testament to a friendship subsumed under the dominant symbolic order, and the expression of a desire at odds with that order. The point of the portrait is not to literally confer the name 'Maréchal' upon Jean as a substitute for that of 'Roland.' Rather, it is to multiply the alternatives to that name, to allow for the emergence of a different desire. The portrait is a signifier that divides the Name of the Father and multiplies the differences to it; it frees desire from the rule of the One. There is no one axis of desire, no one Name, no one paternal law, no one transcendental phallus, unbreachable in its plenitude and totality. Rather, *Pierre et Jean* shows us that the Name of the Father can always be breached, that there is always a desire that escapes its law, and that there is always a return of what the symbolic order had to repress in order to assure its coherence. If the symbolic order has to code woman as lack in order to set up the phallus in its plenitude, this absence will find a way of making itself present. Female desire will not be diverted from its path but always return to it, always arrive at its destination *through the very signifier that supposedly stands for its lack.* The portrait is thus not so much a despotic signifier or signified of lack as a productive sign of a desire that always eludes the law of lack and repression to return as the affirmation of a difference. It is not so much an element that demands a new triangle as one that frees desire from that triangle in order to cause it to flow into a different configuration.[75]

The liberation of a desire that cannot be limited to the despotic familial code of the Oedipal, however, offers little by way of an escape for Pierre.

The Erring of Oedipus

[Q]ue se passe-t-il dans le déchiffrement psychanalytique d'un texte quand celui-ci, le déchiffré, s'explique déjà lui-même? Quand il en dit plus long que le déchiffrant? (dette plus d'une fois reconnue par Freud)? Et surtout quand il inscrit *de surcroît* en lui la scène du déchiffrement? Quand il déploie plus de force à mettre en scène et dérive le procès analytique, jusque dans son dernier mot, par exemple la vérité?

Jacques Derrida[76]

Detective fiction is analytic to the extent that it constitutes a 'backwards' reading of events. For Freud, psychoanalysis and detection are inextricably bound up with each other. The psychoanalyst's reconstruction of the aetiology of neurosis is akin to the detective's reconstruction of the crime and his reading of the patient's symptoms analogous to the detective's interpretation of the clues to a mystery.[77] The comparison between the structure of detective fiction and psychoanalysis holds for the analysand as well – a parallel Freud establishes at the very moment he glimpses the unique status of *Oedipus Rex* as the key narrative of the human psyche. 'The action of the play consists of nothing other than the process of revealing, with cunning delays and ever-mounting excitement, that Oedipus himself is the murderer of Laius, but further, that he is the son of the murdered man and Jocasta.'[78] Like detective work, psychoanalysis is a narrative that seeks to establish a meaningful coherence between beginnings and ends, origin and destination.

By emphasizing the inadequacy of its protagonist's interpretive and narrative power, *Pierre et Jean* problematizes not only the prototypical plot of detective fiction, but the very status of psychoanalysis as a master narrative. Pierre finds himself foiled in his attempts to pierce the enigma of his mother's desire, to know and vanquish feminine alterity. As detective and analyst, Pierre fails both in his attempts to narrate and narrativize. In fact, the analyst himself turns out to be the analysand: Pierre's entire investigation is placed under the sign of a dream sequence, a nightmare: 'Pierre avait ouvert les yeux et regardait, surpris d'être là, réveillé de son cauchemar' (128). And like all dreams, this one will have its own blind spot, its own resisting knot or 'navel.'[79] Oedipal vision runs up against an alterity it cannot master. *Pierre et Jean* shows an Oedipal journey with no redemptive beyond: Pierre's condemnation to the existence of a 'bête errante' refuses to confirm him in the position of a knowing and masterful subject. Maupassant's novel is a telling of the erring of psychoanalysis, the irredeemable exile of its narrative from itself.[80] The psychoanalytical dream is already haunted by the spectre of its impossibility.

Pierre et Jean, while structured according to the Oedipal paradigm whose despotism feminists have denounced, deconstructs its parameters to allow for the expression of an alternative feminine desire. It is thus a text that performs an auto-critique of the Oedipal scenario, the effects of whose deviance and dysfunction are nothing less than cruel for its protagonist. Not content with a subversion of the Oedipal structure, *Pierre et Jean* pushes its critique of the latter to a point where it reveals itself to be an always and already distorted configuration within which desire comes to be trapped. The Oedipal can only generate a despotic and paranoid narrative of desire. The novel's highlighting of the failure of the Oedipal quest for truth, its understanding of the limits of Oedipal vision, and its condemnation of Oedipal desire challenge key feminist assumptions regarding the subjectivity and desire engaged in writing. If there is an Oedipus in *Pierre et Jean*, he is one who seems to have a very difficult time with the Oedipal scenario.

In this sense, a text written by one of the most infamous misogynists of the latter half of the nineteenth century poses a serious challenge to any accusation of narcissism that may be levelled against Oedipus, and asks us to reconsider some feminist assumptions regarding the masculine order's relationship to feminine alterity. It is in order to respond to the demand generated by Maupassant's novel that I would now like to turn my attention to the work of Luce Irigaray, and the myths of Narcissus and Pygmalion in the following chapter.

2 The Error of Narcissus

As we saw in chapter 1, a male-authored text structured according to the paradigm of the Oedipal reveals what one might term a surprising willingness to accommodate feminine difference and, by so doing, questions a fundamental feminist tenet with respect to the solipsistic nature of masculine desire. The narcissism of masculine desire has received its most compelling theoretical elaboration in the work of feminist philosopher Luce Irigaray, whose critique of the phallogocentrism of philosophy and psychoanalysis is based on the premise that they are driven by the desire of and for the self-same. Psychophilosophical speculation (or thought) depends upon a principle of identity and sameness, privileging a single model of (masculine) subjectivity that is constructed at the expense of the feminine. For instance, one of the great dualisms of Western philosophical discourse, that of spirit/matter, is rooted in a denial of the generative powers of the feminine and its exclusion from the scene of representation. Masculine desire works to occlude the feminine and to repress this occlusion.

The purpose of this chapter is to demonstrate the limits of the above theses when applied to literature and to suggest that art and writing do not function as spaces of narcissistic speculation and reflection. To deconstruct the notion of male narcissism, I first show how the psychoanalytical understanding of desire as structured by an illusion inscribes itself within a long line of interpretations that views the relationship of Narcissus to the mirror as determined by falsehood and deception, one which Irigarary's analysis leaves in place. With specific regard to feminist literary criticism, Narcissus and Pygmalion have often been enlisted to understand the dialectics of desire between a male artist and his female creation, a dialectics structured by the dualisms of same/not-same, self/

other, idea/matter, and spirit/nature. Literature and art are seen as mirrors of masculine self-representation, constructed through an appropriation of feminine materiality. For example, Peter Brooks's reading of Pygmalion as emblematic of Western realism builds upon a conception of desire that pits a masculine desire for knowledge against a feminine body that must be known and mastered.

To work through some of the above assumptions, I use a text by one of the founding fathers of nineteenth-century realism, Balzac's *Le chef-d'oeuvre inconnu*. In this tale, which explores the relationship between a male artist and his female creation, I show how the figure of the woman no longer functions as a site of mastery for a narcissistic and solipsistic subject. In fact, the work of art created breaks with representation and signification, ceasing to function as a speculatory surface for a cogito. Balzac, who clearly conceives of artistic activity as a dominance of mind over matter, and of the artist as a being who enters history through his power to become, transform, and negate, writes a text that escapes this thesis. The artist's canvas and work become the loci of an encounter with the alterity of a (feminine) materiality he cannot master. Enlisting the theoretical ideas of Jean-Joseph Goux, I demonstrate that Balzac's artist creates a painting that moves away from the reflective operation of the mirror, thereby instituting a rupture with the Cartesian mirror of self-representation and inaugurating a different mode of subjectivity. The mimetic relation to the materiality gives way to a productive mimesis that Irigarary claims for feminine writing, one in which matter is no longer subjected to idea and spirit. Finally, I show that Balzac's text escapes the philosophy of representation towards a radical alterity irreducible to the dialectics of the same. I conclude the chapter with a call to reconsider the use and usefulness of the myths of Narcissus and Pygmalion in feminist interpretations of male-authored texts.

Looking-Glass Ties

'Women,' wrote Virginia Woolf in 1929, 'have served all these centuries as looking-glasses possessing the magic and delicious power of reflecting the figure of man at twice its natural size.'[1] Nowhere perhaps has the 'woman as looking-glass' metaphor been analysed more painstakingly or argued with greater power than in Luce Irigaray's *Speculum de l'autre femme*. Published forty-three years after Woolf's essay, this bold, irreverent, and ambitious work takes a close 'look' at philosophical thought and at the figures of discourse that work to construct it. Central to Irigaray's thesis is a critique of the 'occulocentrism' of philosophy, of the visual and scopic regimes that subtend its modes of knowledge. In a tradition that runs from Plato to Freud, she argues, the logic of thought is dominated by the visual metaphor. Theoretical discourse anchors itself in the specular ('theory' comes from the Greek *theorein* which means to see or to contemplate), and its epistemological project (to enlighten, clarify, illuminate, and reflect upon) cannot dissociate itself from the visual. Psycho-philosophical speculation depends upon a mirroring effect, on the principle of identity and sameness. Woman functions as a speculum or a mirror for the self-reflexive, solipsistic male subject, but this debt is occluded by the phallocentric order. Her position within the 'echo-nomy' of the narcissistic male subject is that of passive reflexivity. 'Miroir fidèle, poli et vacant de réflexions altérantes. Vierge d'auto-copies. Autre parce qu'au seul service du sujet même auquel il présenterait ses surfaces candides dans leur ignorance de soi.'[2] Philosophical discourse cannot accommodate sexual difference; its supposed neutrality is in fact an unacknowledged male isomorphism driven by the desire of and for the same. The subjectivity denied to women is what enables any theory of the subject to sustain itself through its power to reduce sexual difference to the economy of the same, within 'les systèmes auto-représentatifs d'un "sujet masculin."'[3] As for woman, she is banished, '[h]ors scène, hors représentation, hors jeu, hors je.'[4]

The major philosophical dualism that Irigaray seeks to open up (one which underlies discourses of the subject and subjectivity, of truth, knowledge, and transcendence) is that of the opposition spirit/matter. Once again, in a tradition that begins with Plato, Aristotle, and Plotinus, and runs through Descartes, Kant, and Hegel, Woman is figured as nature/matter. In other words, as the inferior term of the binary. Idea/truth/spirit is associated with the active male principle, while inert matter/earth/nature is associated with the female one. As a passive receptacle incapable of generative powers, matter is a meaningless and unintelligible mass that can only accede to being through an encounter with form. For Irigaray, the split operated by philosophical discourse between the ideal and the material, intelligible and sensible, form and matter, and the inscription of the feminine as the secondary term of each binary excludes woman from the scene of representation. The female capacity to engender and create is obliterated and appropriated by the male term: 'Ils ont montré d'assez loin, mais autant qu'ils l'ont pu, que cette "mère universelle" était stérile et n'était pas, absolument parlant, une femme; elle est femme dans la mesure où la femme reçoit, mais non plus en tant que la femme est capable de procréer.'[5] The site of the feminine is configured as a specular surface that guarantees the autonomy of the masculine economy but is unable to participate in it. Thus, the naming of the feminine within the masculine economy paradoxically constitutes its erasure from it. As such, it is the tain of the mirror, the non-figurable, or rather, a figure that can only exist as an 'excès dérangeant.'

Irigaray's project then becomes to reopen and dismantle the figures of philosophical discourse by questioning the largely occulted and repressed bases of its systems of self-representation and the conditions that render its systemacity possible. Irigarary here outlines a feminist politics of reading that involves a return to the scene of representation, to the 'theatrical' operations at work in its production:

> Ainsi la '*matière*' dont se nourrit le sujet parlant pour se produire, se reproduire; *la scénographie* qui rend praticable la représentation telle qu'elle se définit en philosophie, c'est-à-dire l'architectonique de son théâtre, son cadrage de l'espace-temps, son économie géometrique, son ameublement, ses acteurs, leurs positions respectives, leurs dialogues, voire leurs rapports tragiques, sans oublier *le miroir*, le plus souvent masqué, qui permet au logos, au sujet de se redoubler, de se réfléchir, lui-même. Toutes interventions dans la scène qui, restées ininterpretées, assurent sa cohérence. Il faut donc les faire rejouer, dans chaque figure du discours, pour le déconcerter de son ancrage dans la valeur de "présence". Pour chaque philosophe – à commencer par ceux qui ont déterminé une époque de l'histoire ou de la philosophie – , il faut repérer comment s'opère la coupure d'avec la contiguïté matérielle, le montage du système, l'économie spéculaire.[6]

The strategy through which the feminine can accomplish this project (and one which Irigaray herself employs in *Speculum*) is that of 'le mimétisme.' This consists of a deliberate taking up of one's position within the logic of phallocentric discourse in order to undo its systemacity and to reveal the material operation of the feminine:

> Jouer de la mimésis, c'est donc, pour une femme, tenter de retrouver le lieu de son exploitation par le discours, sans s'y laisser simplement réduire. C'est se resoumettre – en tant que du côté du 'sensible,' de la 'matière' ... – à des 'idées,' notamment d'elle, élaborées dans/par une logique masculine, mais pour faire 'apparaître,' par un effet de répétition ludique, ce qui devait rester occulté: le recouvrement d'une possible opération du féminin dans le langage. C'est aussi 'dévoiler' le fait que, si les femmes miment si

bien, c'est qu'elles ne se résorbent pas simplement dans cette fonction. *Elles restent aussi ailleurs*: autre insistance de 'matière,' mais aussi de 'jouissance.'[7]

In lieu of the flat mirror of mimetic representation (the *speculum mundi*), Irigaray proposes the curved surface of the speculum, with its distortions and anamorphoses. In the feminine disconcerting of language, 'ce "style" ou "écriture" de la femme met plutôt feu aux mots fétiches, aux termes propres, aux formes bien construites ... Son "style" résiste à, et fait exploser, toute forme, figure, idée, concept, solidement établis.'[8] While Irigaray's feminine strategy calls for breaking (with) a certain mode of specularity, she also insists on retaining the metaphor of the mirror and its plane of representation within such a politics of re-reading and rewriting. What Irigaray proposes is not a turning away from the mirror, but a journey through the looking glass, a crossing into its 'other' side in order to uncover what lies behind its surface:

> Et, s'il s'agit bien de briser (avec) un certain mode de spécula(risa)tion, ce n'est pas pour autant qu'il faille renoncer à tout miroir, ni se soustraire à l'analyse de l'emprise de ce *plan* de la représentation qui rend aphasique, et plus généralement atonique, le désir féminin si ce n'est en ses mascarades et revendications phallomorphes. Car l'esquive de ce temps d'interpréta-tion aboutit à ce qu'il se refige, reperde, recoupe. Encore. Mais peut-être qu'au-delà de cette surface spéculaire, qui supporte le discours, s'annonce non le vide du rien mais l'éblouissement d'une spéléologie aux facettes innombrables. Concavité scintillante et incandescante, aussi du langage, qui menace d'ignition les objets fétiches et les yeux aurifiés ... Car là où devrait se retrouver la matrice opaque et silencieuse d'un logos immuable dans la certitude de ses lumières commencent plutôt à briller feux et glaces, qui minent l'évidence de la raison.[9]

Irigaray's sophisticated and compelling use of the mirror metaphor has captivated an entire generation of feminist critics. After all, according to the traditional psychoanalytical view, narcissism was primarily the lot of women. In this respect, the subtle dexterity with which Irigaray turns Freud's speculation upon itself has been a celebratory move for feminism. Feminism's deep-rooted iconoclasm (apparent in the suspi-cion it harbours towards the images of women circulated by and within an oppressive male economy) has no doubt received a strong impetus from the reverse positioning of the male as Narcissus. It has also done much to uncover the disavowed stakes of a largely closed, self-reflexive, and self-referential system of representation.

But what if Narcissus were aware? What curvatures, what anamorphoses might then disturb the specular surface in which both Narcissus and feminism encounter themselves? Or each other? What ripples might disturb the site in and out of which the feminine is inscribed? How else might the 'hom(m)osexuality' of Narcissus be read? And in what other way could his error matter?

Of Narcissus and Narcissism

'Yes, yes, I'm he! I've seen through that deceit:
my image cannot trick me anymore.'

Ovid[10]

Narcissus is aware. Aware of the self-deception he is mired in, aware of the folly of his misplaced desire. Neither blind, nor smug, he 'chooses' to remain prey to an illusion, knowing full well that death is the only outcome that awaits him. Ovid's Narcissus does not stay duped for long; he eventually reaches the moment of self-recognition. He becomes aware of his error.

The psychoanalytical formulations of narcissism (and the feminist appropriation thereof) occlude this instant of awareness in Ovid's narrative. A look at the symbolic history of the myth shows that Freud's concept of narcissism is based on a reading that inscribes itself within an interpretive tradition that has changed very little since classical times.[11] Ovid provides the earliest and most elaborate account of the myth, and his is the only version that divides the narrative into two principal moments: the error and the recognition of error. Other versions of the myth that were either contemporary to or came later than Ovid's, do not mention this moment of recognition. In every other account of the myth, Narcissus remains an unknowing and gullible victim of a delusion. Ovid's *Metamorphoses* provided the most popular and widespread version of the myth but its symbolic use in literature, philosophy, and aesthetic and moral treatises has overwhelmingly ignored his knowing Narcissus – at least, up until the eighteenth century.

Prior to the eighteenth century then, the error of Narcissus is seen as the most important theme of the myth, and it is the stage before the recognition that is privileged. The Narcissus who understands the illusion of which he is the victim, who realizes that it is himself he loves, that it is his own beauty with which he is enamoured, seems to have little, if no interest for writers. The story of Narcissus is read primarily as an allegory of the *vanitas* motif: 'It is not the conscious self-reflection that Narcissus represents to them, but rather the confusion of illusion and reality.'[12]

The two most important readings of the myth in this light are offered by Plotinus and Ficinus, both of whom were deeply influenced by Plato. In a treatise that discusses the relationship between spiritual and material beauty, Plotinus notes:

> When he perceives those shapes of grace that show in body, let him not pursue: he must know them for copies, vestiges, shadows, and hasten away towards That they tell of. For if anyone follow what is like a beautiful shape playing over water – is there not a myth telling in symbol of such a dupe, how he sank into the depths of the current and was swept away to nothingness? So too, one that is held by material beauty and will not break free shall be precipitated, not in body but in Soul, down to the dark depths loathed of Intellective-Being, where, blind even in the Lower-World, he shall have commerce only with shadows, there as here.[13]

For Plotinus, the myth illustrates the idea that material beauty is a deception that can lead to spiritual ruin. According to Louise Vinge, although the allusion to Narcissus is not explicit in the above passage, the 'dupe' referred to by Plotinus has often been understood as Narcissus, and this reading has had a lasting influence in shaping the meaning of the myth. The interpretation of the myth by Plotinus also establishes the mirror as a metaphor for illusory matter. For Plotinus, beauty cannot be attained in the earthly world, for there it is mere image. Material beauty is but a deceptive reflection of a purer, essential beauty.

In the fifteenth century, Ficinus takes up the myth of Narcissus in a similar manner, seeing in it a metaphor for the position of the soul with respect to material and spiritual beauty:

> – our soul alone is so carried away by the enticements of the beauty of the body that it neglects its own and, forgetful of its own beauty, worships the beauty of the body instead, which is the reflection of its own. Hence Narcissus' cruel fate with Orpheus ... *The young Narcissus*, that is to say the soul of the daring and inexperienced man, *does not study his own face*, by no means does he regard his own substance and his real essence. But he tries to reach its reflection in the water and embrace it – that is to say, he admires the

beauty in the body, which is fragile and like running water, and that is the reflection of the soul itself. *But thereby he abandons his own form. The shadow he never reaches.* For the soul forgets itself when striving for the body and is not satisfied with the enjoyment of the body. What it actually strives for is not the body itself but its own beauty, although like Narcissus it is deceived by the bodily beauty, which is the image of its own beauty.[14]

Here as earlier with Plotinus, Narcissus represents the confusion between truth and falsehood. As one who is lead away from true beauty because he is captivated by its material image in the water, he is emblematic of self-ignorance and self-deception.

In an interesting twist, it is the eighteenth century, with its redeployment of the Renaissance engagement with a concept that has its roots in classical antiquity, that moves the myth of Narcissus towards the dictum 'Know thyself.' First, with Diderot and Rousseau (influenced by English thinkers such as Young and Shaftesbury), self-knowledge and introspection become the defining values of the time. Narcissus has become a symbol of conscious self-reflection. Swedenborg later uses the myth to illustrate the idea that man's body constitutes a *parvulus typus mundi* or a smaller model of the world, the understanding of which leads to an understanding of the universe.

In a more interesting development, however, it is with the Schlegel brothers that Narcissus is used to represent the relationship between the self and artistic creation. As a figure of poetic reflection and subjectivity, Narcissus symbolizes the self-knowledge of the artistic genius, of the self-awareness of creative power. Keats employs the drooping narcissus flower as an aesthetic symbol of the striving towards beauty. The Romantic trope of the artist as Narcissus and of the self-consciousness of the poet continues to be seen in Mallarmé, Valéry, and Rilke, but 'moins par une introversion complaisante que pour tenter de saisir et de fixer, au-delà des formes fugitives, leur propre essence.'[15] In this light, the endeavour of Narcissus appears to resemble the Platonic striving towards a spiritual beauty divested of material reality, as opposed to earlier readings by Plotinus and Ficinus, which saw him as entrapped by the material. With the Symbolists, Narcissus once more becomes the figure of aesthetic self-consciousness, of the relationship between the poet and the work of art.

How is it that after being liberated from his illusions in the eighteenth and nineteenth centuries, Narcissus finds himself mired in them once again in the twentieth with Freud and Lacan? And especially by psychoanalytical feminism? While the response to the above questions would necessitate an inquiry that extends beyond the scope of the present one, I would like to explore the spaces opened up by them to go back to the paradoxical duality of Narcissus – a duality that has perhaps been elided in the feminist setting up of the male as Narcissus. I would like to hazard the tentative hypothesis that the male subject does not unthinkingly assume that what is reflected in his specular field is anything other than a symmetrical mirror image. On the contrary, like Narcissus, he displays a surprising (if tormented) awareness of the illusion that undermines the relationship between desire and the object of desire. The specular gaze, in other words, can be self-conscious. Narcissus is not always narcissistic.

It is in order to explore the self-awareness of the masculine gaze that I would henceforth like to turn to two short stories by Balzac, *Le chef-d'oeuvre inconnu* (which will constitute the primary focus of this chapter) and *Sarrasine* (with which I deal in greater detail in chapter 3). The artist's quest for perfect representation forms the key theme of both texts, where the problem of artistic creation functions as a *mise-en-abyme* for the problem of literary representation. In this respect, the narratives may be said to constitute a self-conscious reflection upon the conditions of their own production. To the extent that the representational crisis is lived by the male artist and is centred on the figure of woman in both texts, I would like to suggest that *Le chef-d'oeuvre inconnu* and *Sarrasine* constitute a complex questioning of the scene of representation, of the very kind that Irigaray calls for within a feminist agenda. The mimetic enterprise of the text cannot be dissociated from the mimetic strategy that Irigaray earmarks for the feminine. If the problem of artistic creation serves as a *mise-en-abyme* for that of literary representation, the scene of literary representation functions as a *mise-en-abyme* for that of philosophical representation, where literature seems to undo the figures of discourse that sustain philosophy. In other words, if for Irigaray, philosophical discourse appears to offer little besides an unreflective and solipsistic male subject, literature seems to constitute another matter altogether.

Realism, Representation, and the Question of Woman

In his book *Body Work*, Peter Brooks seeks to disentangle the complex nexus that binds together 'sight, knowledge, truth and woman's body.' He starts out with the premise that in the Western literary tradition (one that goes back to Homer), identity and the body are closely intertwined. The *Odyssey* depicts a scene (made famous by Auerbach in his *Mimesis: The Representation of Reality in Western Literature*) in which the disguised

Odysseus is recognized by his old nurse Eurykleia because of a scar on his thigh. This dramatic moment of recognition (or in Aristotlean terms of *anagnorisis*) comes about through a bodily mark or sign. The passage from non-knowledge to knowledge is effectuated through a reading of what functions as a linguistic signifier. The body is inscribed with a mark that allows it to form part of a signifying process. The marking of the body signals its entry into narrative, first, because the inscribing of the sign onto the body constitutes a story (at this point Homer recounts how Odysseus received the scar), and second, because this marking in turn generates a story. The representation of the body in writing transforms it into both a literary and a narrative body: 'The signing of the body is an allegory of the body become a subject for literary narrative – a body entered into writing.'[16]

For Auerbach, Homer's description of the above scene of recognition emblematizes one of the founding gestures of Western realism. In this sense, the representation of reality seems to be closely tied to the representation of the body. The link between the realist enterprise, narrative, and the body is picked up by Barthes in *S/Z*, when he notes that '[l]e champ symbolique est occupé par un seul objet, dont il tire son unité (et dont nous avons tiré un certain droit à le nommer, un certain plaisir à le décrire et comme l'apparence d'un privilège accordé au système des symboles, à l'aventure symbolique du héros, sculpteur ou narrateur). Cet objet est le corps humain.'[17] According to Brooks, Barthes's intuition can be read 'as a claim that the body is the referent of reference itself, that meaning is always constructed in relation to the body and that all narration is impelled by the desire to transform the body into a text.'[18]

Narrative, in other words, seeks to know and possess the body by mastering the process whereby the body comes to signify. Narrative creates meaning through its effort to semiotize the body. This epistemological project is structured by what Sartre refers to as the 'Actaeon Complex': 'One pulls off the veils of nature, one unveils it ... any research always involves the idea of a nudity that one exposes by putting aside the obstacles that cover it, as Actaeon pushes aside the branches the better to see Diana at her bath.'[19] The positioning of Actaeon as a voyeur finds a curious echo in Barthes's model of classical narrative that, according to him, unfolds through 'un dévoilement progressif [où] toute l'excitation se réfugie dans l'*espoir* de voir le sexe (rêve de collégien) ou de connaître la fin de l'histore (satisfaction romanesque).'[20] By further likening the pleasure afforded by such narrative to an Oedipal pleasure,[21] Barthes reinforces the knot that ties together sight, desire, knowledge, and woman:

Ainsi, un doigt, de son mouvement désignateur et muet, accompagne toujours le texte classique: la vérité est de la sorte longuement désirée et con-
tournée, maintenue dans une sorte de plénitude enceinte, dont la percée, à
la fois libératoire et catastrophique, accomplira la fin même du discours; et
le personnage, espace même de ces signifiés, n'est jamais que le passage de
l'énigme, de cette forme nominative de l'énigme dont Oedipe (dans son
débat avec le Sphynx) a empreint mythiquement tout le discours occiden-
tal.[22]

Barthes's and Sartre's respective uses of the myths of Actaeon and Oedipus posit the epistemic enterprise and the source from which it ema-
nates as predominantly male. Scopophilia and epistemophilia are in-
variably bound up with the figure of woman. That which the epistemic
project seeks to dis-cover is woman.

For Brooks, literature is animated by a desire to recover the materiality
of the body as a site for the inscription of meaning. Writing tries to recuperate the body as a locus of signification, and it does so by stamping it
with a mark or branding it: 'The bodily marking not only serves to recognize and identify, it also indicates the body's passage into the realm of
the letter, into literature: the bodily mark is in some manner a 'character,' a hieroglyph, a sign that can eventually, at the right moment of the
narrative, be read. Signing the body indicates its recovery for the realm
of the semiotic.' The interplay between creative and erotic desire, between the desire to semiotize the body and to possess it through writing,
is perfectly illustrated in the myth of Pygmalion. As a story of 'how the
body can be known, animated and possessed by the artist of desire, and
of how the body marked, imprinted, by desire can enter narrative,' it is
emblematic of the aesthetics of realism, where a desiring subject seeks to
inscribe meaning onto a desired body. While the desiring subject may be
a character within the narrative, it is 'always also the creator of the narrative, whose desire for the body is part of a semiotic project to make the
body signify, to make it part of the narrative dynamic.'[23]

Brooks's understanding of the aesthetics of Western realism thus re-
deploys many of the 'mythical' structures that have served to analyse
masculine desire and its relationship to the (feminine) body. His thesis
echoes Naomi Schor's groundbreaking reading of nineteenth-century
French realism as a representational system founded on the binding of
the female body, a critique strongly influenced by Irigaray's work. 'Realism,' notes Schor, 'is that paradoxical moment in Western literature
when representation can neither accommodate the Otherness of woman

nor exist without it.'[24] Brooks reads the myth of Pygmalion in opposition
to that of Narcissus. To the extent that it is fulfilled under the auspices of
Venus, Pygmalion's desire is a valid, legitimate desire for the other, in
contrast to that of Narcissus, which is a vain and impossible desire for the
self-same. In this respect, argues Brooks, the figure of Pygmalion is that
of an anti-Narcissus.

A closer look at the two myths reveals, however, that they are structured by a similar dynamics of desire. To be sure, the desire of Narcissus
is not only illusory but also placed under the sign of a curse. At the
request of the gods, Nemesis wreaks her vengeance upon Narcissus because he is impassible to the desire of an (other): Narcissus spurns the
love of nymphs and boys alike. His refusal to acknowledge the desire of
the other is viewed as a violation of divine order, a transgression for
which the gods exact their punishment. Pygmalion's desire for Galathea
springs out of a similar gesture of scorn:

> Pygmalion had seen the shameless lives
> of Cyprus' women; and disgusted by
> the many sins to which the female mind
> had been inclined by nature, he resigned
> himself: for years he lived alone, without
> a spouse: he chose no wife to share his couch.[25]

Galathea is first created not out of a desire for the other, but in its very
absence. It is only after the statue is completed that it moves Pygmalion:

> Meanwhile, Pygmalion began to carve
> in snow-white ivory, with wondrous art,
> a female figure more exquisite than
> a woman who was born could ever match.
> That done, he falls in love with his own work.
> The image seems, in truth, to be a girl;
> ...
> He is enchanted and, within his heart,
> *the likeness of a body now ignites*
> *a flame.* (335–6; emphasis mine)

Like Narcissus, Pygmalion's desire is first aroused by an image which is
not that of the other; like Narcissus, Pygmalion is first captivated by an illusion and then moved by the desire to possess it.

While my work in the present chapter owes much to Brooks's insights, it is here that I would like to slightly part company with him. My divergence stems from a small, almost anodyne detail that Brooks's reading seems to ignore – that even if it is made possible by invoking the grace of Venus, it is only after a kiss from Pygmalion that the statue shows signs of life. Although Brooks's reading rightly underscores Pygmalion's debt to Venus, it does so at the expense of the power invested in Pygmalion by Ovid's text. According to Brooks, it is only after Galathea is brought to life by Venus that she can receive the mark of Pygmalion's thumb and take her place within the signifying chain: 'Hands, fingers, thumbs; they make no imprint on the ivory maiden, except in Pygmalion's momentary hallucination. But when she becomes flesh and blood, they leave their imprint, as in wax; and the thumb then feels the pulse throbbing beneath it.'[26] But this is to ignore the fact that it is only after receiving Pygmalion's touch through a kiss that the statue is brought to life. It is this act that literally breathes life into the statue, makes it yield to his mark, and causes its veins to pulsate with blood:

> At once, Pygmalion, at home again,
> seeks out the image of the girl; he bends
> over his couch; he kisses her. And when
> it seems her lips are warm, he leans again
> to kiss her; and he reaches with his hands
> to touch her breasts. The ivory had lost
> its hardness; now his fingers probe; grown soft,
> the statue yields beneath the sculptor's touch,
> just as Hymettian wax beneath the sun
> grows soft and, molded by the thumb, takes on
> so many varied shapes – in fact, becomes
> more pliant as one plies it. Stupefied,
> delighted yet in doubt, afraid that he
> may be deceived, the lover tests his dream:
> it is a body! Now the veins – beneath
> his anxious fingers – pulse. (337)

Venus acts not independently of Pygmalion but through him.

Ovid's myth thus inscribes within its narrative not one but two moments of creation: the first moment when Pygmalion creates his statue, and the second when, after praying to Venus, he comes home and runs his hands over it. It is the second moment that functions as a description of the artistic act, the process whereby a work of art is created, 'brought to life.' We are given no such elaborate depiction of the initial moment of creation, only a statement to the effect that a work has been produced. Ovid's text clearly privileges the second moment as the 'true' scene of the creative act and of artistic power.

The above scene where Pygmalion essentially remoulds and reworks Galathea's statue establishes a powerful metaphor of creation that finds an echo in Plato and Plotinus, and that informs theories of artistic representation for centuries – that the female constitutes the matter (the amorphous wax) on which the male imposes a form. In other words, matter is meaningless in itself and unable to contribute to the creative process; it can only become significant by participating in a form. Initially, Galathea is presented as an image that only appears to be a girl, a mere 'likeness of a body.' Her statue functions very much like the matter that Plotinus describes, one that 'is no more than the image and phantasm of Mass, a bare aspiration towards substantial existence.'[27] In this respect, it is a deception, 'a mirror showing things as in itself when they are really elsewhere, filled in appearance but actually empty, containing nothing, pretending everything.'[28] The space reserved for Galathea in the myth of Pygmalion is that of matter as 'the mere absence of Reality.' Created in the absence of masculine desire, her statue is 'but ivory'; it cannot accede to bodyhood. It is only at the second moment of creation in the narrative of the myth, when she is refashioned according to Pygmalion's desire, that she becomes a body. Only an ideal form dictated by masculine desire can help the statue acquire the status of a body.

Interestingly, after Pygmalion falls in love with his statue, he dares not ask Venus for his ivory girl, but instead, asks for one 'like his ivory girl.' Brought to life as the image of an image, Galathea is thus doubly removed from reality – first as matter, non-being, non-entity; and second, as a creation modelled in the image of an illusory non-other. This leads us to suspect that no mythic figure is perhaps more narcissistic than Pygmalion, or to put it in another way, he is an anti-Narcissus yes, but to the extent that he never steps out of the bounds of an unreflective solipsism.

Narcissus, Pygmalion, and the Metaphors of Feminism

Impregnating discourses of art and philosophy, the myths of Narcissus and Pygmalion resonate with implications for feminism. Feminism's (and notably Irigaray's) challenge to the phallogocentrism of philosophical and literary representation has taken as its starting point an uncovering of the metaphors constructed by these myths. But what could a feminist reading of the myths of Narcissus and Pygmalion conceal of the biases of its own discourse? What might be overlooked in its recuperation of these metaphors? Could an understanding of these omissions avoid petrifying the very figures of discourse that feminism seeks to open up in the first place? These are issues important enough to warrant a return to the metaphors of both phallocentric and feminist discourse, to the myths of Narcissus and Pygmalion. Opening up the myths demands that we read them both with and against phallocentrism, with and against feminism, and more crucially, with and against each other. It is perhaps a more complex Narcissus who can pave the way for a more complex Pygmalion, and perhaps an aware Narcissus who can move us towards an unsolipsistic Pygmalion.

> There was a pool whose waters, silverlike,
> were gleaming, bright. Its borders had no slime.
> No shepherds, no she-goats, no other herds
> of cattle heading for the hills disturbed
> that pool; its surface never had been stirred
> by fallen branch, wild animal, or bird.
> Fed by its waters, rich grass ringed its edge,
> and hedges served to shield it from the sun.[29]

Until Narcissus happens to project his image onto the pool, it remains an empty space that even the sun has not been able to penetrate. Flat, motionless, and mute, it lies awaiting Narcissus to inscribe its surface with an image.

The pool represents the space that Irigaray sees reserved for the feminine within a phallocentric economy – that of a mirror incapable of reflecting anything but the male subject, passive matter that only exists as a possibility for his self-inscription:

> Matière pour reproduction, miroir pour redoublement, la femme du philosophe devra encore assurer cette *caution d'un narcissisme souvent extrapolé dans une dimension transcendantale.* Certes sans le dire, sans le savoir. Ce secret ne devra surtout jamais se dévoiler. Ce rôle n'est possible que par son dérobement ultime à la prospection: une virginité inapte à la réflexion de soi.[30]

Like Plato's *chora*, it is the silent screen for the projection of an image,

the stage of masculine self-representation that guarantees the emergence of the subject. It is on the surface of the pool that we are first given
a complete description of Narcissus:

> ... And he gazes in dismay
> at his own self; he cannot turn away
> his eyes; he does not stir; he is as still
> as any statue carved of Parian marble.
> Stretched out along the ground, he stares again,
> again at the twin stars that are his eyes;
> at his fair hair, which can compare with Bacchus'
> or with Apollo's; at his beardless cheeks
> and at his ivory neck, his splendid mouth,
> the pink blush on a face as white as snow;
> in sum, he now is struck with wonder by
> what's wonderful in him.[31]

The description of the image of Narcissus in the pool functions as that
of a painting,[32] the strategy of *ekphrasis* bringing into play the relationship between the figurative and the written, between painting and literature.

Balzac's *Le chef-d'oeuvre inconnu* is a narrative that goes to the heart of
this relationship. His tale of an artist obsessed with the creation of a perfect painting does more than recruit a visual art to serve as an analogy for
the literary project; it engages the scopic regimes that underlie both en-
terprises to embark on a complex reflection of the issue of representation. And when the central stake of this question is the figure of woman,
we have a narrative that, much like the myth of Pygmalion, functions as
the core at which woman, desire, and representational power intersect.

'Woman and paper are two blank things that suffer everything.'[33] The
body of the woman is conflated with the space where writing occurs,
where knowledge and meaning may be inscribed. In this conceptualization of the relationship between the author and his text, we find echoes
of the cluster of metaphors against which feminism has sought to position itself :

Form	$\Rightarrow$	Matter
Pygmalion	$\Rightarrow$	Galathea
Narcissus	$\Rightarrow$	Image/Pool/Reflection
Artist/Author/Writer	$\Rightarrow$	Woman

Is Balzac's writing then to be yet another illustration of the unequal power relations that feminist critics have denounced in nineteenth-century art?[34] It is in order to determine the response to this question that I would like to read Le chef-d'oeuvre inconnu and Sarrasine in the light of the myths of Narcissus and Pygmalion. As seen earlier, both mythic figures are closely associated with each other, and Pygmalion is often seen as the double of Narcissus.[35] Even if I believe that a simple conflation of the two figures does violence to the complexity of Narcissus, I would nevertheless like to retain the parallel drawn between them. What I wish to suggest is that in both texts, Pygmalion's relationship to Galathea, like that of Narcissus to his reflection, is not quite as unproblematical as one might be led to expect. My reading of the texts will be guided by the supposition that the dialectics of gaze at work in these texts operates within a two-tiered framework – the relationship between the author/narrator and his text and that of the male protagonist with the female character in the narrative. The authors do not exhibit the classical symptoms of male narcissism by simply projecting their desires and fantasies onto a mirror-like other within the space of the text (a role usually reserved for the trope of the feminine), but rather, use the male protagonist to show that such a myopic endeavour is inevitably bound to fail. By drawing attention to the asymmetries that displace the male protagonist's efforts to pin the figure of the woman into a self-same image, they try to accomplish what Narcissus himself was unable to do – detract his gaze and desire towards a true other. In this respect, they perform the same task that Irigaray sets aside for the feminist critic; they reengage with the scene and space of representation in order to recuperate the occluded operation of the feminine, to recover what it has been denied. And what is more, the mimetic project of these texts places itself on the very side of the divide where Irigaray locates feminine writing:

> Chez Platon, il y a deux *mimesis*. Pour aller vite: la *mimesis* comme *production*, qui serait plutôt du côté de la musique, et la *mimesis* qui serait déjà prise dans un procès d'*imitation*, de *spécularisation*, d'*adéquation*, de *reproduction*. C'est la seconde qui va être privilégiée dans toute l'histoire de la philosophie et dont on trouve les effets-symptômes comme latence, souffrance, paralysie du désir, dans l'hystérie. La première semble toujours avoir été réprimée, ne fût-ce que parce qu'elle était constituée comme une enclave dans un discours 'dominant.' Or, c'est sans doute du côté et à partir de cette première *mimesis* que peut advenir la possibilité d'une écriture de femme.[36]

What we see in Balzac is a disruption of the mimetic surface of representation, a stalling of the reproduction of 'auto-copies' by the masculine order. In both both in *Le chef-d'oeuvre inconnu* and *Sarrasine*, the threat to the coherence of psychoanalytical discourse comes through a 'feminine' distortion of the specular surface that serves to reflect and proliferate its self-same images.

Published independently of each other, *Sarrasine* and *Le chef-d'oeuvre inconnu* were subsequently united under the rubric *Romans et contes philosophiques*. How is truth constructed within the duality of a writing project where literature and philosophy intersect? And what is the space occupied by woman within this plane of intersection?

Père, amant et Dieu

In both *Le chef-d'oeuvre inconnu* and *Sarrasine*, the artist is driven by the quest for an absolute that can only be attained in a realm beyond the material. The beauty towards which the artist is impelled also constitutes a search for a spiritual truth that would be uncontaminated by the deceptive metamorphoses of nature/matter. For Balzac, the aesthetic enterprise of the poet cannot be dissociated from the intellectual quest of the philosopher. Artistic creativity is defined as the dominance of mind over matter: 'Ainsi de Gutenberg, de Colomb, de Schwartz, de Descartes, de Raphaël, de Voltaire, de David. Tous étaient artistes car ils créaient, ils appliquaient la pensée à une production nouvelle des forces humaines, à une combinaison neuve des éléments de la nature, ou physique, ou morale.'[37] The artist enters history and imposes himself on posterity through his power to create and mould his material world: 'Les rois commandent aux nations pendant un temps donné; l'artiste commande à des siècles entiers; il change la face des choses, il jette une révolution en moule; il pèse sur le globe, il le façonne' (278). Art is rendered possible by the interiority of thought freed from its dependence on nature. In this respect, art can emerge only from a break with and a move beyond nature: 'La pensée est une chose en quelque sorte contre nature. Dans les premiers âges du monde, l'homme a été *tout extérieur*. Or, les arts sont l'abus de la pensée' (285; emphasis in original).

Frenhofer's conception of art articulates itself on a similar conflict between thought/spirit and nature/matter. Inscribed under the dual sign of the poet and philosopher,[38] Frenhofer seeks (and acquires) the power to invest his creation with the truth of life. Pygmalion's power provides the metaphor for artistic genius – the true artist is one capable of imposing an inner vision and truth upon nature instead of blindly imitating it. Technical mastery and knowledge of the material medium are not sufficient to produce art; only an infusion of the artist's soul into inert and inanimate matter can. Porbus's painting 'sins' because of the soul's inability to triumph over lifeless matter:

> Prr! Il ne suffit pas pour être un grand poète de savoir à fond la syntaxe et de ne pas faire des fautes de langue! Regarde ta sainte, Porbus? ... C'est une silhouette qui n'a qu'une seule face, c'est une apparence découpée, une image qui ne saurait se retourner, ni changer de position ... [m]algré de si louables efforts, je ne saurais croire que ce beau corps soit animé par le tiède souffle de la vie ... Non, mon ami, le sang ne court pas sous cette peau d'ivoire, l'existence ne gonfle pas de sa rosée de pourpre les veines et les fibrilles qui s'entrelacent en réseaux sous la transparence ambrée des tempes de la poitrine. Cette place palpite, mais cette autre est immobile, la vie et la mort luttent dans chaque détail: ici, c'est une femme, là une statue, plus loin un cadavre. Ta création est incomplète. Tu n'as pu souffler qu'une portion de ton âme à ton oeuvre chérie. (46–7)

Needless to say, the vocabulary and tropes of the above passage establish a clear parallel between the figure of the male artist and Pygmalion, wherein Pygmalion's relationship to his statue becomes a metaphor for the artist's relationship to the matter/nature he elevates to the status of art.

In what has become a celebrated manifesto of Romantic aesthetics, Frenhofer affirms the spiritualist mission of artistic creation:

> La mission de l'art n'est pas de copier la nature, mais de l'exprimer! Tu n'es pas un vil copiste, mais un poète! ... Nous avons à saisir l'esprit, l'âme, la physionomie des choses et des êtres. Les effets! les effets! mais ils sont les accidents de la vie, et non la vie. Une main, puisque j'ai pris cet exemple, une main ne tient pas seulement au corps, elle exprime et continue une pensée qu'il faut saisir et rendre. (48)

Artistic vision is one capable of seizing the spirit and principle behind the contingency of matter/nature. The artist has to transform reality in order to express movement and life not as effect, but as cause. The artist's relationship to nature is thus confrontational and adversarial – the transfiguration of reality cannot be achieved without a struggle. Artistic success is cast in terms of a lover's amorous conquest in a discourse that sets up the figure of Woman as a metaphor for nature, as that which must be vanquished in order to create art:

Vous ne descendez pas assez dans l'intimité de la forme,[39] vous ne la poursuivez pas avec assez d'amour et de persévérance dans ses détours et dans ses fuites. La beauté est une chose sévère et difficile qui ne se laisse point atteindre ainsi, il faut attendre des heures, l'épier, la presser et l'enlacer fortement pour la forcer à se rendre. La Forme est un Protée bien plus insaisissable et plus fertile en replis que le Protée de la fable, ce n'est qu'après de longs combats qu'on peut la contraindre à se montrer sous son véritable aspect ... (48–9)

The artist has to battle and overcome the polymorphousness of matter if he is to capture its truthful essence. Matter deceives, and only the vision of the artist can 'see through' her ruses to uncover her spiritual truth. But not only must the artist be capable of seizing the essential truth behind the illusory model of nature, he should also be able to give it a body, to 'incarnate' it in his work. For Balzac, the artistic act is conceived in terms of a certain mode of conception; an idea/spirit that disposes of generative and productive powers and which has to grapple with the material conditions of creation: '*Enfin, c'est l'extase de la conception voilant les déchirantes douleurs de l'enfantement.*'[40]

Frenhofer's completion of Porbus's imperfect canvas resonates with a similar mythic symbolism – Frenhofer's retouching of the painting is placed under the sign of an ardent desire, an 'amoureuse fantaisie.' Interestingly, Frenhofer's recreation of Porbus's painting is assimilated to the harmony of '*O Filii* de Pâques,' a hymn celebrating the Resurrection of Christ. In other words, the symbolic act of spirit reincarnated into flesh.

As an artist 'qui voit plus loin et plus haut que les autres peintres,' Frenhofer's own *La Belle Noiseuse* represents the culmination of an arduous quest for ideal beauty. Frenhofer's creation is no creature of nature; she far surpasses anything nature could produce. She is a pure product of his imagination, a pure creation of masculine desire. Frenhofer believes that he has vanquished nature, that what he has succeeded in capturing on canvas is 'la nature elle-même.' Pygmalion to his Galatea, he covers her with a veil, shields her from the lewd and prying glances of others as would a lover, constantly refers to her as his mistress, and refuses to show her to another man for ten years on the grounds that such a gesture would be akin to prostitution. Frenhofer's possession of

his female creation is complete, total, and solipsistic – she has no existence, no self-consciousness, no alterity outside of the bounds of his
desire: 'Voilà dix ans que je vis avec cette femme, elle est à moi, à moi
seul, elle m'aime. Ne m'a-t-elle pas souri à chaque coup de pinceau que
je lui ai donné? Elle a une âme, une âme dont je l'ai douée' (64). His
painting is the privileged space of his libidinal investment ('Combien de
jouissances sur ce morceau de toile!' Porbus exclaims later), the locus
that affirms his fantasy of mastery: 'Ma peinture n'est pas une peinture,
c'est un sentiment, une passion! Née dans mon atelier, elle doit y rester
vierge et n'en peut sortir que vêtue. La poésie et les femmes ne se livrent
nues qu'à leurs amants' (64). The power of his vision has managed to
unite in art the essence of what was thus far a fragmentary and imperfect
material beauty. But he cannot be sure of his victory until he has satisfied
himself that no earthly being could rival the perfection of his own creation: '[I]l m'a manqué jusqu'à présent de rencontrer une femme irre-
prochable, un corps dont les contours soient d'une beauté parfaite, et
dont la carnation... Mais où est-elle vivante ... cette introuvable Vénus des
anciens, si souvent cherchée, et de qui nous rencontrons à peine
quelques beautés éparses? Oh! pour voir un moment, une seule fois, la
nature divine, complète, l'idéale enfin, je donnerais toute ma fortune'
(57). So prostitute his woman he will, tempted by the beauty of his disci-
ple's mistress, which he wishes to compare to that of *La Belle Noiseuse.*

The figure of the woman thus functions as the site of knowledge for
the male artist – Poussin sells out Gillette to be initiated into the secret of
Frenhofer's art, while Frenhofer prostitutes *La Belle Noiseuse* to reassure
himself that he has indeed triumphed over nature. Woman in this text
seems to play her designated role in a male fiction: object of desire, created, exchanged, and circulated by and within the masculine order.
'Mais n'est-ce pas femme pour femme?' asks Porbus later. The masculine
idealization of feminine beauty reinforces and completes the possession
of the feminine by the masculine.[41] Or does it?

When Frenhofer finally reveals his painting, what Porbus and Poussin
see is not a woman, but 'des couleurs confusément amassées et contenues par une multitude de lignes bizarres qui forment une muraille de
peinture,' a 'chaos de couleurs, de tons, de nuances indécises, espèces
de brouillard sans forme.' And under the layers of paint, they perceive
the figure of a woman, gradually destroyed by the very brushstrokes that
wished to perfect it.

In Balzac's narrative, the feminine refuses to be possessed. Frenhofer's
art, which aimed at the perfect representation of *La Belle Noiseuse* by seek-

ing to 'ôter jusqu'à l'idée de dessin et de moyens artificiels et de lui donner l'aspect et la rondeur même de la nature,' merely ends up flaunting
its own artifice. Frenhofer is convinced that he has created a body, and
not just a work of art: 'Vous êtes devant une femme et vous cherchez un
tableau ... Où est l'art? Perdu, disparu! Voilà les formes mêmes d'une
jeune fille' (69). But he has anything but a body on his canvas, matter
refuses to be shaped by an ideal vision. It cannot be recuperated as a symbol of the male artist's power, and can no longer be contained by it. The
male artist's attempt to reduce the feminine to an idealized construction
is rendered impotent and ineffective. Woman then, will not be misrepresented. Frenhofer's art claims to represent and edify a single, eternal feminine essence. He believes that he has suceeded in creating 'l'introuvable
Vénus des anciens,' that he has given flesh to a beauty which eluded even
the ancients, and to which Gillette is such a poor comparison. But the figure that lies under the brushstrokes is no more the essence of 'woman'
than the undistinguishable mass of lines and squiggles superposed over
it. His spectators cannot recognize this essence on his canvas. The one
discernable shape that remains on it is a foot endowed with a life of its
own, 'un pied délicieux, un pied vivant!' surging from the inchoate scrib-
bles that surround it: 'Ils restèrent pétrifiés d'admiration devant ce fragment échappé à une lente et une progressive destruction' (69). In other
words, not the totality of ideal beauty that Frenhofer wished to capture
and fix, but a fragment that escapes this whole. The mastery of Frenhofer's self-proclaimed status as 'Père, amant et Dieu' is undercut by the
emergence of a force that cannot be reintegrated into the prior vision or
design of the artist. If anything, the foot that surges forth affirms its independence from and impassibility towards its creator.

Not only does the text force the masculine order to confront its mis-
representation and its lack of mastery over the feminine, it challenges the
very possibility of such mastery by henceforth denying it a representational space. Frenhofer's canvas was the locus of a specific movement of
desire, the privileged space where he could project his idealized vision
of woman. This space is now revealed to be empty of this idealization
and desire: '[T]ôt ou tard, il s'apercevra qu'il n'y a rien sur sa toile' (71).
Woman refuses to be contained within the role of a self-same other. And
far from the triumph of masculine self-aggrandization, we are left with its
destruction – Frenhofer dies after burning his paintings.

In *Le chef-d'oeuvre inconnu*, the specular surface of masculine self-representation works not to reaffirm the power of the active male principle of
idea/spirit over the passive female receptacle of matter/nature, but

rather to show how the latter cannot be subjected to the former. Where then is the feminine in Balzac's text? We have seen that it is no longer configured as a term dominated by the masculine. But is it excluded for all that, and if not, how and where does it articulate itself?

The Gesture of Abstract Art

Frenhofer's spectators can discern no recognizable figure on his canvas, nothing that vaguely resembles a body.

> Apercevez-vous quelque chose? demanda Poussin à Porbus.
> – Non. Et vous?
> – Rien. (69)

Frenhofer, convinced that he has eliminated art for life, has to reassure them that they are indeed looking at a work of art, and needs to delineate the spatial configuration of his painting for them, but his audience cannot recognize this artistic space. What Frenhofer has created for them resembles neither reality, nor art: 'Le vieux lansquenet se joue de nous, dit Poussin en revenant devant le prétendu tableau. Je ne vois là que des couleurs confusément amassées et contenues par une multitude de lignes bizarres qui forment une muraille de peinture' (69). For Porbus and Poussin, Frenhofer's painting is just a confused and incomprehensible mass of colours and lines of which no sense can be made. It cannot be integrated into any conceptual framework or a logically coherent system of knowledge. In other words, if *La Belle Noiseuse* means nothing to Porbus and Poussin, it is because it corresponds to no historically contemporary art form. Frenhofer's 'chaos de couleurs, de tons, de nuances indécises, espèce de brouillard sans forme' portends the possibility of another form of painting – that of the antimimetic and the antifigurative. It inaugurates an alternative mode of signification that escapes both its creator and its spectators – a modern abstract art, freed from the object, the representation of the real, and the image.[42]

The iconoclastic gesture of *La Belle Noiseuse* thus warrants a pause. What is being articulated in an art form so radically different from the Flemish realism of which Poussin will become one of the most famous disciples, and which the father of realism so admired? What is the conflict being articulated in this space, between the perfect foot and the chaotic mass of colours and lines? What makes it so problematic that it is destroyed? What tension is being played out in the premonition of an art so different from the dominant historical forms to which it is chronologically contemporary? What gesture is being marked by the rupture of abstract art?

The theoretical formulations of Jean-Joseph Goux offer useful insights into understanding the inscription of feminine difference and materiality within the space of Frenhofer's painting and Balzac's text. According to Goux, what emerges with abstract art is a new relationship with the world of reality, a different articulation of the possibility of knowing and representing it. The epistemological and gnoseological model that characterizes abstract art not only changes modes of representation and signification, it disturbs the sexual archaeology of the classic (idealist) oppositions between spirit and matter, idea and nature. The conflict that pits man against a nature/matter he needs to know and dominate is rewritten in a manner that recasts the sexual terms (and stakes) of this relationship. Specularity yields to a mode of signification in which the alterity of the feminine can no longer be denied, but has to be recognized and acknowledged as such.

In 'The Unrepresentable,' Goux examines the history of the modes of signifying through the forms of painting. His central thesis is that the decision to end representation signals a change in the conceptions of sign and signifier. It marks a departure from the philosophy of representation and reflection and a breach within the conceptions of fantasy and the imaginary.

For Goux, a history of the modes of signification shows a progressive trend towards desemanticization and defiguration, or in other words, a movement towards the dematerialization of the signifier. In the shift from the pictographic to the alphabetic modes of writing, for instance, the concreteness or materiality of the signifier is gradually reduced and sublimated. The relation of the signifier to the signified becomes an increasingly arbitrary one of pure relation. The shift in modes of painting from *symbolist* to *perspectival* to *abstract* is indicative of the same tendency towards desemanticization. In the symbolist (or primitive) mode of production, the signifier is the thing itself, meaning is adherent to the signified material, and everything perceived is overloaded with signification or fetishized; however, in the subsequent perspectival mode of signification, the world is 'deprojected,' i.e., placed in perspective from the point of view of an egocentric subject who now becomes an objective mirror of a world perceived as an objective and coordinated set of facts.

Within the perspectival mode, signs become indifferent to their content and meaning can separate itself from the material signifier or the 'sensuous' element. It is the dematerialization of the sign that makes for the separation between signifier and signified, matter and spirit, object and subject and that corresponds to the birth of the egocentric subject. Meaning, now separated from its signifier, can be transcendentalized into logos, allowing for the notion of an 'objective' representation of the real:

> Only when semantic deprojection is complete can there emerge the notion of the world *reflected* in the mirror of consciousness, the notion of *speculation*, of scientific *theoria*. Only with this deprojection can there be idealism, the philosophical translation of the trend toward matter conceived as *void of sense* and toward the attendant schisms.[43]

The diacritical-reflective mode of signification and its progressive trend towards idealization permits the setting up of philosophical subjectivity, and can be observed in the instauration of the Cartesian subject, the specular idealism of philosophy, in Galilean and Newtonian science, and finally, in pictorial perspective.

In the perspectival mode of signification, painting works for the perception of the spectator; it is aimed at a fixed point of view, that where the subject is situated. It exists not for itself but for a perceiving subject. Abstract art brings about a revolution in this relationship of the spectator to the painting, the subject to the object. For Goux, it is Hegelian idealism that marks this point, as both a culmination of the perspectival mode of signification and as a rupture with it. Hegelian idealism heralds a mode of signification that surpasses the perspectival (bourgeois-capitalist) mode that is Hegel's historical contemporary, and provides the bases on which a Kandinsky is then able to set forth the principles of abstract painting.

Idealism, Materialism, and the Feminine

According to Hegel, art realizes itself through a progressive movement in which it gradually liberates itself from matter. His hierarchy of art places architecture on the lowest rung of the scale, and poetry at the top. Sculpture, painting, and music occupy the successive levels between architecture and poetry. Bound to work with matter, architecture is the most inferior art form, while poetry is the highest because of 'the power with which it subjects to spirit and its ideas the sensuous element from which music and painting begin to make art free.'[44] The perfect art form is the one that is the least material and the most spiritual; in poetry, the sensuous element (sound) is 'but a *sign*, by itself void of significance, a sign of the idea which has become concrete in itself.'[45] Sound is only used in poetry as a 'sign in itself without value or content.' The history of art is thus propelled by a movement towards dematerialization and idealization.

If painting is hierarchically inferior to music and poetry, it is because its content is still limited by nature and matter, which it has to represent through concrete figuration. Painting, in other words, is fettered by the figurative and the representable. Both the form and content of music, on the other hand, express an 'inner life without giving it any outward shape or figure.'[46] If poetry is the most spiritual of arts, it is because it manages to divest itself of the last material element to which music is still attached – sound, which in poetry is pure transparence. With poetry, art that was initially bound to matter gradually frees itself from it to the point of now organizing it. In the organization of matter by art, the former is negated to the point of complete disappearance within the spiritual. The disappearance of the material signifier and the reduction of the sensuous element to a 'sign which has no significance by and in itself' is what elevates poetry to the highest realization of art, that of pure thought.

The 'disappearance' of Frenhofer's art inscribes itself within an analogous drive towards ideality. Cut off from any concrete and recognizable figuration that would correspond to nature, art too seems to have erased itself from the canvas. But if Poussin and Porbus cannot master the painting cognitively, they cannot quite read the absence of figuration on Frenhofer's canvas as a complete failure of art:

> – Il est encore plus poète que peintre, répondit gravement Poussin.
> – Là, reprit Porbus en touchant la toile, finit notre art sur terre.
> – Et, de là, il va se perdre dans les cieux, dit Poussin.[47]

Has Frenhofer's art attained a level of spirituality and ideality such that it has completely assimilated matter within itself, to the point of stanching it of all meaning? In any case, it is clear that for Porbus and Poussin, Frenhofer's art has freed itself from the ties that bind it to the earthly, to the natural, and to the materially recognizable.

With abstract art, Kandinsky affirms the Hegelian conception of the idealist destiny of art. And unlike Hegel, for Kandinsky, it is music which is the ultimate realization of the spiritual in art, because it frees itself completely from nature and matter to devote itself to 'the creation of an autonomous life of musical sound.'[48] Painting, in order to elevate itself to the spirituality of music, must similarly liberate itself from nature and move towards combinations of pure colour and independent form.[49] Here, Kandinsky's articulation of painting as 'pure composition' rejoins the Hegelian notion of pure sound, sound that is dematerialized to the status of pure sign, void of signification, a sign of the idea that has, in its abstraction, become sheer transparence, sound only as a sign in itself without value or content.

In abstract painting, forms and colours must speak a language unconstrained by the natural and the material, in which the materiality of the signifier must yield to the spirituality of meaning and ideas:

> In a conversation with an interesting person, we endeavor to get at his fundamental ideas and feelings. We do not bother about the words he uses, nor his spelling, nor the breath necessary for speaking, nor the movements of his tongue and lips, nor the psychological effect on our brain, nor the physical sound in our ear, nor the physiological effect on our nerves. We realize that these things, though interesting and important, are not the problem. The meaning and ideas are what concerns us. We should have the same attitude when confronted with a work of art if we are to absorb its abstract effect. If this attitude ever becomes general, the artist will be able to dispense with natural forms and colors and to use purely artistic means.[50]

Kandinsky thus inscribes himself within Hegel's idealist trajectory, at the apogee of a mode of signification in which the dematerialization and de-semanticization of the signifier make way for the spiritual transparence of meaning.

Interestingly, Irigaray's distinction between the productive mimesis of music and the reproductive, speculative, and imitative mimesis of idealist philosophy resonates with the terms with which Kandinsky articulates the difference between abstract and imitative, figurative art. In this respect, feminine writing as defined by Irigaray would place itself on the idealist side of the signifying divide. Irigaray's feminine thus appears to paradoxically position itself against the materiality she seeks to claim for it, and situates itself within the very idealism charged with occluding the operation of the feminine.

Irigaray's seemingly impossible affiliation with the latent idealism of a Kandinsky and the assonances between feminine writing and the gesture of abstract art go to the heart of the paradoxical position of the latter. Abstract art is both the realization of the idealist configuration and an

abrupt departure from it. If Kandinsky's conception of painting resonates with Hegelian idealism, it is not idealist in the same manner.
Rather, it situates itself at that oxymoronic moment when idealism makes
a loop back into materialism, or rather, turns back upon itself towards a
different conception of matter.

Abstact Art or the Beyond of the Imaginary?

Abstract art corresponds to a mode of symbolization that is linked to a
different gnoseological configuration and which produces a certain conception of science. As seen earlier, pictorial perspective corresponds to
the diacritical-reflective mode of signification in which a split is operated
between form and matter. Imitative and figurative art thus inscribes itself
within the reflective operation of the mirror because of the power the
latter possesses to separate form from matter. But abstract art breaks with
the speculative and reflexive mode, and indicates a shift from the philosophy of representation and reflection towards 'operation,' a level of abstraction in which the notions of point, line, curve, and surface are separated from the sensory, material, and perceptible element and function
as abstract elements within a system detached from empirical reality. The
elements are not (cannot) be represented visually, but are operable. In
this leap from immediate, perceptible experience to the unrepresentable, 'the mirror not only becomes warped and shattered; it vanishes –
along with representation.'[51]

Abstract painting does away with the egocentric Cartesian subject. The
painting ceases to exist for the perception of a subject and function as a
mirror of the real. The surface of the painting dismantles perspective to
allow for the emergence of an internal organization:

> The [pictorial surface] is no longer a flat mirror of preexisting reality, pre-
> sented again from the point of view of a subject or even simultaneously
> from multiple points of view; with the leap of nonfiguration, it becomes a
> specific arrangement of a diacritical field of form-colors, with the laws of its
> composition being produced in the very process of its generation.[52]

The pictorial surface is no longer reflective and specular, it becomes
'life, generation, auto-development.' 'We see a rejection of any metapi-
ctorial guarantee ensuring the meaning and order of the canvas, any
centralized reflection of something already there. No longer does a stable, focused aspect of the subject repeat in pictorial space a referential

given that preordains the painted signifiers; the dislocated subject is invaded, so to speak, by its own operative and generative capacity.'[53] And to the extent that it does away with the mirror of (self) representation, abstract painting takes us beyond the realm of the specular, beyond the image and illusion, beyond fantasy.

This precisely is the tension articulated on Frenhofer's canvas, in the opposition between the 'pied vivant' and the 'chaos de couleurs' and the 'multitude de lignes bizarres' that surround it. Frenhofer's painting ceases to exist for a spectator/creator; its pictorial surface cannot be organized for one. There is no logos, no world reflected faithfully on his canvas. The realism of linear perspective is eliminated; Porbus and Poussin are unable to comprehend the meaning of the painting. They are incapable of seizing its meaning either for themselves or for Frenhofer. Frenhofer himself cannot explain his creation to his spectators. He cannot guarantee its meaning for them. His lengthy and numerous descriptions of what he believes to be reflected on his canvas fail to convince Porbus and Poussin. The very space of his specular surface is dispersed beyond delimitation. Frenhofer tries in vain to map out its boundaries for his disciples; for them, it is but a 'prétendu tableau.' Frenhofer can neither bestow meaning onto his canvas nor ensure it for its spectators; the 'Père, amant et Dieu' is disjuncted from his creation. His painting was the space where he could control knowledge, pierce and possess the secret of nature. But he is disclocated from this logos. Finally, what the space of the canvas seems to affirm is an art capable of self-invention and self-organization.[54]

As we saw earlier, the ideality of Frenhofer's art leads to a dissolution of the material object. '[T]ôt ou tard, il s'apercevra qu'il n'y a rien sur la toile.' Pygmalion is unable to recuperate a body for meaning, knowledge, and truth. Matter refuses to be subjected to systems of meaning and truth. But can we take Porbus's and Poussin's contention that there is nothing on the canvas at face value? Even if on Frenhofer's canvas we find nothing that corresponds to an art form historically contemporary to its spectators, it is not for all that totally empty. In addition to the perfect foot, it does contain 'un chaos de couleurs, de tons, de nuances indécises, espèce de brouillard sans forme'; 'des couleurs confusément amassées et contenues par une multitude de lignes bizarres qui forment une muraille de peinture.' In other words, if not a material object of art, at the very least, the *materiality* of art. For the unbridled mass of colours and lines that impose themselves upon the figure that lies beneath them substitute for the object a process of generation and organization that the artist cannot claim as his own. The artist cannot recognize himself in his creation – it remains wholly other to him. And what is this other power of generation but the operation of the feminine as defined by Irigaray, a materiality which 'résiste à et fait exploser toute forme, toute figure, idée, concept, solidement établis'?[55] What *La Belle Noiseuse* confirms is not matter as object, subject to an organizing male principle, but matter as activity itself, as production, matter capable of its own generative and organizational powers.

The feminine is no longer deprived of its creative capacity or subjected to idea and form. What it affirms on the contrary is its capacity to generate its own lines and forms, to organize itself. The feminine is not characterized by sterility, specularity, and reflection, but is life, production, jouissance. 'Que de jouissances sur cette toile!' exclaims Poussin. A plurality irreducible to the one, a materiality free of the logic of the same. From the reflective and imitative to the productive. Mimesis as production, not reproduction, from the representable to the unrepresentable, from the image to the non-figurable, and in a move that exceeds Irigaray, beyond the image and fantasy, beyond the flat mirror of the *speculum mundi*, beyond the curvatures and distortions of the speculum.

Towards (An)other Matter

As noted earlier, with abstract art, the reflective mode gives way to the 'operable.' The realism of linear perspective yields to 'a combination of pure colour and independent form.' From the concrete figuration of the object, the pictorial surface moves towards an organization dictated by internal necessity. Abstract art thus situates itself within a mode of signification that inaugurates a new relationship to matter, affirming the 'internal powers that compose and organize the "mind."'[56] Hegel occupies this paradoxical moment – his philosophy, which marks the apogee of the Cartesian split between two worlds and makes reflexive duplication in philosophy and pictorial representation possible, also dismantles it by the thesis of the unity of concept and reality, a thesis that continues into dialectical materialism as the unity of thought and being.[57] Hegelianism at its peak both culminates in and puts an end to the transcendental subject of classical philosophy; it now announces the 'living subject, organized and organizing.'

Abstract art is characterized by the same gesture, situating itself within a new mode of symbolization that Goux terms the *epigenetic*. The epigenetic mode sets forth an alternative conception of matter, that is, matter not as object, but as activity. Materialism can no longer be reduced to vulgar realism or empiricism; it is practical, sensory activity: 'Perfected spiritualism, idealism at its apogee, at the diametric pole of the objective material base, ends up turning back upon itself in a dialectical loop, affirming the practical unity of subject and object in a rooted productivity.'[58]

How else can we define the new conception of matter that informs abstract art and the epigenetic mode to which it belongs? As mentioned earlier, idealist philosophy sets up the dualities between form and matter, thought and nature, by rooting them in sexual difference. According to Aristotle, for example, matter desires form as male desires female. Man constitutes the form, woman the matter. Matter has no organizing principle, no order. Thought and meaning are 'other' to matter. (Female) matter is amorphous, transitory, and inessential. It is this idealist 'conception' that codes law, order, permanence, and organization as male, while placing matter outside of meaning. The epigenetic mode overcomes these oppositions by defining thought as a product of highly organized matter. In other words, matter and its organizational powers are conceived of as one, or rather, matter organizes itself. Thought, mind, and consciousness are conceived of as products of nature, as matter organized in a certain way.

To think of mind as a product of matter is to return to an 'other' matter, to an (other) femininity. The dialectical reunion with the 'other' matter is conceived in terms of the negation of a negation – the negation of that which estranges matter from its generative potency, from order and meaning. The epigenetic mode and the concurrent move from idealism to dialectical materialism thus lead us towards feminine alterity, from woman to woman as other.

Certainly, one could argue that it is this feminine that irrupts so strikingly on the surface of Frenhofer's painting. It appears as matter that is 'other' to the drive towards ideality, as matter that cannot be severed from its immanent meaning. As seen earlier, the pictorial surface shows both a scission from the fetishistic and symbolic modes of signification, and a departure from the specular and perspectival. The idealism and spiritualism of Frenhofer run up against a materiality they cannot master. The work of art affirms creative powers that are not wholly localizable in the creating subject: the work of art is not quite the same as that of its creator. And yet, for all that, does Frenhofer's painting fit neatly and unproblematically into the epigenetic mode within which Goux positions abstract painting?

'And the work, finally, knows him not'[59]

> Jamais l'oeuvre la plus belle ne peut être comprise. Sa simplicité même repousse parce qu'il faut que l'admirateur ait le mot de l'énigme. Les jouissances prodiguées aux connaisseurs sont enfermées dans un temple et le premier venu ne peut pas toujours dire: 'Sésame, ouvre-toi!'
>
> Balzac[60]

In his intuition of an antimimetic and antifigurative art, one that frees itself from the image and can no longer be explained in terms of the specular, Balzac glimpses the iconoclasm of modern art. *Le chef-d'oeuvre inconnu* hints at the possibility that the temple that houses the work of art, or rather, the temple that is itself the work of art could be empty of the imaginary. Placed under the sign of an epigraph that contains neither words nor images, Balzac's text echoes the iconoclastic gesture of its protagonist's painting. It undermines its status as a *speculum mundi* as well as the mimetic enterprise of realism. The paper, much like woman, refuses to be inscribed with a plenitude of meaning. What remain are the blanks of an alterity it can neither reduce nor possess, an alterity that remains unknown, other.

'L'art du romancier consiste à bien matérialiser ses idées,' writes Balzac.[61] *Le chef-d'oeuvre inconnu* problematizes the notion of matter as a pliant medium capable of being negated (in the Hegelian sense of the term, i.e., transformed) through an active operation of a human will to production. Matter resists the overcoming power of thought, and art is not created by a conscious application of will. Let us recall Balzac's definition of the artist:

> Les rois commandent aux nations pendant un temps donné, l'artiste commande à des siècles entiers; il change la face des choses, il jette une révolution en moule, il pèse sur le globe, il le façonne. Ainsi de Gutenberg, de Colomb, de Schwartz, de Descartes, de Voltaire, de David. Tous étaient artistes, car ils créaient, ils appliquaient la pensée à une production nouvelle des forces humaines, à une combinaison neuve des éléments de la nature, ou physique, ou morale.[62]

Clearly for Balzac, art is a means of active intervention in the world, a realization of human endeavour. The artist is envisioned as one who labours, who moulds and shapes his world. He is a historical being, capable of exercising knowledge and effective action. But, as we have seen, in

Le chef-d'oeuvre inconnu, the site occupied by the subject/spectator is not one of action or cognition. Frenhofer is a far cry from the dynamic and transforming figure that forms Balzac's conception of the artist. *Le chef-d'oeuvre inconnu* does not affirm the creative powers of an individual consciousness; what imposes itself in the narrative is rather (in Heideggerian terms) the 'createdness' of the work.

The end of Balzac's text offers no dialectalized reunion of mind and matter, no harmonious unity that would overcome the adversarial relationship of man and nature. The work of art that Frenhofer has created remains strange, uncanny, and alien to him. There is no redemptive resolution of oppositions, no messianic and totalizing negation of negation. Goux's epigenetic mode is still light years away, or perhaps in a realm from which *La Belle Noiseuse* is completely removed.

La Belle Noiseuse is a work that tears itself asunder from its time, a work that is almost achronological and ahistorical. It cannot be easily categorized into a cognitive system or take its place within a logically ordered narrative of a history of the modes of production.

Let us repeat Goux's definition of the shift effectuated by the epigenetic mode:

> Corresponding to speculative metaphysical philosophy is reflective, realistic art; but when idealism itself, in the very act of its completion, at its zenith, becomes dialectical and affirms the infinite productivity of 'spirit' as demiurge and driving force, it is no longer enough for art itself passively to reflect reality; it also affirms internal powers that compose and organize the 'mind,' beyond the scope of immediate positive data. In the process, art tears itself away from nature, both in the content signified and in the means of signifying.[63]

Balzac's description of artistic genius does depict the artist as moved by forces not completely centred within himself. As we have seen, for Balzac, art is an exercise of the transforming power of mind:

> Une oeuvre d'art est une idée tout aussi puissante que celle à laquelle on doit les loteries, que l'observation physique qui a doté le monde de la vapeur, que l'analyse physiologique au moyen de laquelle on a renoncé aux systèmes pour coordonner et comparer les faits. Ainsi, tout va de pair dans tout ce qui procède de l'intelligence, et Napoléon est un aussi grand poète qu'Homère; il a fait de la poésie comme le second a livré des batailles.[64]

And yet, the artist is one whose powers derive from a source not wholly identifiable to himself: '[I]l est reconnu qu'il [l'artiste] n'est pas lui-même dans le secret de son intelligence. Il opère sous l'empire de certaines circonstances, dont la réunion est un mystère. Il ne s'appartient pas. Il est le jouet d'une force éminement capricieuse' (281).

The figure of Frenhofer is marked by the same duality. On the one hand, we see a ferocious, demiurgic subjectivity that seeks to rival God's creative powers ('Tudieu! je suis donc chez le dieu de la peinture,' says Poussin), and on the other, we see the intuition that this demonic power originates in an elsewhere: '[P]our le jeune Poussin, il semblait qu'il y eut dans le corps de ce bizarre personnage un démon qui agissait par ses mains en les prenant fantastiquement contre le gré de l'homme' (52); 'Ce vieillard aux yeux blancs, attentif et stupide, devenu pour lui plus qu'un homme, lui apparut comme un génie fantasque qui vivait dans une sphère inconnue' (56); 'Ainsi, pour l'enthousiaste Poussin, ce vieillard était devenu, par une transfiguration subite, l'Art lui-même, l'art avec ses secrets, ses fougues et ses rêveries' (57). Where earlier in the text, art was that which resulted from the organizing power of spirit, here, in an unexpected twist, it is the artist who is now subjected (assimilated) to the organizing power of art. Art becomes a reunion of the mind with the powers that organize it.

In the reintegration of the driving force of 'spirit' within that which it seeks to modify, Balzac's Romantic aesthetic (like Goux's epigenetic mode), ultimately places itself within a historical process of transformation and negation.[65] Romanticism, as Blanchot remarks, thus extends the double move of the modern moment, one which can be traced back to Descartes and is distinguished by 'a perpetual play of exchange between an existence that becomes an increasingly pure, subjective intimacy and the ever more active and objective conquest of the world according to the aims of the realizing mind and the productive will. Hegel was the first to account fully for this double movement; and thereby, joined to Marx, he made its culmination possible.'[66]

For Blanchot, the Romantic vindication of the self and ego, of a subjectivity and inner life opposed to the world, and of the uselessness of art is humanistic to the extent that Romantic art becomes a means of self-recognition and self-realization. Romanticism sets up the poetic as the subjective: 'Art appears as the artist and the artist as man – as man in the most general sense.'[67] But Romanticism's celebration of poetic creativity could also be seen (like realist imitation), as another expression of the universal will to production:

Just as Cartesian representation contains in itself the power of science (the

power of conquest, the ability to conquer reality by negating and transforming it), so the artist becomes he who by representing transforms. He
becomes the one who creates, the creator, but always, nonetheless, man the
creator – creation at the level of man, of man understood as the ability to
produce and act, as the will to exert power, whose true nature is revealed by
commitment to goals, by thought's need of objects in order to find its way.
The fact that art is glorified in the creative artist is indicative of a great
change in art. Art accepts subordination to him who practices it, consenting
to be no more than he.[68]

Romanticism, like Hegelianism and Marxism, is still Cartesian, and for
Blanchot, the reciprocal incorporation within one another or the perfect union of art and artist remains bound within the dialectics of the
negating power of spirit. And yet, *La Belle Noiseuse* resists the Romantic
conflation of art and the artist. It offers no harmonious synthesis of the
work of art and its creator. Rather, what it affirms (to borrow Blanchot's
words), is art itself.

'Sometimes,' writes Blanchot, the notion of the creator 'gives art the
right to compete for authority in the world, by defining the artist as the
realizer, the superlative maker whom it claims, moreover, to protect
against the anonymity of collective tasks by assuring him that he remains
the exemplary individual, or man on a grand scale. For the creator is
always unique, he aims to remain what he is irreducibly within himself,
a treasure which cannot be compared even to the greatest action.'[69]
Certainly, in 'Des artistes,' Balzac reserves such a space for the artist. And
yet, *Le chef-d'oeuvre inconnu* rejects the Romantic valorization of artistic
genius. Frenhofer's work is associated with failure; it does not overthrow
the world but ends up being destroyed within it. In this sense, it exceeds
the modernism of Romanticism (and even realism), where the intensifi-
cation of subjectivity leads to an increasing objectivization of the world.
Rather, its modernity lies in its being in excess of this world. Art is that
which escapes the totalizing drive of spirit and is removed from a world
completely known and transformed.

Le chef-d'oeuvre inconnu is thus marked by a double articulation: Balzac,
who inscribes artistic endeavour within the active movement of history
finds himself impelled towards that which cannot be assimilated to it.
The author who clearly conceives of artistic activity as part of a process of
conquest and transformation seems to project himself towards that
moment when 'art has become a thing of the past,'[70] to the 'after' of the
instant when art has itself been incorporated and integrated into the historical process as 'real, purposeful activity.' In *Le chef-d'oeuvre inconnu*, art

frees itself from this enterprise. What we see in Frenhofer is the artist undone by the work. But in this undoing, a work nevertheless is created, one that cannot be accommodated into a logically significant conceptual system for its historically situated subject and spectators. It 'emerges as the unaccustomed, the unwonted, that which has no relation to this world or with time.'[71] *La Belle Noiseuse* others its creator: 'In the work man speaks, but the work gives voice in man to what does not speak: to the unnameable, the inhuman, to what is devoid of truth, bereft of justice, without rights. Here man does not recognize himself; he does not feel justified. No longer is he present, either as man for himself, or before God, as a god before himself.'[72]

Le chef-d'oeuvre inconnu thus moves towards a different conception of the relationship between the artist and his work, the writer and his writing. It is a conception that is closer to the Blanchotian articulation of the poetics of modernity. The work of art is outside the relationship of identity and difference. It is the space (or rather, the non-space) of the non-identical, that which (once again in Heideggerian terms) simply is. The work is strange and thinglike, self-contained and uncommunicative. It is not of this world, it is the presence of 'the other of all worlds, that which is always other than the world.'[73] The work of art is thus an encounter with an alterity that is irreducible to the same. To write is to experience its pure exteriority (what Blanchot designates as 'l'inconnu'). It is an otherness that is not negative (i.e., subject to the transformation of a totalizing consciousness). Rather, it attests to the impossibility of negation and historical transformation. It is an alterity of pure refusal, one that cannot be assimilated into the discourse of subjectivity.

Blanchot does put a face onto the otherness that constitutes the work of art – that of Eurydice.[74] The site of the terrible, irrecuperable alterity is thus a feminine one. 'Comme Orphée, je descendrais dans l'enfer de l'art pour en ramener la vie,' cries Frenhofer. And like Orpheus, he fails in the endeavour. But it is in the space of this impossible desire – the encounter with pure otherness – within the failure of this move that a work of art is created. Art places itself on the hither side of power, mastery, and knowledge.[75] Art is thus the feminine that lies on the hither side of the dialectics of possession, or perhaps even more simply, art is always, already, feminine.[76]

Noli me legere?

Le chef-d'oeuvre inconnu is inscribed under a non-mimetic, non-figurative epigraph, one that contains neither word nor image. The discourse of the text is thus placed under the sign of a blank, a silence, of that which does not speak. For the epigraph, with its marked absence of word and image is not even a hieroglyph dense with an ultimately recuperable meaning. Rather, it situates itself outside the possibility of meaning. And with this simple gesture, the representational status of the text is called into question. Language divests itself of the power to negate, to know, to construct, and to transform. Language veers away from philosophy, from the ability to name, order, reason, and conceptualize. It takes leave of the domain of philosophy to enter that of poetry or literature: 'Literature now dispenses with the writer: it is no longer this inspiration at work, this negation asserting itself, this idea inscribed in the world as though it were the absolute perspective of the world in its totality. It is not beyond the world, but neither is it the world itself: it is the presence of things before the *world* exists, their perseverance after the world has disappeared, the stubbornness of what remains when everything vanishes and the dumbfoundedness of what appears when nothing exists.'[77]

'[T]he stubbornness of what remains when everything vanishes and the dumbfoundedness of what appears when nothing exists': this, one might say, is the very poetic (non) space of *La Belle Noiseuse*. The work of art is what others the philosophical enterprise of its creator. *Le chef-d'oeuvre inconnu* depicts the unpredictability and unexpectedness of the work of art. More crucially perhaps, the work of art is not a space for the articulation of an estranged self that can be ultimately reintegrated. Neither does it constitute the space of an alienation that would lead the author/ creator towards a greater understanding or possession of self. Rather, it is that which renders such self-mastery and self-appropriation impossible. The relationship of Narcissus to the mirror is no longer the same.

In the course of this chapter, we reexamined Irigrary's thesis that masculine desire is caught in a structure of specularity that requires the erasure of feminine corporeality and difference in order to erect itself. Linking her deconstruction of one of the founding dualisms of Western metaphysics, that of spirit and matter to the myths of Narcissus and Pygmalion, we reviewed recent literary criticism that considers the marking of the female body as an enabling condition for the aesthetics of nineteenth-century realism. Following Irigaray's scenography of masculine desire, as well as the mirror metaphor, and deploying her strategy of 'productive mimesis' as a mode of feminine resistance to the narcissistic systems of masculine self-representation, we saw how the spaces of painting and writing problematize the inscription of a self-same subjectivity, revealing the very productive mimesis that Irigaray claims for the feminine. The theoretical formulations of Goux allowed us to understand how the aesthetic rupture of Balzac's text corresponds to a break with a specular mode of reflection and representation, participating in a mode of signification in which feminine materiality is no longer subjugated to idea or spirit. Finally, Blanchot's conception of art and literature as sites of an alterity outside of the dialectics of identity and specularity invites us to rethink the validity of Irigaray's scenography of thought, desire, and representation. *Le chef-d'oeuvre inconnu* is thus a text that raises a serious question: to what extent is psychoanalytical feminism's understanding of 'male desire' mired in and distorted by the systems of mythic representation it inherits from psychoanalysis? This issue will be discussed in detail in the next chapter.

3 The Three Virtues of Imperceptibility, Indiscernibility, and Impersonality

> The poet is Narcissus to the extent that Narcissus is an anti-Narcissus.
>
> Maurice Blanchot[1]

The present chapter takes as its starting point the following query: how and why do male-authored texts structured according to the myths accused of perpetuating the narcissism of masculine desire reveal themselves to be non-narcissistic by allowing for the expression of feminine difference? My investigation proceeds according to a threefold approach. First, I use Maurice Blanchot's reading of the figure of Narcissus to arrive at an alternative view of the relationship between writing and difference. Second, I examine some of the blind spots of Irigaray's conception of the unconscious that lead to an unhappy disjunction between the theory and practice of desire in literary texts. Third, I appeal to a theory of desire that can explain the unconscious in terms other than those of the signifying systems of myth, namely, the model laid out by Deleuze and Guattari. I conclude with a consideration of the interpretive pitfalls that their concepts could help avoid within the practice of feminist literary criticism.

Narcissus Revisited

The feminist use of the myth of Narcissus as an explanatory model for male-authored narrative needs some rethinking. As we saw with *Le chef-d'oeuvre inconnu*, the spaces of art and writing do not function as specular surfaces for the constitution of a subject present and adequate to itself. The text reveals workings that the feminist reading of the myth fails to account for. What is at stake in these operations is the very model of (masculine) subjectivity elaborated by Irigaray, as well as the economy of desire in which that subjectivity is held to be constructed. The literary text calls into question the assumptions that underlie Irigaray's challenge to psychoanalysis, namely, that subjectivity is exclusively masculine and narcissistic, that it needs the detour of the occlusion of the feminine to constitute itself, that it can only function through a desire for the same, that it is predicated on the logic of the One, and that it cannot accommodate feminine difference. To the feminist critic who claims the sole privilege of knowing how the male economy actually works, the text responds with what appears to be a knowledge of its error.

The question thus arises: does the text's inability to conform to the mythic paradigm stem from an erroneous application of the myth (i.e., a misunderstanding of how the myth actually works) or is it just the failure of the myth itself (as a system of signification) to account for the workings of desire? In other words, is it a skewed reading of the myth that results in an unsatisfactory application of it (in which case, one need only arrive at a proper understanding of the true meaning of the myth in order to apply it correctly to a body of literature), or is it rather that the myth itself produces a skewed and distorted version of the operations of desire at work in literature? The first possibility deserves serious consideration (see chapter 2). Undeniably, Irigaray's formulation of male narcissism has nothing to do with Ovid's Narcissus. Narcissus is not a dupe; he becomes aware of his error. In fact, he does not seem to need either psychoanalysis or psychoanalytical feminism to realize what his problem is, he knows how the illusion works, he knows how his desire operates. It would appear that Ovid's Narcissus has been psychoanalysed and can psychoanalyse:

> Yes, yes, I'm he! I've seen through that deceit:
> my image cannot trick me anymore.
> I burn with love for my own self: it's I
> who light the flames – the flames that scorch me then.
> ...
> If I could just be split from my own body!
> The strangest longing in a lover: I
> want that which I desire to stand apart
> from my own self.[2]

The recognition by Narcissus of his error does not lead to a greater mastery of self, nor does it restore the unity of the schism between the body and the image. The recognition of error does not eliminate the duality, nor permit a dialectical mediation of the two:

> ... Even when
> the world below became his home, he still
> would stare at his own image in the pool
> of Styx.[3]

Ovid's Narcissus appears to be the psychoanalytical subject par excellence – split into two, desiring in vain, impelled by a desire born of lack, captivated by an image he can never possess. What is more, he knows how it works. He has been demystified.

It is precisely the conflation between Narcissus and narcissism that Blanchot questions in a few pages devoted to the myth in *The Writing of the Disaster*. He notes:

> It is typical of narcissism, defined carelessly or subtly, that, like la Rochefoucauld's *amour-propre*, its effect is easily discernible in everything everywhere. It suffices to form the adjective from the noun: what is there that isn't narcissistic? All the positions of being are narcissistic, and of non-being. Even when being is totally renounced – denied to the point of becoming not-being – it does not cease (with the element of ambiguity which then obscures it) to be passively active. Thus the rigors of spiritual purification, even the absolute withdrawal into the void can be seen as narcissistic modes: relatively undemanding ways for a disappointed subject, or one uncertain of his identity, to affirm by annulling himself. This doubt cast upon selflessness is not to be ignored. We encounter it in the dizzying occidental tendency to link all values back up with the Same, and this tendency is all the more pronounced when it is a matter of an ill-constituted 'same' – the self – an evanescent identity which is lost even as it is grasped (here we recognize a favorite theme for certain dialectical meditations).[4]

For Blanchot, it is easy to see narcissism everywhere as long as we are under the spell of a logic that subsumes the other to the same. To talk of narcissism is to necessarily postulate the primacy and identity of the self, which is why even a fissured, double, and vainly desiring subject eventually brings us back to the unity of the one and the same.

This is what Blanchot is suspicious of. For him, Narcissus is precisely the one who lacks self-presence. He is the one turned away from himself by virtue of the decrees 'Thou shalt not know thyself' and 'Thou shalt not see thyself.' Lacking the identity of the self-same, he is anything but a self-reflexive and self-present subject: '[T]he aspect of the myth which Ovid finally forgets is that Narcissus, bending over the spring, does not recognize himself in the fluid image that the water sends back to him. It is thus not himself, not his perhaps nonexistent "I" that he loves or – even in his mystification – desires.' Which is why for Blanchot, Narcissus is solitary, but not solipsistic: 'Narcissus is said to be solitary, but it is not because he is excessively present to himself; it is rather because he lacks, by decree (you shall not see yourself), that reflected presence – identity, the self-same – the basis upon which a living relation with life, which is other, can be ventured.'[5] Narcissus, therefore, is not narcissistic.

For Blanchot, then, the image that Narcissus sees in the water is not a reflection of the same or even a likeness to anything. The image resembles nothing, it is the unknown, an alterity that cannot be grasped. And it is the encounter with alterity that brings about the disappearance of Narcissus: '[M]an – is it man? – can make himself in accordance with the image, but this means that he is still more apt to unmake himself in accordance with the image.' The pool into which Narcissus gazes is not a space for the self-constitution of a subject, nor a space for complacent self-representation and self-reflection. The water is a surface that blurs the very categories of subject and object, the distinction and separation attributed to beings. What Narcissus sees is an alterity beyond being. The pool is not the space of an object that offers itself to a specular subject. It is no longer a question of vision and reflection: 'The water in which Narcissus sees what he shouldn't is not a mirror, capable of producing a distinct and definite image. What he sees is the invisible in the visible – in the picture the undepicted, the unstable unknown of a representation without presence, which reflects no model: he sees the nameless one whom only the name he does not have could hold at a distance.'[6] It is only when we name Narcissus, when we see him as a doubled same, that we are able to do the same to the image in the water. It is when we postulate a self-presence of Narcissus that we are able to attribute to Narcissus a schism between self and other, of the other within the same. But for Blanchot, what Narcissus sees in the water goes beyond the schism of a divided self; what he sees in the pool is an alterity irreducible to being and non-being. What he sees is the forbidden, the divine and the sacred. The water is not the space of mediation between self and other, but the realm of the relation of non-relation to the other. In other words, the realm of fascination, or the very space of literature.

Writing is thus a break with specularity; it is non-identification. It is the relation to the unknown, what Blanchot calls the neuter, an alterity beyond ontology, irreducible to dialectics. Writing and poetry do not constitute a space for the recognition of a subjectivity. It is when the writer ceases to say 'I,' when s/he enters the realm of fascination that writing becomes possible: 'To write is to pass from the first to the third person, so that what happens to me happens to no one, is anonymous insofar as it concerns me, repeats itself in infinite dispersal. To write is to let fascination rule language.'[7] 'Fascination is fundamentally linked to the neutral, impersonal presence, to the indeterminate They, the immense, faceless Someone.'[8] Writing is the domain of the anonymous, the impersonal and the asubjective.[9] To write is to enter this domain, to respond to the call of the neuter.

To the extent that he enters the realm of fascination, Narcissus encounters the neuter in the water; he sees the nameless one who cannot be subordinated to the unity of totality and being, and who cannot be recuperated by the dialectics of one and the same. What Narcissus sees in the water then, is the multiple and the fragmentary.

Blanchot thus radically rewrites a whole tradition of readings of the myth of Narcissus, and by so doing, challenges the classic identification of Narcissus to the writer, poet, and artist:

> Schlegel is supposed to have said: 'Every poet is Narcissus.' We should not be content simply to rediscover in this statement the superficial mark of a certain romanticism according to which creation – poetry – is absolute subjectivity and the poet a living subject in the poem that reflects him, just as he is a poet by virtue of having transformed his life into poetry by incarnating it in his pure subjectivity. One ought, no doubt, to understand Schlegel's statement in another way too: in the poem, where the poet writes himself, he does not recognize himself, for he does not become conscious of himself. He is excluded from the facile, humanistic hope that by writing or 'creating,' he would transform his dark experience into greater consciousness. On the contrary: dismissed, excluded from what is written – unable even to be present by virtue of the non-presence of his very death – he has to renounce all conceivable relations of a self (either living or dying) to the poem which henceforth belongs to the other, or else will remain without any belonging at all. The poet is Narcissus to the extent that Narcissus is an anti-Narcissus: he who, turned away from himself – causing the detour of which he is the effect, dying of not re-cognizing himself – leaves the trace of what has not occurred.[10]

Blanchot, following a whole line of philosophical thinking before the eighteenth century, privileges the moment of non-recognition, the moment of error, but assigns a radically different value to it. The moment of non-recognition has nothing to do with blindness and insight, with knowledge and ignorance. It is removed from the domain or the faculty of sight and vision, of the gaze and the look. It marks the entry into writing, into the realm of fascination. For Blanchot, Narcissus's lack of recognition in the water is not an error, but the very essence of the (non) relation between the poet and the work. He pulls Narcissus away from narcissism, away from the lack of an encounter with otherness, away from the logic of the one and the same. Poetry and writing are the spaces of alterity, not narcissistic subjectivity. Literature has to do with the asubjective and the apersonal. For him, the error, if any, lies with Ovid's narrative – 'as if Narcissus could speak, speak "to himself," utter a soliloquy.'[11] Ovid's rendition of the myth of Narcissus is already steeped in a Platonic tradition of thought that is predicated on the unity of the one and the logic of the same and structured by its dualisms (spirit/matter, self/image, body/shadow, truth/reflection, truth/illusion, idea/matter, and yes, subject/object of knowledge), from whence have come all the successive readings it spawns (from Plotinus and Ficinus, to psychoanalysis and psychoanalytical feminism). But Blanchot's reading of Narcissus does not address the question of desire, or rather, if it does, leaves the psychoanalytical formulation of desire in place.

A Narcissistic Unconscious?

The unexpected convergence between psychoanalysis and Ovid's Narcissus warrants a pause. Psychoanalysis, then, ultimately inscribes itself within the trajectory of a long Platonic tradition; it can only conceive of a desire driven by a lack predicated on the originary unity of a whole. In this sense, Ovid's narrative functions according to a model of desire that needs to posit a lost totality in order to proceed. If Irigaray recognizes this for a fact,[12] she is unable to fully theorize an alternative to it. Her critique of Freud and Lacan remains bound by what she inherits from them; her model of the economy of (male) desire can, like psychoanalysis, only elaborate a desire that is illusory, deceptive, and displaced. She has to postulate a (male) unconscious that necessarily functions through a distorting mechanism – masculine desire has to suppress the feminine, and repress the suppression in order to work. The only way out of this skewed hall of mirrors is the operation of the feminine, as a disruptive excess that cannot be recuperated within the self-representations of the masculine economy. In other words, Irigaray needs to posit an unconscious of the male unconscious.

Interestingly, Irigaray grapples with this very question in *Ce sexe qui n'en est pas un*.[13] When asked whether over and beyond the deconstruction of the Freudian theory of femininity, one could formulate an alternative unconscious of the feminine, Irigaray responds with a call to historicize the concept of the unconscious. This would require a consideration of that which, in the current designation of the unconscious, would be the repressed feminine. In other words, she wonders what in the psychoanalytical understanding of the unconscious constitutes the captured and repressed feminine of history. In order to determine this, one would need to study the feminine specificity that was occluded by the formulation of the unconscious. As for the question of a feminine unconscious, she asks whether a feminine symbolic could even have something like a repressed, let alone require a space for it. Even if one accepted that the unconscious was the repressed and censured feminine of history, it was still an unconscious that remained inscribed within the domain of discourse, as an object or theme to be studied and recuperated by the systems of the former. In other words, reluctant to imprison the elaboration of 'un inconscient de femme' within the logic of discourse, unwilling to theorize it as a content, Irigaray asks what the psychoanalytical theorization of the unconscious itself contains of the unconscious. Not wishing to go as far as to define a specifically feminine unconscious, she wants to consider what a masculine elaboration of the unconscious represses of the feminine. Her project of psychoanalyzing the psychoanalysts and the philosophers is subtended by the premise that the feminine is the repressed of the masculine unconscious. In short, the unconscious of an unconscious.

We do see that male-authored texts are capable of articulating this unconscious. The operations of the feminine can be clearly discerned in these texts; the excess, the power to disturb and irrupt through the systems of representation, they are all there. Assuming that writing speaks a desire, that writing is desire, male authors can evidently make a space for the feminine and can speak it. The unconscious of male-authored texts, far from being repressed, hidden, buried, and distorted, works at the very level of their conscious structures; it exists along with them, it functions alongside them, it disturbs and destabilizes them. No, if masculine desire can manifest its unconscious, it does not mean that male authors are better psychoanalysts than feminist critics. There is more at issue here than the tempting, but facile, opposition between the blindness of the critic and the insight of the text. If the feminist reading of male-authored texts that draw upon certain myths can only take us up to a specific point beyond which it encounters workings and operations that shatter its assumptions about how the economy of desire operates, or if it finds an unexpected convergence between these operations and its elaboration of the feminine, this does not mean that feminism is a poor reader of myth. It could be that there is something in myth that can only render a poor reading of how desire works. Myth, perhaps, has very little to tell us about desire. As a system of signification, it can perhaps only give us a displaced and distorted view of it. And to compound matters, we quickly realize there is no Oedipus in the Oedipal, nor a Narcissus in narcissism. Ultimately, it is not even a question of a difference between a knowing Narcissus or Oedipus and an unknowing one, between a duped one and an aware one, between one who has been psychoanalysed and one who has not. Desire seems to be uncaring of what it knows or does not know, what it is aware of or unaware of, so that it is no longer a question of a conscious desire opposed to an unconscious one, or a male unconscious opposed to the feminine, but of multiple movements and flows of one and the same economy of desiring-production.[14]

In the sections that follow, I will examine the model of the unconscious elaborated by Deleuze and Guattari and outline the manner in which their ontology of desire circumvents the theoretical traps of psychoanalysis and structuralism. I will also explore the value of an ontology of difference that retains materiality and corporeality for sexuality while rescuing it from the traditional dualisms (such as mind/body, idealism/materialism, truth/illusion) with which feminist thought has contended for the past three decades.[15]

Deleuze and Guattari: Towards an Anoedipal, Anarcissistic Unconscious

In *Anti-Oedipus*, Deleuze and Guattari offer a conception of the unconscious that enables us to grapple with the question that both *Pierre et Jean* and *Le chef-d'oeuvre inconnu* raise: how and why is it that desire in male-authored texts escapes the mythic paradigms of psychoanalysis and psychoanalytical feminism? They permit us to theorize the presence of the feminine in male-authored texts in a more satisfactory manner by trying to account for why myth is inadequate to desire.

Deleuze and Guattari propose a materialist theory of the unconscious that ceases to view it in terms of a split or schism between a deep and surface structure. Instead of considering the unconscious primarily in terms of the oppositions between truth and error, reality and illusion (that is, in terms of representation and signification), they wish to understand it in terms of the real, understood as non-representative, asignifying movements and flows of desire. For Deleuze and Guattari, Freud's genius and modernity lay in his discovery of the sheer materiality of unconscious drives, of the productive force of the unconscious. What they reject in psychoanalysis is its attempt to enclose the productive power of desire within the abstraction of the Oedipal triangle. By confining desire to the sterile structure of the symbolic, and by subjecting it to the law of the absent phallus as a master signifier, psychoanalysis 'territorializes' or codes the unconscious within a structural representation that condemns it to lack and impossibility. Desire is deformed within a signification in which it can only desire what is missing, impossible, or out of reach. Psychoanalysis stumbles upon the positive material forces and drives of the unconscious only to imprison them within the rigid structures of representation and signification. The unconscious becomes a theatre for the playing out of the same tiresome family drama, the same Greek tragedy of incest, castration, and lack:

> The great discovery of psychoanalysis was that of the production of desire, of the productions of the unconscious. But once Oedipus entered the picture, this discovery was soon buried beneath a new brand of idealism: a classical theater was substituted for the unconscious as a factory; representation was substituted for the units of production of the unconscious; and an unconscious that was capable of nothing but expressing itself – in myth, tragedy, dreams – was substituted for the productive unconscious.[16]

Deleuze and Guattari refuse the meaning that Freud ascribes to the unconscious. For them, there is nothing to interpret in the unconscious, nothing there that represents, nothing that signifies. The unconscious is a factory, not a theatre, it is machinic (an assemblage of parts that work and produce), non-representative, and asignifying. 'No problem of meaning, only of usage.'[17] The unconscious is neither dyadic nor triangular in structure; its multiplicity cannot be shored up within the three sides of the Oedipal triangle. It is a plane of immanence, a surface of multiple flows, movements, and connections. It cannot be reduced to binary or biunivocalized structures. Desire can be distributed according to the different series or terms of a structure, but will always escape them to produce the multiple communications, connections, and syntheses of what they term 'assemblages.' Desire can be captured and stratified within the large categories of the 'molar,' but will always elude them on the lines of escape of 'molecular *becomings*.'[18]

For Deleuze and Guattari in *Anti-Oedipus*, then, the unconscious is an orphan; it is asubjective and anoedipal. Its impersonal and subjectless force can always break apart the narrow parameters of the Oedipal triangle, 'a poorly closed triangle, a porous or seeping triangle, an exploded triangle from which the flows of desire escape in the direction of other territories.'[19] If there is a structure to the unconscious, it is one that multiplies polygons rather than restricting itself to dyads and triads: '(not even 3+1, but 4+n).' It is not determined by the lack or absence of an empty signifier. Rather, any structure of the unconscious (and they can be multiple!) is a machinic production of *signs*, as forces of desire that know of no lack:

> [The sign] is a production of the real and a position of desire within reality ... [T]he sign of desire is never a sign of the law, it is a sign of strength (*puissance*) ... [T]he sign of desire is never signifying, it exists in the thousands of productive breaks-flows that never allow themselves to be signified within the unary stroke of castration. (111–12)

There is no signifying chain to the unconscious, no single and overarching code or law of desire. Desiring-signs are multiple; 'these indifferent signs follow no plan, they function at all levels and enter into any and every sort of connection' (38).

In *Anti-Oedipus*, Deleuze and Guattari offer a more nuanced conception of structure by inviting us to explore the positivity of the reverse side of the one that Lacan establishes for the unconscious. And it is here that they forcefully push Lacan's intuition of the Oedipal as a fiction of the imaginary towards its full implications for the unconscious. For Deleuze and Guattari, Lacan's radicality lay in his understanding of the Oedipus as an imaginary structure of representation within which the unconscious comes to be trapped, but within which the unconscious cannot be completely enclosed. It is at this point of auto-critique that Deleuze and Guattari wish to step in, 'where desire is shifted into the order of production, related to its molecular elements, and where it lacks nothing, because it is defined as *the natural and sensuous objective being*, at the same time as the Real is defined as *the objective being of desire*' (311; emphasis in original).

By viewing the unconscious as a machinic assemblage of production, Deleuze and Guattari offer us a way out of the mythic structures and distortions from which psychoanalysis is unable to rescue desire. Instead of understanding the unconscious as a stage for self-representation (as Lacan and Irigaray essentially do), they consider it as a force of asignifying production. In other words, for the scenography of the unconscious, they substitute the power of desiring-production, and for the negative drama of the self-same, the positive and asubjective multiplicity of the real. The unconscious for them is no more narcissistic than it is Oedipal:

> If desire produces, its product is real. If desire is productive, it can be productive only in the real world and can produce only reality ... Desire does not lack anything; it does not lack its object. *It is, rather, the* subject *that is missing in desire, or desire that lacks a fixed subject; there is no fixed subject unless there is repression.* Desire and its object are one and the same thing: the machine, as a machine of a machine. Desire is a machine, and the object of desire is another machine connected to it ... The objective being of desire is the Real in and of itself. (26–7; emphasis mine)

In *Anti-Oedipus*, Deleuze and Guattari allow us to break out of the categories of truth, falsehood, and illusion as applied to the unconscious in order to deal with the real as the force and movement of becomings. It is important to note that they do not deny that distortions can be effectuated upon desire. What is pernicious about the Oedipus is that it operates precisely through a disfiguring or displacement of desire. Not only does it repress desire by forcing its multiplicity within the configuration of the family triangle, but it also dissimulates the real nature of what is repressed. It leads us to believe that what is repressed is incestuous desire when, in fact, what is repressed is the multiple and anoedipal nature of desire: 'The law tells us: You will not marry your mother, and you will not kill your father. And we docile subjects say to ourselves: so *that's* what I wanted!' (114; emphasis in original). For Deleuze and Guattari, one cannot infer the nature of what is repressed from the law that represses: 'Oedipal desires are the bait, the disfigured image by means of which repression catches desire in the trap. If desire is repressed, this is not because it is desire for the mother and for the death of the father; on the contrary, desire becomes that only because it is repressed, it takes on that mask only under the reign of the repression that models the mask for it and plasters it on its face' (116).

Like Lacan and Irigaray, Deleuze and Guattari recognize that a fiction or an idea is imposed upon the unconscious by psychoanalysis (and the Oedipal). But they push this line of thought much further than either Lacan or Irigaray by refusing to see the unconscious as essentially or fundamentally distorted. Where both Lacan and Irigaray operate for the most part within the terms of this distortion, Deleuze and Guattari do not. The driving concern of their thought is to theorize the moments when desire escapes its distortions, to rescue the positive and multiple force of the unconscious from the despotic meanings inscribed upon it. For them, the unconscious is always capable of escaping the skewed mechanism of the Oedipal. The materiality of desire and sexuality can always break through systems of representation and signification: '[S]exuality and love do not live in the bedroom of Oedipus, they dream instead of wide-open spaces, and cause strange flows to circulate that do not let themselves be stocked within an established order' (116). And as I will argue a little later during the course of this study, by refusing to consider these places of escape as anything other than moments of positive affirmation of desire, Deleuze and Guattari offer us a way out of some of the impasses into which psychoanalytical feminism may be led.

Like Irigaray, Deleuze and Guattari wish to account for the materiality of desire but, unlike her, do so without claiming it exclusively for one sex while denying it for the other. That is to say, they do not partition this materiality between two mutually exclusive sexes (or statistical aggregates). They do not free sexuality for one sex by enclosing the other within its fictions. They avoid the move whereby a distinction has to be made between a masculine and a feminine unconscious or a male and female one, a move that would necessarily reimpose the binary organizations of representation and signification upon the unconscious. Instead of a rigid separation into two molar sexes, in *Anti-Oedipus* they call for the communicating multiplicity of a molecular sexuality:

[E]verywhere a microscopic transsexuality, resulting in the woman containing as many men as the man, and the man as many women, all capable of entering – men with women, women with men – into relations of production of desire that overturn the statistical order of the sexes. Making love is not just becoming as one, or even two, but becoming as a hundred thousand. Desiring-machines or the nonhuman sex: not one or even two sexes, but *n* sexes ... beyond the anthropomorphic representation that society imposes on this subject, and with which it represents its own sexuality. The schizoanalytic slogan of the desiring-revolution will be first of all: to each its own sexes. (295–6)

Refusing a molar and anthropomorphic representation of sexuality, they propose one that, from a statistical distribution of two sexes, enables us to theorize multiplicity in an inclusive rather than an exclusive manner. But more important, by so doing, they allow us to understand and affirm desire as a positive and multiple force. *Anti-Oedipus* and *A Thousand Plateaus* provide us with powerful (and crucial) intellectual tools that enable desire and thought to break out of the sterile circle of representation in which they may be imprisoned in order to confront the real, to think in terms of the real and the possible.

Towards the Imperceptible, the Indiscernible, and the Impersonal

Deleuze and Guattari break with phenomenology and humanism to construct a different ontology of desire. As we saw with *Anti-Oedipus*, theirs is a materialist thought that ceases to consider forces in terms of the anthropomorphic and the subjective. For Deleuze and Guattari, desire is a force that extends beyond the realm of the human, and further than the domain of sexual or gender relations. As a machinic production of heterogeneous connections and syntheses, it expresses a vitalism that includes the animal and the vegetal, the animate and the inanimate, the 'solidity' of the material, as well as the evanescence of the imperceptible and microscopic – an ontology of the geological. To be is to desire and become, but to become is to 'happen,' to synthesize and produce new relations and connections. Spinoza's notion of 'substance' becomes an important tool in the elaboration of this different ontology of desire. For Spinoza, all beings and things derive from a single, absolute, and infinite substance (God). Different individual entities derive from different modifications of substance, but these organizations are in themselves not eternal and fixed forms; they express the ever-changing relations of a singular substance. In other words, for Spinoza, it is substance that is eternal and essential, not form. Or rather, the very dualism between form and substance is abolished, because form and substance, mind and body are immanent to each other. The individuality of different entities derives from the relations into which they enter among themselves, but these modifications constitute a constantly fluid and dynamic process.

Deleuze and Guattari replace the Spinozist notion of substance with a 'plane of immanence' in which being is defined by its modes, or events of modification. Being is an event, and 'to be' is 'to happen.'[20] From the domain of fixed essences, entities, and beings, we now move towards the relations and modifications of beings, or towards the world of events.

In *A Thousand Plateaus*, Deleuze and Guattari invite us to reconsider Spinoza's notion of the body in the following manner:

> Arrive at elements that no longer have either form or function, that are abstract in this sense even though they are perfectly real. They are distinguished solely by movement and rest, slowness and speed. They are not atoms, in other words, finite elements still endowed with form. Nor are they infinitely divisible. They are infinitely small, ultimate parts of an actual infinity, laid out on the same plane of consistency or composition. (253–4)

What Deleuze and Guattari find interesting in Spinoza is that he understands bodies not as fixed forms or essences, but as relations of speed, movements, pauses, and rests: '[D]epending on their degree of speed or the relation of movement and rest into which they enter, they belong to a given Individual, which may itself be part of another Individual governed by another, more complex, relation, and so on to infinity' (254). The usefulness of Spinoza's conception of substance lies in its ability to encompass the materiality of the infinitely small and the infinitely large. Once again, it accomplishes this by understanding materiality in terms of relations of forces rather than in terms of organic entities, essential qualities, and characteristics.

This Spinozist understanding of substance becomes essential to Deleuze and Guattari in the construction of their thought of an 'incorporeal materiality' – the concept of the plane of consistency, which is a plane of life that encompasses the animate and the inanimate, the natural and the artificial. The plane of consistency is constituted by an infinity of particles and their relations of speed and movement, or their modifications. On this plane of immanence, '[t]he One is said with a single meaning of all the multiple [and] Being expresses in a single meaning all that differs.'[21] Deleuze and Guattari avoid the exclusive disjunction of either/or set up between the one and the other or between the one and the multiple by conceiving of being as the one *and* the multiple, of the one *as* the multiple.[22]

As mentioned earlier, the construction of the plane of immanence allows for a different (Spinozist) conception of the body. Rather than as organic entities defined according to form or meaning, bodies are grasped in terms of the relations into which they enter with one another. They are understood as affects or intensities, as potentialities to affect and be affected by other bodies. They are distinguished from each other only by relations of movement and rest, and by the connections they form. The plane of immanence is abstract because it is a plane where there are no longer any forms, functions, or organizations, only the movements of anonymous molecules that form different connections with each other. This, then, is a plane of affects and intensities, a plane of becomings, events, and haecceities.

The plane of consistency has another side that is copresent or coextensive to it: this is a plane of organization that concerns the development of structures, forms, functions, and subjects. But it is not a question of a separation or opposition between two types of planes. Rather, they are to be thought of as two sides of a surface that extend into one another, and that are immanent to each other. While the plane of organization is a plane of stratification of forms, subjects, organs, and functions, the plane of consistency or immanence is a plane of destratification, of the extraction or liberation of asignifying particles and elements from the strata. This extraction or production of particles can also be effectuated by the most 'artificial' of means (art being one such example), none of which detract from their being real.

In other words, the plane of consistency is not a prior source or principle, an initial ground from which the plane of organization is later extracted. Rather, as Philip Goodchild notes, the planes of consistency and organization are in a state of 'inclusive disjunction,'[23] simultaneous, yet not quite coincidental.[24] The copresence of the two planes has an important implication for the conception of desire – it is no longer an originary principle or reservoir, but an effect that is produced: '[T]he plane is a state of desire, but far from being a natural, primal, spontaneous or chaotic state, it is quite the opposite. Desire exists only when assembled or machined. The plane exists only when constructed. Far from being an abstract, universal subject, desire is nothing other than the set of passive syntheses or specific assemblages which construct it.'[25]

It is important to note that for Deleuze and Guattari, forms, functions, and stratifications are not always oppressive or destructive; on the contrary, they prevent the plane of consistency from disappearing into the undifferentiated emptiness of the void. '[S]o much caution is needed to prevent the plane of consistency from becoming a pure plane of abolition or death, to prevent the involution from turning into a regression to the undifferentiated. Is it not necessary to retain a minimum of strata, a minimum of forms and functions, a minimal subject from which to extract materials, affects, and assemblages?'[26] It is on the plane of organization that forces are captured, coded, and territorialized (forms and functions extracted), but on the plane of consistency that they are set free. In other words, it is the immanence of the planes of consistency and organization to each other that permits the positive relations and connections among forces to occur, and which makes becomings possible. The planes of consistency and organization, or rather, the two poles of the plane of immanence together ensure the production of assemblages and becomings.

Deleuze and Guattari's engagement with Spinoza results in the laying out of a new ethics of desire, one that is concerned with the following problems: What is the plane of composition that will permit the production of becomings? At what point does the plane of organization become despotic and destructive enough to impede the creation of new and different syntheses, affects, and becomings? And how does one prevent a becoming from veering into the void of chaos, where the speeds and movements are so fast and furious that no relations can be entered into?

Central to Deleuze and Guattari's 'philosophy of the event' is the notion of 'becomings.' Becomings are to be understood as productive relations or connections between bodies that flee the rigidity and stasis of organization. In other words, they are expressions of forces that do not allow themselves to be restricted or limited by the categories, forms, and functions of strata. It is here that Deleuze and Guattari mark their difference from structuralism, which tends to view relations between forces according to the principles of identity, opposition, equality, and analogy, and primarily understands forces in terms of fixed and immutable structures.[27] Deleuze and Guattari view relations between forces in terms of dynamic becomings. A becoming for them is neither a correspondence between relations (as with the structuralists), nor an imitation or an identification. Becoming is the production of a process of desire, of subjectless relations and syntheses. Becoming lacks both a subject and terms, since terms only exist to the extent that they are taken up in another becoming which forms a block with the first, and with which it coexists. Becomings are movements of forces that evade fixed forms and categories, but are no less real for all that:

> Becoming can and should be qualified as becoming-animal even in the absence of a term that would be the animal become. The becoming-animal of the human being is real, even if the animal the human being becomes is not; and the becoming-other of the animal is real, even if that something other it becomes is not.[28]

Becoming is thus not so much an ability to transform oneself from one entity into another as a process of desire that is independent of subjects

and forms. To become is to form compositions that distend the boundaries between organic entities; it is to create and enter zones of indiscernibility:

> Starting from the forms one has, the subject one is, the organs one has, or
> the functions one fulfills, becoming is to extract particles between which
> one establishes the relations of movement and rest, speed and slowness that
> are *closest* to what one is becoming and through which one becomes ... It
> indicates as rigorously as possible a zone of proximity or copresence of a
> particle, the movement into which any particle that enters the zone is drawn
> ... Becoming is to emit particles that take on certain relations of movement
> and rest because they enter a particular zone of proximity. Or, it is to emit
> particles that enter that zone because they take on those relations.[29]

The zone of a becoming is the space of the in-between, a no-man's-land
of the middle. Again, becoming is not the evasion of a self from one identity into another; it is the creation of an intermediate zone that escapes
both terms. But more important, becoming is a matter of being enveloped in the middle of the productive power of 'the three virtues of imperceptibility, indiscernibility, and impersonality': 'One is then like grass:
one has made the world, everybody/everything, into a becoming, because one has made a necessarily communicating world, because one has
suppressed in oneself everything that prevents us from slipping between
things and growing in the midst of things.'[30] And it is on the surface of
the plane of consistency that renders possible the charting out of becomings, on the plane of desire of the 'Body without Organs' (the BwO) that
Deleuze and Guattari define the possibility of a new freedom and ethics.
   As we saw earlier, for Deleuze and Guattari, desire is neither an originary cause nor a principle of the human; it is not even something to be
understood in the image of the human. It is a plane of immanence, a vast
surface field of movements, speeds, flows, and intensities. It is a 'Body
without Organs,' opposed not to organs as such, but to the organism, or
the meaningful organization of organs. The BwO is a continuum of asignifying flows that can be stratified into signifying bodies and subjects,
and sedimented according to forms, meanings and functions, but which
also flees its organization towards the plane of consistency of becomings.
The BwO is a plane that is constructed for the creation and syntheses of
ever new and different relations, a surface for the passage of becomings,
intensities, and affects.[31]
   The concept of the Body without Organs allows Deleuze and Guattari
to articulate a new possibility for the material and the corporeal, giving

rise to a different ethics of desire. Desire is seen as the productive force of the multiplicities and becomings of the real; it expresses the potential of the productive (and anorganic) power of life forces. As such, it demands an ethics of expression rather than representation. In other words, it is not a matter of determining whether a given force of desire is true or false; it is one of ascertaining whether it will allow an organism to create new and productive syntheses, or if, on the contrary, it will immure the organism in a stasis that will either destroy or impede that process. The only questions one need ask are: How can we free the organism from despotic subjectifications? How can we construct a BwO that will liberate the productive flows of desire, and how do we exercise enough sobriety and caution to prevent desire from turning into a deadly and destructive fascist force? How can we make sure that a Body without Organs will not be an empty or catatonic one, on which nothing can come to pass and on which nothing can be produced? Their entire ethic can thus be summarized as follows:

> It is a problem not of ideology but of pure matter, a phenomenon of physical, biological, psychic, social, or cosmic matter. That is why the material problem confronting schizoanalysis is knowing whether we have it within our means to make the selection, to distinguish the BwO from its doubles: empty vitreous bodies, cancerous bodies, totalitarian and fascist. The test of desire: not denouncing false desires, but distinguishing within desire between that which pertains to stratic proliferation, or else too-violent destratification, and that which pertains to the construction of the plane of consistency (keep an eye out for all that is fascist, even inside us, and also for the suicidal and the demented).[32]

An entire ethic that demands an entirely different way of thinking about what bodies can do.[33]

In summary, during the course of this chapter, I detailed some of the shortcomings of the paradigm of masculine narcissistic desire articulated by Irigaray and questioned the validity of applying this model to explain male-authored literary texts. Arguing for the need to understand desire in terms other than those of myth, and drawing upon Deleuze and Guattari's notion of the unconscious as anoedipal and anarcissistic, I highlighted their concept of 'becoming' in order to foreground the ethics of expression that they render possible for desire, materiality, and corporeality.

In light of the above considerations, I would like to read Balzac's *Sarrasine* through the myths of Narcissus and Pygmalion in the following chapter. As with *Le chef-d'oeuvre inconnu*, the text not only resists the application of a feminist reading of the myth of Narcissus; it rejects even the narcissism of the myth of Pygmalion to reveal workings of desire that neither of the myths can fully contain. It is *Sarrasine* that enables us to articulate the surprising manner in which Blanchot's reading of Narcissus, and his conception of literature as the encounter with the alterity of the neuter (as the asubjective and the apersonal), rejoins the conceptions of writing and desire put forth by Deleuze and Guattari. Writing breaks with specularity in order to unleash movements and forces for which mythic paradigms are inadequate. Desire decomposes the sexual categories and dualist oppositions of the molar to free and affirm itself along the asubjective lines of the molecular and the imperceptible.

4 Becoming-flower, Becoming-imperceptible: Oedipus, Narcissus, and Their Lines of Flight in *Sarrasine* and *Le chef-d'oeuvre inconnu*

The point is to get out of it, not in art, in other words, in spirit, but in life, in real life ... Of course, this requires all the resources of art, and art of the highest kind ... But art is never an end in itself; it is only a tool for blazing life lines, in other words, all of those real becomings that are not produced only *in* art, and all of those active escapes that do not consist in fleeing *into* art, taking refuge in art, and all of those positive deterritorializations that never reterritorialize on art, but instead, sweep it away with them toward the realms of the asignifying, asubjective, and faceless.

Gilles Deleuze and Félix Gauttari[1]

In this chapter, I once again take up the presuppositions whose inconsistencies were exposed through our readings of *Pierre et Jean* and *Le chef-d'oeuvre inconnu*: first, that (male) narrative speaks uniquely of an Oedipal desire that obliterates feminine difference; second, that the myths of Narcissus and Pygmalion are crucial to the analysis of how feminine alterity is erased by the masculine order; and third, that the signifying systems of art and literature effectuate a repression of feminine materiality and desire. Focusing primarily on Balzac's *Sarrasine*, a short story that depicts the dynamics of desire between a male artist and his female model, and which has been read as an illustration of the moral implicit to the myth of Narcissus (that of the superiority of the Platonic ideal over the deceptions of matter), as well as in the light of an Oedipal will to knowledge, I will show how the text deconstructs both mythic paradigms to affirm the power of a materiality that cannot be confined to the idea, and the productivity of a desire that will neither Oedipalize nor be Oedipalized. I will argue that in so doing, the text undercuts both Peter

Brooks's hypothesis that realist narrative constructs itself by recuperating materiality for meaning and signification, and Naomi Schor's feminist corollary that the aesthetics of realism imposes its systems of signification through an occlusion of feminine difference and an appropriation of female corporeality. The female body escapes the dualisms of sexual oppositions to create machinic assemblages and becomings that are signs of productive forces and movements. Deviating from an implacable progression towards the unveiling of the truth of castration, the narrative flees the unilinear movement towards the revelation of the Oedipal secret and breaks with the Oedipal drama of the recognition of lack. The dialectics of identity and recognition give way to the expression of the non-representative, asignifying forces of the real. My chapter concludes with a survey of the implications of the above findings for a feminist politics of reading.

An Aesthetics of the Sensible

As mentioned before, *Sarrasine* is a novella that explicitly draws on the myth of Pygmalion to structure the relationship between a male sculptor and his female creation, between the artist and the ideal beauty towards which he aspires. Sarrasine's stormy and turbulent temperament is specifically linked to that of Pygmalion. We are told that Sarrasine is brought up by his master Bouchardon in an 'ignorance profonde sur les choses de la vie.'[2] Sarrasine's life of isolation and withdrawal is reminescent of that of the mythic sculptor: 'Fanatique de son art ... il se levait au jour, entrait dans l'atelier pour n'en sortir qu'à la nuit, et ne vivait qu'avec sa muse ... [I]l préféra rester seul, et répudia les plaisirs de cette époque licencieuse' (56). The parallel between the two is a little more explicit in the description of the scene where Sarrasine sees la Zambinella for the first time: 'Sarrasine dévorait des yeux la statue de Pygmalion, pour lui descendue de son piédestal' (58). For him la Zambinella incarnates the Grecian ideal of beauty as a unified, organic, and harmonious whole, one that surpasses the fragmentary perfections of nature:

> Sarrasine poussa des cris de plaisir. Il admirait en ce moment la beauté idéale de laquelle il avait jusqu'alors cherché çà et là les perfections dans la nature, en demandant à un modèle, souvent ignoble, les rondeurs d'une jambe accomplie; à tel autre, les contours du sein; à celui-là, ses blanches épaules; prenant enfin le cou d'une jeune fille, et les mains de cette femme, et les genoux polis de cet enfant, sans rencontrer jamais sous le ciel froid de

Paris les riches et suaves créations de la Grèce antique. La Zambinella lui montrait réunies, bien vivantes et délicates, ces exquises proportions de la nature féminine si ardemment désirées, desquelles un sculpteur est, tout à la fois, le juge le plus sévère et le plus passionné. (57–8)

The sculptor's reaction to la Zambinella is cast in terms of a desire of possession that is complete and total: 'Sarrasine voulait s'élancer sur le théâtre et s'emparer de cette femme ... Bien mieux, il n'existait pas de distance entre lui et la Zambinella, il la possédait, ses yeux, attachés sur elle, s'emparaient d'elle' (58–9). Sarrasine's desire for la Zambinella resonates with elements of Ovid's account of the myth of Pygmalion: 'Une puissance presque diabolique lui permettait de sentir le vent de cette voix, de respirer la poudre embaumée dont les cheveux étaient imprégnés, de voir les méplats de ce visage, d'y compter les veines bleues qui en nuançaient la peau satinée' (59). Here we encounter the topoi set up by Ovid's narrative: the (male) artist's desire for and power over (female) matter. Indeed, Sarrasine's passion for la Zambinella finds its initial satisfaction in the sculptor's ability to 'materialize' the object of desire by capturing it within a system of significations offered by art:

> En proie à cette première fièvre d'amour qui tient autant au plaisir qu'à la douleur, il voulut tromper son impatience et son délire en dessinant la Zambinella de mémoire. *Ce fut une sorte de méditation matérielle.* Sur telle feuille, la Zambinella se trouvait dans cette attitude, calme et froide en apparence, affectionnée par Raphaël, par le Giorgion et par tous les grands peintres. Sur telle autre, elle tournait la tête avec finesse en achevant une roulade, et semblait s'écouter elle-même. Sarrasine crayonna sa maîtresse dans toutes les poses: il la fit sans voile, assise, debout, couchée, ou chaste ou amoureuse, en réalisant, grâce au délire de ses crayons, toutes les idées capricieuses qui sollicitent notre imagination quand nous pensons à une maîtresse. (59–60; emphasis mine)

Again, we detect the mechanisms at work in the myth of Pygmalion, mechanisms that, according to Peter Brooks, constitute the hallmark of realist narrative - art as a means of recuperating materiality for signification, art as a system of signification that assigns meaning and narrative to bodies. This mechanism is evident in one of Sarrasine's reactions to la Zambinella when he sees her for the first time: 'C'était plus qu'une femme, c'était un chef-d'oeuvre!' (58).

Sarrasine first perceives and understands la Zambinella's body within a framework of representation: 'Tout à coup des applaudissements à faire crouler la salle accueillirent l'entrée en scène de la *prima donna*. Elle s'avança par coquetterie sur le devant du théâtre, et salua le public avec une grâce infinie. Les lumières, l'enthousiasme de tout un peuple, l'illusion de la scène, les prestiges d'une toilette qui, à cette époque, était assez engageante, conspirèrent en faveur de cette femme' (57). Immediately, and as we saw earlier, each line, each contour of her body and face is brought back to an ordered organization of Greek statuary. Body and face have meaning and beauty insofar as they can be integrated into the harmonious unity of Greek art, and to the extent that their corporeality is composed, organized and arranged into the signifying system of classic art: '[J]oignez à ces détails, qui eussent ravi un peintre, toutes les merveilles des Vénus révérées et rendues par le ciseau des Grecs ... C'était plus qu'une femme, c'était un chef-d'oeuvre!' (58).

The traits and lines of la Zambinella's face and body are simultaneously 'subjected' to a system of signifiance that operates through binaries: whole/part; feminine/masculine; idea/nature. La Zambinella is the unified subject composed of scattered parts, the body that unifies the fragmented organs, as opposed to the dispersed organs without the unified body with which Sarrasine has had to make do thus far. Bodies are hence understood as a function of the way they are coded. If art is one such coding machine, social codes such as dress, gestures, mannerisms, and gender conventions equally constitute a network of signs, which, when read correctly, permit access to the meaning of the body. And whatever codes the body also codes sexual desire, as we are told by the narrator during his recounting of Sarrasine's rendezvous with la Zambinella:

> Oh! comme son coeur battit quand il aperçut un pied mignon, chaussé de ces mules qui, permettez-moi de le dire, madame, donnaient jadis au pied des femmes une expression si coquette, si voluptueuse, que je ne sais pas comment les hommes y pouvaient résister. Les bas blancs bien tirés et à coins verts, les jupes courtes, les mules pointues et à talons hauts du règne de Louis XV ont peut-être un peu contribué à démoraliser l'Europe et le clergé. – Un peu! dit la marquise. Vous n'avez donc rien lu? (64)

Desire is aroused by a body enveloped in and interpreted through a tissue of signs:

> Elle avait quitté ses habits de théâtre, et portait un corps qui dessinait une taille svelte et que faisaient valoir des paniers et une robe de satin brodée de

fleurs bleues. Sa poitrine, dont une dentelle dissimulait les trésors par un luxe de coquetterie, étincelait de blancheur. Coiffée à peu près comme se coiffait Mme du Barry, sa figure, quoique surchargée d'un large bonnet, n'en paraissait que plus mignonne, et la poudre lui seyait bien. La voir ainsi, c'était l'adorer. (64–5)

During the course of the hours that Sarrasine spends with la Zambinella, because the latter displays all the signs of 'feminine' behaviour – fear at the sight of a serpent, starting at the sound of a champagne cork, weakness, frailty, ignorance, and superstition, Sarrasine unhesitatingly reads her as 'woman.' In fact, the signs of her womanliness are all he sees:

Cette matinée s'écoula trop vite pour l'amoureux sculpteur, mais elle fut remplie par une foule d'incidents qui lui dévoilèrent la coquetterie, la faiblesse, la mignardise de cette âme molle et sans énergie. C'était la femme avec ses peurs soudaines, ses caprices sans raison, ses troubles instinctifs, ses audaces sans cause, ses bravades et sa délicieuse finesse de sentiment. (71)

When la Zambinella suggests to him that she may not be a woman, Sarrasine's faith in his 'eye' remains unshakeable: 'Crois-tu pouvoir tromper l'oeil d'un artiste? N'ai-je pas, depuis dix jours, dévoré, scruté, admiré tes perfections? Une femme seule peut avoir ce bras rond et moelleux, ces contours élégants' (70). Sarrasine conceives of the body as a simple container with a commensurate content; to a specific body, a specific meaning: 'Ô frêle et douce créature! comment peux-tu être autrement? Cette voix d'ange, cette voix délicate, êut été un contresens si elle fût sortie d'un corps autre que le tien' (72).

Sarrasine believes that his power as an artist resides in his knowledge and mastery of 'woman.' The realization that la Zambinella is a castrato deconstructs this belief. The figure of la Zambinella and the statue that Sarrasine sculpts do not function as sites of mastery for the male creator, nor are they surfaces for the inscription of a self-same, narcissistic subject. As with Le chef-d'oeuvre inconnu, the artist cannot recognize himself in his art. It appears as that which is other to a certain movement of desire – Sarrasine's desire to 'territorialize' la Zambinella's body, to fix it within a set of signifying codes and to integrate it into a meaningful, artistic whole results in the production of a statue that cannot be recuperated within such a despotic or totalizing system. For Sarrasine, la Zambinella's body reunites the fragments of an originary, lost (Platonic) ideal, and is immediately integrated into that whole. But the statue appears as other to the drive towards the unity of the ideal. It is already the movement or the line of flight away from it, away from the signifying body that it represented for Sarrasine. The body of la Zambinella has a material alterity that escapes the signifying systems of art and artist. It is a material that fragments the unity even as it escapes it, that sweeps it away in its movement. Art is now the encounter with alterity as materiality.

As mentioned earlier, Sarrasine's artistic power grounds itself in his capacity to know the body and essence of woman, and it is a knowledge that bases itself on the primacy of the sculptor's vision, not touch. With Sarrasine, the hand is subordinated to the eye and vision is invested with the power of the tactile: 'Sarrasine dévorait des yeux la statue de Pygmalion, pour lui descendue de son piédestal ... [B]ien mieux, il n'existait pas de distance entre lui et la Zambinella, il la possédait, ses yeux, attachés sur elle, s'emparaient d'elle' (58–9). When he learns that la Zambinella is not the woman he thought she was, he denounces the statue as an illusion because it calls into question the power of his vision. The sculptor's hand has created something that has escaped the eye.

Henceforth, Sarrasine can only perceive la Zambinella's body as a lack, a desert: 'Monstre! toi qui ne peux donner la vie à rien, tu m'as dépeuplé la terre de toutes ses femmes' (76). For him, la Zambinella's body is a monstrous chimera because its appearance is deceptive – her body is but an illusory shadow of the ideal beauty his art wished to reach. Insofar as the body does not correspond to the signification he assigns to it, its materiality can only be lived by Sarrasine as a deceptive illusion.

Sarrasine could be (and has been) read as an illustration of the Platonic philosophy of art – that beauty can only be attained in the realm of the ideal and not in that of the material. In her book *The Impact of Art on French Literature*, Helen Borowitz views *Sarrasine* as a retelling of the myth of Narcissus. According to her, Balzac was very much influenced by the Neoplatonism of Friedrich Creuzer, a mythographer who, like Plotinus, interpreted the myth as exemplifying the fall of the soul from the spiritual and divine to the material and earthly: 'To Creuzer Narcissus' pursuit of the visible world reflected in the water was analogous to the soul's attachment to beauty without substance, an attachment that lures the soul away from spiritual truth.'[3] Creuzer's explanation of the myth, a key text for followers of Swedenborg, appeared in his introduction to a new edition of Plotinus's *On Beauty*, which was published in 1814 and was followed by Hoffman's *Der Sandmann* a year later. Borowitz reads Balzac's epigraph to the first edition of Sarrasine[4] and his dedication of the 1844 edition to Charles de Bernard du Grail[5] as a testament to the influence

Hoffman had on him and on *Sarrasine* in particular. She argues that *Sarrasine*, like Hoffmann's *Der Sandmann*, illustrates the theme of the artist's confusion between the ideal and the material. The artist's passion for the material incarnation of the ideal can only end in a delusion. Because Sarrasine forgets the truth of spiritual beauty and becomes enamoured of its material embodiment, he fails to reach the ideal through the superior senses of vision, hearing, and reason.[6] Neglecting to avail himself of his 'second sight,' i.e., of his visionary powers as an artist in order to attain the spiritual, he falls to the depths of the lower senses of taste, touch, and smell that dominate the corporeal and the material. *Sarrasine* is thus a demonstration of the progressive descent from the superior senses of vision, hearing, and reason to the base voluptuousness of the inferior senses of taste, smell, and touch.[7] It is a fall that can only be devastating, for it leads to the loss of love and creativity, and mires the artist in the domain of the sensual and the bestial. For Borowitz, Balzac's novella is a lesson about the degradation to which art submits in its movement from the Platonic to the Ovidian banquet, from the sphere of the spiritual to the domain of the material, from the higher sense of sight to the lower sense of touch, or in other words, from the idea to the sensation.

There is certainly much to warrant the reading of *Sarrasine* as an exemplum of the moral philosophy of Plotinus and an illustration of the Platonic vision of art – Sarrasine is punished with death because he, like Narcissus, is the one who lets himself be captivated by the illusion of the material. And yet, the statue persists in its materiality. It survives its creator to whom it emerges as other – Sarrasine cannot destroy it. Not only does it escape its creator, but it is part of the production of several other works of art, and, let us not forget, one that Balzac admired enormously – Girodet's *Endymion*. Far from stalling the production of art, the statue attests to the emergence of works to which Balzac's novella assigns a material history. Furthermore, these works arise in the domain of the senses, as a materiality that eludes the organizing power of the eye. They surge forth as a *sensible*, wherein the tactile cannot be subordinated to or subjected by an overarching organization of vision. The hand ceases to be dominated by a signifying eye or, rather, the eye itself acquires a tactile function. In this respect, the materiality of the statue and that of la Zambinella's body cannot be dismissed as empty and deceptive illusions. For Sarrasine, the statue is an illusion because it cannot be 'explained' by la Zambinella's body – perfect feminine beauty has been created from the body of a castrato. Its 'truth' therefore, cannot be guaranteed by its model. But neither can the model be explained by the ideal – nature has exemplified the ideal in a materiality far removed from it. And yet, model and copy form parts of a series of material works that typify the ideals of masculine and feminine beauty. All of these – la Zambinella, Sarrasine's statue, the statue that Cardinal Cicognora has executed in marble, Vien's *Adonis,* and Girodet's *Endymion* – are not endless and empty plays of a signifier disjuncted from its signified but nevertheless attesting to its (w)hole,[8] nor are they bodies devoid of all materiality, save that of the linguistic and the discursive. They cannot be reduced to the question of a simple Platonic dualism between the ideal and the material, the intelligible and the sensible, the idea and the body. These bodies are receptive to the idea and can represent ideal beauty, but they also point to what flees the idea and the representation of the ideal: 'It is a more profound and secret dualism hidden in sensible and material bodies themselves. It is a subterranean dualism between that which receives the action of the Idea and that which eludes this action. It is not the dualism between the Model and the copy, but rather between copies and simulacra.'[9] The different works of art are not just bodies opposed to the idea or fixed and stratified entities that are separated from or antithetical to it. Rather, they form a line of movement that distends the limits of the two, moving in both directions at the same time – in other words, a 'becoming': 'Pure becoming, the unlimited, is the matter of the simulacrum insofar as it eludes the action of the Idea and insofar as it contests *both* model *and* copy at once.'[10] They are the workings of whatever in the material cannot be reduced to the meaning and signification imposed by the idea, a becoming that is not the transformation of a form, but the rebelliousness of matter. If there is a lesson to be learnt from Balzac's novella, it is that it is not a question of what the body means, but of what it does. What la Zambinella's body signifies (plenitude of the whole or lack of castration) is irrelevant to what it produces. The art machine churns out its productions uncaring of what stalls or jams the machinery of signification.[11] Balzac's novella does not tell us that there is nothing behind social codes, no essence, no nature, no materiality behind signifying systems. La Zambinella's body is not a nothingness or lack – it is part of a real and material production (and several works of art are produced in *Sarrasine*). It is just a body that is not reducible to an organic whole or to an organism (the meaningful organization of organs). It does not represent a sexuality that is biunivocalized into male and female, or that can alternately be one or the other, but is instead the indice of a sexuality that has the power to sweep away the very binarisms set up by the great systems of signification.

The Lines of Escape of Narrative Desire

The narrative of *Sarrasine* may be defined as an attempt to elucidate the mystery surrounding the figure of la Zambinella, or rather, to explain the relationship between la Zambinella and the figure of Adonis represented in a painting by Vien. The narrator attends a ball with a young woman, Mme de Rochefide, who is both fascinated and repulsed by a strange old figure that makes a sudden appearance among the guests. Escaping to a boudoir in the mansion, she chances upon a painting of Adonis and is immediately entranced by the beauty of the young man represented in it. The jealous narrator offers to tell her the story of the secret surrounding the bizarre personage at the ball. His story turns out to be a demystification of the beauty represented in art – the model for the Adonis that has so captivated the young woman (and which was responsible for the creation of another classic painting, Girodet's *Endymion*), was none other than the ugly old creature of the ball.

What sets off the story related by the narrator is the desire that Vien's Adonis arouses in Mme de Rochefide. The figure of la Zambinella is what serves to link the frame and framed narratives. The entire narrative of *Sarrasine* could thus be considered as a structure that seeks to reveal, explain, and give coherence to the series of sculptures and paintings that starts out with la Zambinella and ends with Girodet's *Endymion*; in other words, a narrative that traces the line of a progression that begins with la Zambinella and moves through the points constituted by the successive works of art to which it leads (Sarrasine's statue, the marble copy that Cardinal Cicognara has made, Vien's *Adonis,* and finally, Girodet's *Endymion*.) Each work of art could be viewed as an element of a series, as part of a system of signification that assigns to it a specific place and meaning. *Sarrasine* could thus be understood in terms of a binary movement that, starting out with a secret and progressing towards its revelation, seeks to integrate the various works of art into the cohesive, meaningful whole of narration.

It is in this sense that the narrative structure of Balzac's novella appears as a correlate of the classic representative and figurative art it depicts:

Le figuratif (la représentation) implique en effet le rapport d'une image à un objet qu'elle est censée illustrer; mais elle implique aussi le rapport d'une image avec d'autres images dans un ensemble composé qui donne précisément à chacune son objet. La narration est le corrélat de l'illustration. Entre deux figures, toujours une histoire se glisse ou tend à se glisser, pour animer l'ensemble illustré.[12]

Narration, representation, and signification are functions of each other in classic art (and writing?) bound to the representative and the figurative.

And yet, in *Sarrasine*, both the form and content of the narrative are traversed by lines that point to what flees figuration and signification. The different statues and paintings no longer serve as coordinating points on a single line of narration, or rather, the line drawn through each term in the series is marked by break and rupture. La Zambinella cannot fully illustrate the ideal essence Sarrasine assigns to it. She cannot justify the statue that Sarrasine creates. Nor can the statue illustrate the body of la Zambinella. The model defies the Idea and the copy defies the model. Vien's *Adonis* and Girodet's *Endymion* create perfect masculine beauty from the figure of a woman. In this respect they cannot be completely accounted for by Sarrasine's and Cardinal Cicognara's statues either. There is thus a becoming that evades both model and copies. The marble statue commanded by Cardinal Cicognara already captures la Zambinella within a flow of desire that is not Sarrasine's, as do Vien's *Adonis* and Girodet's *Endymion*. Each work of art attests to a different position of desire and is part of a different desiring-machine. Even more than the terms of a series captured within the homogeneous flow of a single desire, model and copies are heterogeneous elements of a multiplicity, a collective assemblage of desire. The bodies are not signifying signs within a system of meaning but productions of the real, multiple positions of desire within reality: 'The one vocation of the sign is to produce desire, engineering it in every direction.'[13]

The movement from one work of art to another is not linear, continuous, and necessary, with each successive figure deriving from the previous one. The relationship 'between' them is rather one of 'asignifying rupture' – each figure breaks with the figuration and organization of another to make way for something that cannot completely find its narrative origin and meaning in the previous term of the series. They do not just function as links on a chain, as coordinates in the tracing of a genealogy or lineage. They also map out a line of flight that eludes the latter, a line of becoming in which the figure as representation of an object gives way to the emergence of the Figure as event.[14] The Figure is thus what arises after the rupture with representation, narration, and illustration has been made.[15]

To be sure, each figure in the series remains captured within a coding and territorialization – it is categorized by beauty, as man, woman, feminine, or masculine perfection, but it also charts out an accompanying line of escape, a movement of deterritorialization. La Zambinella's body draws the line of flight from the ideal body that it represents for Sarrasine and institutes a movement of becoming in which it 'involves'[16] the others. The bodies in *Sarrasine* are not simply fixed elements in a series governed by a relationship of resemblance or the repetition of an identical principle or quality. Nor is the relationship between them structured by the way in which they differ from a single model. They form a block of becoming whose line does not lead from one point to another, but passes in a travsversal movement 'between' things and points, or in Deleuze and Guattari's words, '"between" the terms in play and beneath assignable relations.'[17] The block of becoming constituted by the figures is not the traversing of a Zambinellean essence or even the constant of a Zambinellean body that would persist across all of them. Rather, it is a body that makes itself take flight, that is itself the force of a movement of flight. This movement is not the transformation of an abstract form, but is the deformation of the body as a force that seeks to escape the meaningful arrangement of the organism. As we shall see a little later, the signifying chain of the narrative is itself susceptible to a becoming. The line that would lead from la Zambinella to the other bodies as localizable entities, or that would bring them all back to itself as a localizable centre is interrupted by a multiplicity of lines and connections that extend it into other assemblages with which it converges and from which it flees. The narrative chain, in other words, shoots off into a rhizome.

Of Bodies and Meaning

What makes the body want to escape? From what is it escaping? The body tries to reach the Body without Organs, an anorganic field of intensities opposed to the organism. As we noted earlier, the BwO is a plane of consistency on which bodies are stratified, signified, and subjectified, but also a plane on which bodies are dismantled and set free. In other words, the BwO oscillates between the surface of stratification and sedimentation and the plane of consistency that destratifies, deterritorializes, and liberates the movements and flows of pure intensities.[18]

At work everywhere in *Sarrasine* is the machinic assemblage of interpretation, signification, and meaning to which bodies are subjected, especially that of la Zambinella. Castration territorializes the body and voice to extract needed labour. Sarrasine's desire for her imprisons her within a despotic code of femininity. In Paris, castration becomes the dirty and shameful secret to which the body is consigned. Old age, ugliness and decrepitude constitute the tyrannical categories used to understand (and condemn) the body:

> For the judgment of God weighs upon and is exercised against the BwO; it is the BwO that undergoes it. It is in the BwO that the organs enter into the relations of compositions called the organism. The BwO howls: 'They've made me an organism! They've wrongfully folded me! They've stolen my body!' The judgment of God uproots it from its immanence and makes it an organism, a signification, a subject.[19]

Balzac shows us the violence and cruelty inherent in the signifying apparatus and the suffering that it brings about: 'J'abhorre les hommes encore plus peut-être que je ne hais les femmes. J'ai besoin de me réfugier dans l'amitié. Le monde est désert pour moi. Je suis une créature maudite, condamnée à comprendre le bonheur, à le sentir, à le désirer, et comme tant d'autres, forcée à le voir me fuir à toute heure' (69). La Zambinella recoils from the categories to which she is forced to submit and where her inability to fit clearly into either side of their demarcations necessarily entails a blocking and drying up of the flows of desire. The body can only live the strata of meaning to which it is subjected as a bondage:

> Elle leva les yeux au ciel. En ce moment son regard eut je ne sais quelle expression d'horreur si puissante, si vive, que Sarrasine en tressaillit. "Seigneur Français, reprit-elle, oubliez à jamais un instant de folie. Je vous estime; mais, quant à de l'amour, ne m'en demandez pas; ce sentiment est étouffé dans mon coeur. Je n'ai pas de coeur! s'écria-t-elle en pleurant. Le théâtre sur lequel vous m'avez vue, ses applaudissements, cette musique, cette gloire, à laquelle on m'a condamnée, voilà ma vie, je n'en ai pas d'autre. Dans quelques heures vous ne me verrez plus des mêmes yeux, la femme que vous aimez sera morte. (70)

'You will be organized, you will be an organism, you will articulate your body – otherwise you are just depraved. You will be signifier and signified, interpreter and interpreted – otherwise you are just a deviant. You will be a subject, nailed down as one, a subject of the enunciation recoiled into a subject of the statement – otherwise you're just a tramp.'[20] This indeed, is the very operation that Sarrasine performs on la Zambinella's body, and to a point where he absolutely effaces it: 'Mais, reprit-il avec un dédain froid, en fouillant ton être avec un poignard, y trouverais-je un sentiment à éteindre, une vengeance à satisfaire? Tu n'es rien. Homme ou femme, je te tuerais! mais ...' (75). But of course, the most despotic territorialization of the body is carried out by fixing it within a signifying landscape: 'Un coeur de femme était pour moi un asile, une patrie. As-tu des soeurs qui te ressemblent? Non? Et bien, meurs!' (75) The heart as a metaphor for a signifying body grounds la Zambinella within the totality of an 'earth' and a genealogy. And it is precisely the deviance and the sterility of what cannot be rooted into an earth that she represents for Sarrasine: 'Monstre, toi qui ne peux donner la vie à rien, tu m'as dépeuplé la terre de toutes ses femmes' (76).

Sarrasine suffers no less the consequences of the large 'molar' structures and categories within which he too is stratified. The deterritorialization effectuated by la Zambinella is too intense for him and carries with it the same danger of blocking the flows of desire, or of plunging him even deeper into their stratifications: 'Plus d'amour! je suis mort à tout plaisir, à toutes les émotions humaines' (76) – a destructive and annihilating BwO.[21] Mme de Rochefide's revulsion at the end of the narrator's story is reminiscent of Sarrasine's:

> Vous m'avez dégoûtée de la vie et des passions pour longtemps. Au monstre près, tous les sentiments humains ne se dénouent-ils pas ainsi, par d'atroces déceptions? Mères, des enfants nous assasinent ou par leur mauvaise conduite ou par leur froideur. Épouses, nous sommes trahies. Amantes, nous sommes délaissées, abandonnées. L'amitié! existe-t-elle? ... Laissez-moi seule ... Personne ne m'aura connue! J'en suis fière. (77–8)

Mme de Rochefide's diatribe is striking not only because it parallels that of Sarrasine, but because of the manoeuver by which it extricates la Zambinella from the sculptor's judgment and condemnation, thereby exculpating her. To Sarrasine's sentence of guilt, Mme de Rochefide responds with an ardent declaration of innocence. Her empathy for and defence of la Zambinella base themselves on the violence perpetrated against the members of her sex through the various categories by which womanhood is defined: mothers, wives, lovers. Ultimately then, Mme de Rochefide will recuperate la Zambinella into the large molar structures and strata of the human: 'sentiments humains,' 'mères,' 'epouses,' 'amantes,' Her decision to isolate herself, her embracing of the principles of religion (although she is prudent enough to just stop short of the nunnery) do risk a complete and possibly catastrophic rejection of life.

Is Balzac's novella then a writing machine that imprisons and calcifies the real (defined as productive, non-representative flows of desire) within its molar workings? Is it just another part of the despotic 'realist' assemblage that subjects all to the domination of representation and signification[22] and, above all, to the tyranny of castration, the master signifier of the phallus as (w)hole? In and among the strata and rigid sedimentations of *Sarrasine*, does there lurk a cancerous and malignant Balzacian BwO?

Not really. For all its great realist codings and territorializations, Balzac's *Sarrasine* is also a wonderful delving into the worlds of the molecular and the imperceptible. It is a great little machine of deterritorialization. What starts out as a straight, unilinear chain of narrative structure multiplies lines, establishes multiple connections, constructs multiple assemblages, and expands into the rhizomatic workings of a becoming. To the binarisms of structure, Balzac opposes multiplicity; to the signifier of lack, the polyvocality of the real and the productions of desiring-machines; to the rigidity of molar strata, the movements and flows of intensities. His BwO is for real.

Of Bodies and Becomings

The famous (and oft analysed) beginning of *Sarrasine* sets up the dualisms and binaries that will serve as entryways into the narrative, with antithesis functioning as the dominant figure of discourse. The opening scene is thus structured with the oppositions inside/outside, death/life, nature/culture, darkness/light, immobility/movement, the world of the fantastic/the world of reality, sterility/fertility, death/desire – oppositions that are also inscribed in a filigree throughout the novella. These binaries will soon be echoed by other dualities: the pairings and mirrorings of the text become increasingly complex and virtuosic.[23] *Sarrasine* essentially establishes two sets of couples – the narrator and the young woman he escorts to the ball, and Sarrasine and la Zambinella. The novella could thus be divided into two lines of narrative that deal with two different movements of desire and seduction, with the figure of la Zambinella functioning as a common point of intersection. Very quickly, however, the couples and couplings make way for movements of doubles and doublings. The relationship between la Zambinella and Sarrasine (itself parallelling the relationship between another sculptor and his

ideal, i.e., Pygmalion and Galatea) curiously echoes that of the narrator
and Mme de Rochefide: 'Oh! vous me faites à votre goût. Singulière tyr-
annie! Vous voulez que je ne sois pas *moi*' (52; emphasis in original). We
find that the narrator gives into the same kinds of judgments and obser-
vations regarding women as Sarrasine. Mme de Rochefide's defence of la
Zambinella is an outcry that la Zambinella herself could not utter. But by
the same token, Mme de Rochefide's repudiation of the narrator and his
story is couched in terms very much like those of Sarrasine's rejection of
la Zambinella. Finally, let us not forget that the narrator's recounting of
the story behind the painting of Adonis is sparked by his jealousy of the
beauty of the figure depicted in it. The body represented in the painting
has aroused a desire in Mme de Rochefide that he himself could not. In
other words, his jealousy of a rendering of la Zambinella could be read as
an (inverse) identification of the narrator with her. In any case, it is
apparent that the parallel lines of narrative now intersect and criss cross
at several junctures, and that the fixed centre of narrative (la Zambinella) burgeons and spreads into other directions, to a point where it
ceases to be clearly localizable.

Echoes, parallels, formal relations, and correspondances. Evocations,
recallings, resemblances, and identifications. Certainly, all of these can
be found in abundance in Balzac's story. If anything, the narrative is
impelled towards the drawing up of such a network. *Sarrasine* could
always be read as a tireless play of a chain of language and signification.
But does not its force lie precisely in its ability to always not quite coincide with that chain, to somehow leave it hanging awry? Or rather,
beyond the signifying structures, do we not hear the rumblings of assemblages in and of the real, movements of territorialization, deterritorialization, and reterritorialization that have in them the power to make the
links in the chain take flight? In other words, the stuff of rhizomes and
becomings?

Zambinella is first presented to us as a figure that interrupts the carefully
ordered world of Parisian aristocracy; he appears in the midst of balls
and concerts as that which does not belong, as that which is outside of
this society. He is confined to a space away from the public sphere but
emerges to haunt its boundaries and parameters. He is thus a figure of
bordering; we are told that the old man 'n'apparaît qu'aux équinoxes ou
aux solstices.' He is labelled as a man ('C'était un homme,' 'L'étranger
était simplement un *vieillard*' [40]), but defined by all that is non-
human:

> Sans être précisément un vampire, une goule, un homme artificiel, une espèce de Faust ou de Robin des bois, il participait, au dire des gens amis du fantastique, de toutes ces natures anthropomorphes. (40)

> Il semblait que ce fût une personne enchantée de qui dépendissent le bonheur, la vie ou la fortune de tous ... Caché pendant des mois entiers au fond d'un sanctuaire inconnu, ce génie familier en sortait tout à coup comme furtivement, sans être attendu, et apparaissait au milieu des salons comme ces fées d'autrefois qui descendaient de leurs dragons volants pour venir troubler les solennités auxquelles elles n'avaient pas été conviées. (42)

For the narrator, Zambinella is the bearer of an abnormal humanity – he is described by categories that are predicated on the permanence of the human and measured by the degree to which they vary from the latter. Fairies, ghouls, and vampires are not really other to human, but anthropomorphic. They are different to the extent that they deviate from a human constant. Zambinella's slowness of motion and lack of coherent speech place him on the side of an enfeebled humanity. He is also compared to an obstinate and capricious child and his outward appearance is not without its share of femininity. Zambinella then, is a composite blend of man, woman, and child. The predominance of verbs such as *ressembler, caractériser, se comparer,* and the frequent use of the conjunction of comparison *comme* serve to enumerate a list of specific and generic characteristics that make up a realist description premised on the identity of the human to itself.

It is his voice, however, that dehumanizes Zambinella: 'Sa voix cassée ressembla au bruit que fait une pierre en tombant dans un puits' (45). '[Aussitôt] qu'elle eut touché le vieillard, elle entendit un cri semblable à celui d'*une crécelle.* Cette aigre voix, *si c'était une voix,* s'échappa d'*un gosier* presque désséché. Puis à cette clameur succéda vivement une petite toux d'enfant, convulsive et d'une sonorité particulière' (48; emphasis mine). The depiction of Zambinella undertakes a slight shift from the realm of the non-human towards the inhumanity of the stone and animal, and the impersonality of the thing. The cracked voice is a deterritorialization of Zambinella, who ceases to be portrayed in terms of the human and anthropomorphic, and is now inhabited by the animal and the thing-like. To be sure, the little 'toux d'enfant' reterritorializes the sound emanating from him onto the human. But the voice opens up a space that leads out of its territorialization as the former: 'Sa voix cassée ressembla au bruit que fait une pierre en tombant dans *un puits.*

La jeune femme me pressa vivement la main, comme si elle eût cherché à se garantir d'*un précipice*, et frissona quand cet homme, qu'elle regardait, tourna sur elle deux yeux sans chaleur, deux yeux glauques qui ne pouvaient se comparer qu'à de la nacre ternie' (45; emphasis mine). Zambinella's eyes resist the inscription of a subjectivity through the look, and their gaze does not map out a phenomenological field for the recognition of one. The transparence and reflection of the young woman's eyes and face are what the narrator finds reassuring after the unnerving opacity of those of Zambinella, 'cette créature sans nom dans le langage humain, forme sans substance, être sans vie, ou vie sans action' (45). Throughout the portraiture, Zambinella is cast as the first term of every antithesis that is set up in the opening scene.

The description of the old man constructs a grid of meaning within which the face and body are interpreted, and subjectivity is assigned. The face and body are (over)coded according to a system of binaries and distributed along a surface/depth dimension: 'Ce visage noir était anguleux et creusé dans tous les sens. Le menton était creux; les tempes étaient creuses; les yeux étaient perdus en de jaunâtres orbites. Les os maxillaires, rendus saillants par une maigreur indescriptible, dessinaient des cavités au milieu de chaque joue' (46). The angles and hollows of the face represent signifying spaces within a coordinated landscape that attests to either the presence or the pregnant absence of a meaningful subjectivity. Zambinella's face is inscribed with the depth of a meaning waiting to be read: 'Puis les années avaient si fortement collé sur les os la peau jaune et fine de ce visage qu'elle y décrivait partout une multitude de rides ou circulaires, comme des replis de l'eau troublée par un caillou que jette un enfant, ou étoilées comme une fêlure de vitre, mais toujours profondes et aussi pressées que les feuillets dans la tranche d'un livre' (46–7). The body too is facialized,[24] i.e., cast as a network of signs, where each bodily trait is an index that points to a corresponding signification:

Quoique le petit vieillard eût le dos courbé comme celui d'un journalier, on s'apercevait facilement que sa taille avait dû être ordinaire. Son excessive maigreur, la délicatesse de ses membres, prouvaient que ses proportions étaient toujours restées sveltes. Il portait une culotte de soie noire, qui flottait autour de ses cuisses décharnées en décrivant des plis comme une voile abattue. Un anatomiste eût reconnu soudain les symptômes d'une affreuse étisie en voyant les petites jambes qui servaient à soutenir ce corps étrange. Vous eussiez dit de deux os mis en croix sur une tombe. Un sentiment de profonde horreur pour l'homme saisissait le coeur quand une fatale attention vous dévoilait les marques imprimées par la décrépitude à cette casuelle machine. (46)

The verbs *s'apercevait, prouvaient, eût reconnu, eussiez dit,* and *dévoilez* delimit the body as an aggregate of signs that must be deciphered. The body offers symptoms that the science of anatomy must interpret. Dress and ornamentation complete the process of semiotic coding:

Heureusement pour la vue attristée de tant de ruines, son crâne cadavéreux était caché sous une perruque blonde dont les boucles innombrables trahissaient une prétention extraordinaire. Du reste, la coquetterie féminine de ce personnage fantasmagorique était assez énergiquement annoncée par les boucles d'or qui pendaient à ses oreilles, par les anneaux dont les admirables pierreries brillaient à ses doigts ossifiés, et par une chaîne de montre qui scintillait comme les chatons d'une rivière au cou d'une femme. (47)

Again, the verbs *trahissaient* and *était annoncée* anchor the body within a semiotic of signifying codes in which an object or jewel is indexed onto the quality it represents.

Zambinella's face is thus organized by a series of dualities: European/ Oriental, masculine/feminine, human/artificial, death/life, surface/ depth. 'The abstract machine of faciality' proceeds through biunivocalization, according to the alternatives of either/or. Divergences are calculated by taking into account the degree of deviance from the normal term.[25] The computation of normalities and the measurement of deviance are thereby subtended by one and the same authoritarian operation that integrates difference into identity.[26] After all, vampires, ghouls, and fairies are still human, only less so. Denoted as anthropomorphic natures, their power of difference is captured and defused by the principle of sameness.

The abstract machine of faciality neutralizes the immanence and corporeality of the body, which is separated from the real. Faces are produced by assemblages of power that act through signifying and subjectifying systems: 'Bodies are disciplined, corporeality dismantled, becomings-animal hounded out ... The face is a politics.'[27] Natural sciences and natural history, with their methods of classification and ordering, also collude to stratify bodies as organisms. What is repressed in the process is the immanence of the BwO, its intensive speeds and movements of territorialization and deterritorialization – in short, the polyvocality of the real.

Balzac's 'realism' does erect such assemblages of power. But Zambinella's face is already on a line of escape from the territorializations to which it is subjected, on a movement of flight towards the inhuman, the asignifying and the asubjective: 'Ces gibbosités, plus ou moins éclairées par les lumières, produisirent des ombres et des reflets curieux qui achevaient d'ôter à ce visage les caractères de la face humaine' (46). It delineates a zone of imperceptible movements and speeds: 'Si le vieillard tournait les yeux vers l'assemblée, il semblait que les movements de ces globes incapables de réfléchir une lueur se fussent accomplis par un artifice imperceptible; et quand les yeux s'arrêtaient, celui qui les examinait finissait par douter qu'ils eussent remué' (47). As we saw earlier, what is disconcerting about Zambinella's eyes is that they are removed from the delimiting and plotting of a field of vision for the reflection and recognition of a subjectivity. They resist the limpidity of the gaze, and they are not transparent to it either. Their speed and intensity cannot be captured by the faculty of vision: 'Il semblait être sorti de dessous terre, poussé par quelque mécanisme de théâtre. Immobile et sombre, il resta pendant un moment à regarder cette fête, dont le murmure avait peut-être atteint à ses oreilles. Sa préoccupation, presque somnambulique, était si concentrée sur les choses qu'il se trouvait au milieu du monde sans voir le monde' (44). Is this the stasis of somnambulism, or rather, the apparent immobility of imperceptible velocity of movement? The old man manages to give the guard who watches over his apartments the slip and come into the salon unnoticed. This makes his apparition even more striking, because it is undetected at first: 'Caché pendant des mois entiers au fond d'un sanctuaire inconnu, ce génie familier en sortait tout à coup comme furtivement, sans être attendu, et apparaissait au milieu des salons comme ces fées d'autrefois qui descendaient de leurs dragons volants pour venir troubler les sollenités auxquelles elles n'avaient pas été conviées' (42). And the very first time that Zambinella's presence is perceived, it is as an *affect*,[28] an intensity:

La première fois qu'il se montra dans l'hôtel, ce fût pendant un concert, où il semblait avoir été attiré vers le salon par la voix enchanteresse de Marianina.

   'Depuis un moment, j'ai froid', dit à sa voisine une dame placée près de la porte.

   L'inconnu, qui se trouvait près de cette femme, s'en alla.

   'Voilà qui est singulier! j'ai chaud, dit cette femme après le départ de l'étranger. Et vous me taxerez peut-être de folie, mais je ne saurais m'empêcher de penser que mon voisin, ce monsieur vêtu de noir qui vient de partir, causait ce froid.' (40)

Zambinella is initially individuated not as·a person or subject, but as a haecceity, a capacity to affect other bodies. 'A degree of heat, an intensity of white, are perfect individualities; and a degree of heat can combine in latitude with another degree to form a new individual, as in a body that is cold here and hot there depending on its longitude.'[29] It is the narrator who captures Zambinella within the individuations of person, subject, thing, and substance, if only to determine the degree to which Zambinella departs from these modes or cannot fit into them as 'une créature sans nom dans le langage humain, forme sans substance, être sans vie, ou vie sans action' (45). Subjective and personal modes of individuation operate through a mechanism of representation that proceeds by means of contrast and opposition. Mme de Rochefide and Zambinella are pinned in one such coding apparatus:

Il [Zambinella] avait surgi sans cérémonie auprès d'une des plus ravissantes femmes de Paris, danseuse élégante et jeune, aux formes délicates, une de ces figures aussi fraîches que l'est celle d'un enfant, blanches et roses, et si frêles, si transparentes, qu'un regard d'homme semble devoir les pénétrer, comme les rayons du soleil traversent une glace pure ... Voir, auprès de ces débris humains, une jeune femme dont le cou, le bras et le corsage étaient nus et blancs; dont les formes pleines et verdoyantes de beauté, dont les cheveux bien plantés sur un front d'albâtre inspiraient l'amour, dont les yeux ne recevaient pas mais répandaient la lumière, qui était suave, fraîche, et dont les boucles vapoureuses, dont l'haleine embaumée semblaient trop lourdes, trop dures, trop puissantes pour cette ombre, pour cet homme en poussière; ah! c'était bien la mort et la vie ... (44–8)

The opposition between Zambinella and Mme de Rochefide is structured by the dualisms old age/youth, death/life, stasis/movement (the above passage is preceded by a reference to Zambinella's somnambulism). But as we saw earlier, Zambinella escapes the major categories by which the narrator marks him: to old age, Zambinella opposes the mutinousness of a child, to death, the longevity of a hundred years, and to immobility, the celerity of movement. And neither is it a question of him being defined by the second term of the opposition – his relation to it is not one of correspondance, identification, or imitation. Zambinella does not imitate or mimic a child, he does not represent life as essence nor movement as a quality. Youth, life, movement are not fixed terms within which Zambinella is lodged. Rather, he is involved in a block of becoming, where each term is simultaneously taken up in another becoming that is coexistent with the first. The exclusionary logic of binarisms gives way to a phenomenon of fusion and crossing over that blurs the demarcation between both terms, without effacing either:

> Ils étaient là, devant moi, tous deux, ensemble, unis et si serrés que l'étranger froissait et la robe de gaze, et les guirlandes de fleurs, et les cheveux légèrement crêpés, et la ceinture flottante. (44)

> [A]h! c'était bien la mort et la vie, ma pensée, une arabesque imaginaire, une chimère hideuse à moitié, divinement femelle par le corsage. (48)

The barriers erected by the narrator between Mme de Rochefide and Zambinella dissolve in favour of an unnatural union of heterogeneities in which no term can be assimilated to the other. Respectively organized within the molar codings of old man and young woman, Zambinella and Mme de Rochefide are deterritorialized and reterritorialized within a hermaphroditic assemblage that involves both in a becoming – a becoming-woman of Zambinella and a becoming-chimera of Mme de Rochefide. Zambinella (as a set of affects) interlinks with another set of intensities (vaporous curls, perfumed breath) and is metamorphasized into an assemblage that is simultaneously inserted into the composition of another via a fragment of thought:

> [J]e résumais, dans une dernière pensée, mes réflexions mélangées de noir et de blanc, de vie et de mort. Ma folle imagination autant que mes yeux contemplait tour à tour et la fête, arrivée à son plus haut degré de splendeur, et le sombre tableau des jardins. Je ne sais combien de temps je méditai sur les deux côtés de la médaille humaine; mais soudain, le rire étouffé d'une jeune femme me réveilla. Je restai stupéfait à l'aspect de l'image qui s'offrit à mes regards. Par un des plus rares caprices de la nature, la pensée en demi-deuil qui se roulait dans ma cervelle en était sortie, elle se trouvait devant moi, personnifiée, vivante, elle avait jailli comme Minerve de la tête de Jupiter, grande et forte, elle avait tout à la fois cent ans et vingt-deux ans, elle était vivante et morte. (43–4)

The narrator, no less than Zambinella and Mme de Rochefide, is shunted along an expanding block of becoming-woman and becoming-chimera that carry away polarities on an ever-extending line of flight. He is himself an interesting figure of bordering. We are given no physical description of him, and we know nothing of his age or name. He has no significant qualities and is set apart from all characterization and particularization. In this sense, he evades conventional narrative representation as an individual or subject. All we know of him are his affects, i.e., his capacity to affect and be affected by other bodies – desire for a woman, jealousy of beauty, narrative agency. The absence of subjective modes of individuation renders the first person singular pronoun of narrative almost impersonal. If anything, the narrator is defined only as a set of intensities and spatiotemporal relations: seated on a window-sill, between inside and outside, alternately hot and cold, on the edge of night and day, between movement and immobility, winter and spring, life and death.[30] In other words, rather than a self or subjectivity, he is a haecceity 'inseparable from an hour, a season, an atmosphere, an air, a life':

> You are longitude and latitude, a set of speeds and slownesses between unformed particles, a set of nonsubjectified affects. You have the individuality of a day, a season, a year, *a life* (regardless of its duration) – a climate, a wind, a fog, a swarm, a pack (regardless of its regularity) ... It should not be thought that a haecceity consists simply of a decor or backdrop that situates subjects, or of appendages that hold things and people to the ground. It is the entire assemblage in its individuated aggregate that is a haecceity; it is this assemblage that is defined by a longitude and a latitude, by speeds and affects, independently of forms and subjects, which belong to another plane ... Climate, wind, season, hour are not of another nature than the things, animals or people that populate them, follow them, sleep and awaken with them ... 'The thin dog is running in the road, this dog is the road,' cries Virginia Woolf. That is how we need to feel. Spatiotemporal relations, determinations, are not predicates of the thing but dimensions of multiplicities ... We are all five o'clock in the evening, or another hour, or rather two hours simultaneously, the optimal and the pessimal, noon-midnight ... [31]

The narrator is a set of positions within a continuum of nature and culture, and with regard to a 'pack' (Parisian high society). He is the anomalous that occupies the fringes, he is the *intermezzo* as an agent of becoming and deterritorialization. He cannot be characterized by a list of traits and qualities, but participates in phenomena of unnatural couplings and reproduction: 'Par un des plus rares caprices de la nature, la pensée en demi-deuil qui se roulait dans ma cervelle en était sortie, elle se trouvait devant moi, personnifiée, vivante, elle avait jailli comme Minerve de la tête de Jupiter, grande et forte' (44). Here, the connections between the narrator, Zambinella, and Mme de Rochefide multiply through modes of propagation and expansion that have nothing to do with a linearity that departs from a single point of origin and is punctuated by others on a unidirectional progression towards an end. The desire with which narration (and by extension, writing) are invested cannot be tied to a filiation or genealogy. Nor can the sexuality that is the index of desire be strictly structured by biunivocal polarizations – sexuality is not just divided along the line of male and female, masculine and feminine, but includes the animal and floral as well.[32] Thought constitutes a mode of procreation cut off from genitality, and both the form and content of narration are fused within a hybridization that breaks through the barriers of rigid and exclusive binaries. '[A]h! c'était bien la mort et la vie, ma pensée, une arabesque imaginaire, une chimère hideuse à moitié, divinement femelle par le corsage' (48). Thought, narration (and writing) are composed of multiplicities and carried along a movement that breaks with the unidimensionality and unidirectionality of a line with an original and end point. The narrator exists as a term in a series or a dualistic opposition only to the extent that he is deterritorialized and reterritorialized, captured within simultaneous blocks of becoming that disperse all origin and establish multiple connections. Any association with the imaginary is quickly dispelled; his relations to Zambinella and Mme de Rochefide are alliances of desire within the real: '"Il y a pourtant de ces mariages-là qui s'accomplissent assez souvent dans le monde," me dis-je' (48). A desire that has nothing to do with an economy organized by hereditary reproduction stemming from a simple union of two sexes, but rather, a desire that proliferates through multiplicities, '[l]ike hybrids, which are in themselves sterile, born of a sexual union that will not reproduce itself, but which begins over again every time, gaining that much more ground. Unnatural participations or nuptials are the true Nature spanning the kingdoms of nature ... That is the only way Nature operates – against itself.'[33] This is why the heterosexual economy to which Sarrasine restricts himself fails to work: positing itself as true and natural, and rejecting as monstrous all sexuality that falls outside of its narrow scope, it cuts itself off from the immense field of desiring-production. The flows of desire cannot but be blocked and sealed off. In any case, even though *Sarrasine* is governed by dualistic structures, binary oppositions, and rigid molar segments and stratifications, it is accompanied by coexistent movements of the molecular that reconfigu- rate the former in assemblages of becoming. There is always a line of flight that leads one out of the impasses in which desire may be cornered.

We started out with a consideration of the significations to which the body is subjected, as well as the territorializations effected on a body by the abstract machine of faciality. As mentioned before, it is la Zambinella who bears the brunt of their despotism in *Sarrasine*. What affords the body a means of escape, and what is its principal recourse?

As we saw a little earlier, castration territorializes Zambinella's voice, and by so doing, situates his body in a certain position within a sexual economy. With old age, his cracked and raspy voice displaces him from the category of the human and cannot accommodate him within its economy of desire. But it is Marianina's voice that will act as a crucial agent of deterritorialization; it will draw the old man out from his con- finement and interject him into the collective space from which he has been excluded. Her singing exercises a fascination on Zambinella that he cannot resist, and it is primarily to her voice, not her physical appear- ance, that he is attached. It is music and sound that link them both, not her face or body (unlike Zambinella's attraction for Mme de Rochefide). And it is with music that Zambinella's desire is freed, that the line of flight that leads out of the corpselike body is drawn:

> Avant de confier le vieillard à ce gardien mystérieux, la jeune enfant baisa respectuesement le cadavre ambulant, et sa chaste caresse ne fut pas exempte de cette câlinerie gracieuse dont le secret appartient à quelques femmes privilégiées.
>
> '*Addio, Addio!*' disait-elle avec les inflexions les plus jolies de sa jeune voix.
>
> Elle ajouta même sur la dernière syllabe une roulade admirablement bien exécutée, mais à voix basse, et comme pour peindre l'effusion de son coeur par une expression poétique. Le vieillard, frappé subitement par quelque souvenir, resta sur le seuil de ce réduit secret. Nous entendîmes alors, grâce à un profond silence, le soupir lourd qui sortit de sa poitrine: il tira la plus belle des bagues dont ses doigts de squelette étaient chargés, et la plaça dans le sein de Marianina. (50–1)

What is non-musical in a non-human body (Zambinella's broken voice) combines with a fragment of musical sound from a child-woman and disappears on a sigh. To be sure, one could always read this moment of the narrative as a sign pointing to Zambinella's shameful past as a castrato singer.[34] One could always tie down the memory fragment to the weight of a secret that must be deciphered within a signifying landscape of the past. But as we shall see later, it is the secret itself that will be freed, both from the facialized body and the signifying landscape, set on a line of flight towards the asignifying and the asubjective.

Desire as the Real

Before dealing with the question of the secret, however, there is a larger issue that needs to be addressed in some detail, that of desire and its place within the split between the ideal and the material. Is *Sarrasine*, as Borowitz contends, a tale that privileges the ideal and the spiritual over the material and sensual? Is Sarrasine punished because he is captivated by the illusory desire for the material? And, in a related line of inquiry, does *Sarrasine* put forth a conception of desire as condemned to lack and impossibility?

To see *Sarrasine* as a valorization of the Platonic ideal over the sensual is to ignore the materiality of desiring-production at work in the novella. As we saw to some extent earlier, desire in *Sarrasine* is firmly anchored within the real. If anything, it is Sarrasine's stubborn and tyrannical privileging of the signifying systems of the ideal that brings about suffering and the rejection of life. Balzac's world is one that is resolutely permeated by the voluptuousness of desire.[35] Sexual energy is everywhere; it suffuses everything from the ballrooms and boudoirs of France to the halls, hidden corridors, and underground rooms of the theatres in Italy. Artistic production proceeds from an unbridled licentiousness that cannot be contained by religious or spiritual austerity, and from which the latter is not entirely exempt: we are told that even the Jesuit priests looked upon Sarrasine's irreverent creations with some indulgence. It is the sculptor Bouchardon who tempers Sarrasine's 'blasphemous' energy; art constitutes one means of coding and territorializing desiring-production: 'Les longues et laborieuses études exigées par la sculpture domptèrent pendant longtemps le caractère impétueux et le génie sauvage de Sarrasine. Bouchardon, prévoyant la violence avec laquelle les passions se déchaîneraient dans cette jeune âme, peut-être aussi vigoureusement trempée que celle de Michel-Ange, en étouffa l'énergie sous des travaux continus' (55). Artistic study cuts and channels the flows of sexual desire to extract required labour:

Sarrasine était depuis dix ans le commensal de Bouchardon. Fanatique de
son art comme Canova le fut depuis, il se levait au jour, entrait dans l'atelier
pour n'en sortir qu'à la nuit, et ne vivait qu'avec sa muse. S'il allait à la
Comédie-Française, il y était entraîné par son maître. Il se sentait si gêné
chez Mme Geoffrin et dans le grand monde où Bouchardon essaya de
l'introduire, qu'il préféra rester seul, et répudia les plaisirs de cette époque
licencieuse. (56)

·Sarrasine's encounter with la Zambinella constitutes a momentous
event where, once again, it is music and the voice that function as crucial
agents of deterritorialization. As Barthes also points out, it is with music
that erotic desire in Sarrasine is freed.[36] Furthermore, the encounter
with la Zambinella initially takes place through the faculty of hearing
rather than that of vision. Instead of being individuated according to the
categories of person, subject or object, la Zambinella is apprehended as
part of an assemblage within a collective field of desire, as a set of affects
and intensities: 'Zambinella! Jomelli!' The absence of the definite article
indicates nothing more than this: freed from personal subjectification,
Zambinella is nothing other than a set of effects produced in and on a
field of intensities. 'The proper name does not indicate a subject; nor
does a noun take on the value of a proper name as a function of a form
or species. The proper name fundamentally designates something that is
of the order of the event, of becoming or of the haecceity. It is the mili-
tary men and meteorologists who hold the secret of proper names, when
they give them to a strategic operation or a hurricane.'[37] The assemblage
'Zambinella! Jomelli!' emerges as a haecceity, as an event that involves
Sarrasine in an opening up to a multiplicity: 'Les sens du jeune sculpteur
furent, pour ainsi dire, lubrifiés par les accents de la sublime harmonie
de Jomelli. Les langoureuses originalités de ces voix italiennes habile-
ment mariées le plongèrent dans une ravissante extase ... Son âme passa
dans ses oreilles et dans ses yeux. Il crut écouter par chacun de ses pores'
(57). Music has a deterritorializing and depersonalizing effect on Sarrasine: 'Gloire, science, avenir, existence, couronnes, tout s'écroula'
(58). With their collapse comes the violent liberation of the flows of
desire:

Quand la Zambinella chanta, ce fut un délire. L'artiste eut froid; puis il sen-
tit un foyer qui pétilla soudain dans les profondeurs de son être intime, de
ce que nous nommons le coeur, faute de mot! Il n'applaudit pas, il ne dit
rien, il éprouvait un mouvement de folie, espèce de frénésie qui ne nous

agite qu'à cet âge où le désir a je ne sais quoi de terrible et d'infernal ...
Enfin cette voix agile, fraîche et d'un timbre argenté, souple comme un fil
auquel le moindre souffle d'air donne une forme, qu'il roule et déroule,
développe et disperse, cette voix attaquait si vivement son âme qu'il laissa
plus d'une fois échapper de ces cris involontaires arrachés par les délices
convulsives trop rarement données par les passions humaines. (58–9)

Sarrasine's delirium is thus the index of a becoming in which desire is
freed and destratified onto the fields of intensities of the BwO: "There is
no longer a Self that feels, acts and recalls; there is "a glowing fog, a dark
yellow mist" that has affects and experiences movements, speeds.'[38] It is
in one such sense that Sarrasine's movement towards la Zambinella can
be understood:

Sarrasine voulait s'élancer sur le théâtre et s'emparer de cette femme. Sa
force, centuplée par une dépression morale impossible à expliquer,
puisque ces phénomènes se passent dans une sphère inaccessible à l'obser-
vation humaine, tendait à se projeter avec une violence douloureuse ... Il
était si complètement ivre qu'il ne voyait plus ni salle, ni spectateurs, ni
acteurs, n'entendait plus de musique. Bien mieux, il n'existait pas de distance entre lui et la Zambinella, il la possédait, ses yeux, attachés sur elle,
s'emparaient d'elle. (58–9)

There is a movement of interpenetrating and fusional multiplicities in
which breath, voice, powder, perfume, facial planes, and blue veins form
disparate elements and impersonal singularities: 'Une puissance
presque diabolique lui permettaient de sentir le vent de cette voix, de
respirer la poudre embaumée dont ces cheveux étaient imprégnés, de
voir les méplats de ce visage, d'y compter les veines bleues qui en
nuançaient la peau satinée' (59). Face and body no longer refer to the
overarching network of meaning into which they were earlier integrated,
but become so many autonomous traits freed from the signifying whole.
Face and body are deterritorialized from the abstract machine of faciality, and corporeality is released and reterritorialized through a becoming
that dismantles both self and other within a heterogenous assemblage
that flees organization and subjectification. In this movement, the eyes
take on a tactile function, intermingling with taste, smell, touch, and
hearing. Instead of a clear separation or hierarchy of the senses, there
are convergences and crossings-over in a burst of affects and sensations.
The opposition between self and other is fused in the construction of a

plane of immanence, a BwO for the passage of intensities, odours, sounds, and colours: 'A continuum of all substances in intensity and of all intensities in substance.'[39]

Sarrasine's subsequent experimentation with different bodily states can thus be understood as part of a deliberate program, that of the fabrication of a BwO. The collapse of a self, the delirium and hallucinations are not illusory fantasies but operations of the real, the making of a BwO for the passage of intensities and affects. Sarrasine's experiences are fuelled by a desire that is a radical departure from the psychoanalytical conception, which sees desire as inscribed by 'the negative law of lack, the external rule of pleasure and the transcendent ideal of phantasy.'[40] Pleasure in fact, is what deprives desire of the joy immanent to it by interrupting its flows: 'Il avait eu tant de plaisir, ou peut-être avait-il tant souffert, que sa vie s'était écoulée comme l'eau d'un vase renversé par un choc. Il sentait en lui un vide, un anéantissement semblable à ces atonies qui désespèrent les convalescents au sortir d'une forte maladie. Envahi par une tristesse inexplicable, il alla s'asseoir sur les marches d'une église' (59). Art is an unsatisfactory means of recapturing the intensity of the encounter with la Zambinella. Subordinated to memory, it offers a reterritorialization of desire through a pleasure that is ultimately deceptive: 'En proie à cette première fièvre d'amour qui tient autant au plaisir qu'à la douleur, il voulut *tromper son impatience et son délire* en dessinant la Zambinella de mémoire' (59–60; emphasis mine). Sarrasine has to find another way, which is through the deliberate construction of a BwO. Fantasy here is not self-delusion; it is the real production of a desiring-machine for the drawing up of a BwO, for the freeing of desire onto a plane of affects and intensities: '*Mais sa pensée furieuse alla plus loin que le dessin.* Il voyait la Zambinella, lui parlait, la suppliait, épuisait mille années de vie et de bonheur avec elle, en la plaçant dans toutes les situations imaginables, en essayant, pour ainsi dire, l'avenir avec elle' (60; emphasis mine). Desire is not determined by lack nor propelled by an ideal to be attained; Sarrasine traverses an 'âge d'or de l'amour, pendant lequel nous jouissons de notre propre sentiment et *où nous nous trouvons heureux presque par nous-mêmes*' (60; emphasis mine). Sarrasine seeks less to satisfy desire than to intensify it; what he is involved in is the fabrication of a BwO, of a plane of desire immanent to itself, which lacks nothing, and which is not subordinated to an external pleasure or jouissance:

Le soir, installé de bonne heure dans sa loge, seul, couché sur un sofa, il se faisait, semblable à un Turc enivré d'opium, un bonheur aussi fécond, aussi prodigue qu'il le souhaitait. D'abord, il se familiarisa graduellement avec les émotions trop vives que lui donnait le chant de sa maîtresse; puis il apprivoisa ses yeux à la voir, et finit par la contempler sans redouter l'explosion de la sourde rage par laquelle il avait été animé le premier jour. Sa passion devint plus profonde en devenant plus tranquille. (61)

In fact, it is the acquisition of the love object that is deferred and put off; Sarrasine is reluctant to embark on the course of action that would interrupt the state of affects:

En commençant à entrevoir qu'il faudrait bientôt agir, s'intriguer, demander où demeurait la Zambinella, savoir si elle avait une mère, un oncle, un tuteur, une famille; en songeant enfin aux moyens de la voir, de lui parler, il sentait son coeur se gonfler si fort à des idées si ambitieuses, qu'il remettait ces soins au lendemain, heureux de ses souffrances physiques autant que de ses plaisirs intellectuels. (61)

What counts is the flow of desire itself, of a desire sufficient unto itself and whose joys are not measured by the norms of pleasure or suffering. In other words, Sarrasine does not suffer in order to obtain pleasure, and neither is suffering a means towards the attainment of pleasure. It is not a question of ends and goals. Rather, suffering and pleasure are intensities, affects on a body without organs: 'The renunciation of external pleasure, or its delay, its infinite regress, testifies on the contrary to an achieved state in which desire no longer lacks anything but fills itself and constructs its own field of immanence.'[41]

Sarrasine's love for la Zambinella is an index of the revolutionary force of desire, of its power to overturn sexual oppositions and binarisms, as well as the divide between self and other. Zambinella is a set of affects that sweeps Sarrasine onto the interpenetrating multiplicity of a becoming-feminine, a becoming-woman: '[I]l se para comme une jeune fille qui doit se promener devant son premier amant' (63). His name itself bears the effect of this becoming; Sarrasine is after all a feminine name. It delineates the region that belongs to the outside, the Anamolous that occupies the fringe of the France/Italy dichotomy – Sarrasine the Arab, Sarrasine the Moor. But the revolutionary (and schizophrenic) pole of desire does end in an impasse, or rather, desire swings back towards its rigid stratifications and significations. Sarrasine's condemnation of la Zambinella will imprison it within the reactionary and despotic structures of the molar.

Why does Sarrasine fail? Why on its way to being freed on the Body without Organs is desire plugged up, choked and reterritorialized? At what point on its line of flight of a becoming does desire become destructive? Or did the BwO already carry with it the seeds of destruction? Was it a BwO of the organism and not that of the plane of consistency? Was it always the cancerous BwO of the strata, fascist instead of revolutionary? Or was it just that the process of destratification was too quick and sudden for the organism? Were the lines of flight too swift?

Perhaps all of the above. But the essential is that it is a matter of real desire, not that of an illusory or delusional one.[42] *Sarrasine* is not a defence and illustration of the truth of the spiritual over the falsity of the material. It is traversed by the real and material workings of a desire that render the above binary moot. Balzac's world and writing remain firmly entrenched within the flows of a matter that cannot be contained by the meaning of spirit. To every totalizing structure of spirit corresponds a movement of becoming – a becoming-woman, a becoming-molecular, a becoming-imperceptible. Art can be despotic, reactionary, and fascist, but it also has its schizophrenic and revolutionary side, one that frees desire on multiple lines of flight. And it is the dangers of the fascist and reactionary pole of desiring-production that are clearly enunciated in Balzac. If Frenhofer and Sarrasine fail, it is because their desire could never quite attain the plane of immanence of the BwO – art always stopped short of that limit. Or perhaps, desire was freed all too violently. To go back to *Le chef-d'oeuvre inconnu*, the chaotic mass of lines and colours that breaks through the signifying systems of art in *La Belle Noiseuse* liberates the flows of desire in too brusque a movement, and risks plunging art into a void. And if *La Belle Noiseuse* teeters on that brink of destruction, it is not because the lines of escape could only go up to a certain point, it is because they were not allowed to go far enough. They were not extended further, and this, through the use of caution and restraint. Deterritorialization was effected too swiftly. But if Frenhofer himself was unable to fully stretch out that line of escape, if he was unable to save *La Belle Noiseuse*, art nevertheless survives through him. Through Frenhofer, Balzac does allow something to escape for a Cézanne.

Oedipus, Narcissus, and Their Lines of Flight

Is *Sarrasine* an Oedipal narrative? In other words, is it a narrative structured by a linear progression towards the resolution of an enigma (centred on the figure of woman)? Is it impelled by the desire for a truth and knowledge that are ultimately the nothingness and lack of castration?[43]

In 'Three Novellas, or "What Happened?"' Deleuze and Guattari note that the novella as a literary genre has an essential relationship to secrecy, unlike the tale, which is bound to the question of discovery. The novella is organized around the question of what happened, while the tale is organized around the question 'what is going to happen?' The novella is tied to secrecy as form, not to the secret as a content to be discovered. In other words, the novella is linked to an unknowable and an imperceptible, and so it has to do with a forgetting rather than a memory.[44] The novella in short, plays upon the becomings of a secret.

Deleuze and Guattari distinguish between three stages or states of the becoming-secret. In the first, the secret is a simple content enclosed in a container, an object hidden in a box. At this stage, 'the secret is opposed to its discovery as in a binary machine having only two terms, the secret and disclosure, the secret and desecration.'[45] But the becoming of the secret impels it towards the acquisition of an infinite form. The secret as a content concealed in a container becomes the secret as secrecy, as secretion. The secret as matter can no longer be contained in its box, it escapes its container, it oozes and spreads. 'We go from a content that is well defined, localized, and belongs to the past, to the a priori general form of a nonlocalizable *something* that has happened.[46] We don't know what exactly happened, just that something did. Instead of opening up boxes to check their contents, we anticipate the perception of a secret – something happened that we must perceive. And the advance perception of the imperceptible leads to the paranoid judgment of 'guilty a priori.' It is this stage of the secret that psychoanalysis holds onto, or rather, the stage at which it is stuck. Emptied of all content, the secret is elevated to the tyranny of pure form.[47]

But the secret does not remain immobile. It continues on a trajectory in which both form and content collapse in a becoming-feminine, a becoming-molecular, and a becoming-imperceptible: 'Oedipus, the phallus, castration, 'the splinter in the flesh' – that was the secret? It is enough to make women, children, lunatics, and molecules laugh.[48]

The secret moves from the virility and rigidity of the molar towards the suppleness of the molecular, onto the 'pure moving line' of the imperceptible. No longer is there anything left to hide or conceal – the clandestine becomes pure transparence. One is innocent a priori. There is nothing left to perceive but the imperceptible, or rather, it is the becoming-imperceptible of the secret that has been perceived. The secret as a matter to be known and understood is dispersed in the movements of a becoming-imperceptible where there is no longer a secret to pierce and discover, just the abstract line of flight of a secret becoming, of the becoming-secret: 'From the gray eminence to the gray immanence.'[49]

This is precisely the course charted by Balzac's novella. Undeniably, what is at stake in *Sarrasine* is a secret and its uncovering. But the secret is far from static; it cannot be confined within a structure determined by the binaries of the secret and its discovery. The novella maps out a complex assemblage of lines that disperse its unilinear narrative chain towards the multiplicity of a becoming-molecular and a becoming-imperceptible. The secret, therefore, is no less susceptible to a becoming; it cannot be restricted to a unidirectional line that begins with the mystery and ends in its solution. Rather than tracing a single line punctuated by a fixed set of points, the novella constructs a rhizome; it draws up a BwO on which it charts multiple lines of movements and escapes.

The opening scene, as noted earlier, sets up the binary machine of polarities and antitheses. It is a world of large molar aggregates and rigid segments, of classes, social ranks, individuals, and persons within well-defined positions. And it is a world governed by secrets. There is always a knowledge to be sought after and gained by 'cette gent curieuse qui, à Paris, s'occupe exclusivement des *Pourquoi? des Comment? D'où vient-il? Qui sont-ils? Qu'y a-t-il? Qu'a-t-elle fait?*' (37; emphasis in original). It is the paranoid form of the secret that dominates here. What matters is the structure of the secret, not its content. Or rather, in a society where the flows of desire have been completely abstracted and axiomatized,[50] the content of the secret has also been abstracted to the point where it is the perception of what cannot be perceived that acquires prominence. There is something to be perceived, even if one does not know what it is: 'Jamais mine plus féconde ne s'était ouverte aux chercheurs de mystères. Personne ne savait de quel pays venait la famille de Lanty' (37).

Already, however, there is a molecularization of the secret. The origin of the Lanty family is scattered on multiple lines of dispersal – its members speak several languages and have lived among different peoples. Zambinella's identity or rather, his 'vie dérobée à toutes les investigations' induces the same paranoia, but at the same time as one attempts to tie him to a fixed origin, his identity is molecularized along supple lines of deterritorialization – he could be a famous criminal in the service of the Prince of Mysore, 'une *tête génoise*,' Balsamo, the Count of Saint-Germain. It is the narrator who tries to fix Zambinella within a stable identity: 'L'étranger était simplement un *vieillard*' (40; emphasis in original).

His recounting of the story of Sarrasine and la Zambinella seeks to integrate and unify the hypotheses surrounding the strange creature at the
ball into a single and logical solution. *Sarrasine* seems to set up nothingness and lack of castration as the answer to the enigma of Zambinella's
identity. In this sense, it does appear to be a narrative that, premised on
the judgment of guilty a prioiri, progresses towards the uncovering of
the dirty and shameful secret of castration.

The novella that would imprison Zambinella within the condemnation of its rigid line of segmentarity, however, also draws a line of escape
on which no sentence of guilt can come to pass. We have already noted
that Mme de Rochefide's final judgment is not against Zambinella, but
against the assemblages of power that seek to subjugate him/her. In fact,
all judgment is suspended on the narration's final line of flight: 'Et la
marquise resta pensive' (78). On this line of escape, there is nothing left
to tell, no one left to condemn. Everything has been revealed, but not
everything has been explained or integrated into a meaningful (w)hole.
Zambinella cannot really be captured within the guilt of castration.[51]
The form and the content of the secret have both collapsed into the
imperceptibility of silence. The suspension of Mme de Rochefide's
speech is the silence of the becoming-imperceptible of the secret, of the
movement of the narrative towards its abstract line of flight. Zambinella
cannot be seized within a fixed identity, s/he will always escape the molar
categories of self and subject, and the judgment brought against them:
'To become imperceptible oneself ... to no longer be anybody.'[52]

Sarrasine is thus a narrative that refuses to Oedipalize or to be Oedipalized. To the accusation of guilty a priori, it responds with a declaration of
innocence a priori: 'It is because we no longer have anything to hide that
we can no longer be apprehended.'[53] For is not the story of Oedipus a
story of the innocence of the becoming-imperceptible? Does not Oedipus
chart this very line of escape for himself and for us? '*Oedipus passes through
all three secrets*: the secret of the sphinx whose box he penetrates; the secret
that weighs upon him as the infinite form of his own guilt; and finally, the
secret at Colonus that makes him inaccessible and melds with the pure
line of his flight and exile, he who has nothing left to hide, or, like an old
No actor, has only a girl's mask with which to cover his lack of a face.'[54] And
like that of Oedipus, the story of Narcissus is also a tale of becomings, of
a becoming-flower and a becoming-imperceptible, of the movement of
the pure, abstract line of flight towards the realms of the asubjective and
the asignifying. Both Oedipus and Narcissus escape the self; they make the
self escape the condemnation brought to bear against it.

Le chef-d'oeuvre inconnu Revisited

We are now perhaps in a better position to understand the becomings at work in *Le chef-d'oeuvre inconnu*. To recapitulate, our initial reading of the text revealed that the figure of the woman ceased to operate as a locus of power in the service of a solipsistic or narcissistic subject. The rupture of the work of art with representation and signification signalled the emergence of a non-specular mode of subjectivity. The artist's canvas becomes the locus of a materiality that cannot be reduced within a dialectics of mastery between a self and an other. Frenhofer, who wished to capture the perfect body of a woman, brings forth instead the workings of a materiality that cannot be contained by idea and spirit. What we have in the painting is not the perfect figurative rendition of an object, but colours, lines, and strokes that evade figuration and meaning. Frenhofer's attempts to integrate the canvas within a narrative, explanatory, and illustrative function run into forces that flee them. His painting does not function as a mirror for the self-representation of a subject. Art escapes the organizing power of an eye/I. Matter eludes the totalizing powers of spirit, and is irreducible to its representational and signifying systems. Art affirms its independence from its creator, impassible and neutral to its 'père, amant et Dieu.'

What we have on Frenhofer's canvas then, is not an object of reference, but a burst of antimimetic and antifigurative lines and colours. In other words, what we have is the power of non-narrative, non-illustrative and asignifying forces of desire. *La Belle Noiseuse* affirms itself not as representation, but as sensation. The body cannot be fixed within a meaningful essence; it is force and movement. It eludes capture within despotic stratification and signification; it is deterritorialized from the organization to which it is subjected on a non-organic line of flight towards the Body without Organs. The chaotic lines and colours destroy figuration and escape intentionality; they constitute a field of intensities and affects. They are the forces of a becoming, of a becoming-molecular, a becoming-imperceptible. What is rendered on canvas is not the stasis of woman as object, woman as spectacle, or even woman as abstraction. It is not a simple matter of the transformation of a form from the realm of the figurative to that of the abstract. Rather, it is the deformation of the body as movement, as the material force of a becoming-woman. With *La Belle Noiseuse*, it is not a question of rendering the visible, but of rendering visible, of rendering perceptible the forces of a becoming-imperceptible.

We identified three pictorial elements contiguous to one another on the surface of the painting: first, a perfect figure of a woman; second, brushstrokes that destroy this figuration to constitute a zone of indiscernibility; and last but not the least, a foot that surges forth from the chaos of lines and colours. There is, then, on Frenhofer's canvas, a figuration that is still preserved. But following Deleuze, I will argue that this is a figuration that differs in nature from the first; it is a figuration that marks a movement from the figurative to what Deleuze terms the *figural*.[55] The initial figure is destroyed by the asignifying and non-representative brushstrokes to now emerge as Figure, as sensation. The body undergoes a deformation within the zone of indiscernibility and chaos, surfacing as that which is irreducible to a preexisting whole or totality of meaning. The foot escapes the prefigured design or intention of a logos to instead emerge as the accidental, the contingent and the improbable: 'Ce pied apparaissait là comme le torse de quelque Vénus en marbre de Paros qui surgirait parmi les décombres d'une ville incendiée' (*Le chef-d'oeuvre inconnu*, 70). In other words, it returns as difference, as that which cannot be recuperated by the principle of the same. It affirms its difference from essence and idea, it returns as the affirmation of chance. The figure of the woman yields to the woman as Figure, to a becoming-woman that is of the order of the event, of difference. What arises to the surface is an effect, a simulacrum as a force that cannot be contained by the idea. What returns is the power of life forces that can no longer be denied by the negating values of truth and spirit.[56] What returns is thus the false in the Nietzschean sense of the term,[57] what is affirmed is the power of art as falsehood. It is in this sense that the affirmation of *La Belle Noiseuse* may be said to be double: it escapes the ownership of both creation and destruction. It does not dissipate into the void, but affirms itself as a neutral and impassible production of desire.[58]

To reiterate, in his intuition of the non-mimetic and non-figurative, Balzac expresses an aesthetics of sensation in which art is freed from the domain of representation and signification towards the movements and flows of asignifying material forces. Balzac's non-narrative and non-illustrative epigraph extends the line of deterritorialization mapped out by its protagonist's painting. Art and writing escape the dialectics of identity and recognition. They are an encounter with the alterity of the impersonal and the asubjective. And in a more compelling manner than *Pierre et Jean*, *Sarrasine* and *Le chef-d'oeuvre 'inconnu* challenge the feminist assumption that male writing works for the construction of a narcissistic subjectivity. They are texts that raise the following important questions: How much does a feminist critique that is unable to wrest itself from the representational system of the dialectic misunderstand of the real forces of desire at work in writing? And how much does its faithfulness to the terms of the dialectic blind it to the multiplicity and difference, to the becoming-woman that even male authors are capable of charting?

A Way Out of the Feminist Impasse?

We have seen that *Sarrasine* and *Le chef-d'oeuvre inconnu* call into question psychoanalytical feminism's assumptions regarding the narcissistic desire of the male economy and, by extension, those that provide the basis for feminist readings of male-authored texts. Irigaray's critique of psychoanalysis does not prevent her from buying into its theory of desire in order to explain the occluded place of the feminine within what she considers to be a uniquely male economy. This generates a feminist critical practice that is founded on a distorted conception of (male) desire in its turn. Such an interpretive framework is driven by the belief that desire is exclusively masculine, narcissistic, illusory, and idealistic, and that it is impelled by the nostalgia for a whole that causes it to repress the feminine. The feminine, in other words, is repressed to cover the lack upon which male subjectivity is founded.

Irigaray's most important contribution to feminism is her project to restore the materiality of desire and to understand how systems of representation repress the materiality of desiring bodies. But by reclaiming this materiality only for the female body, or rather, by seeking to recover it uniquely for the female sex, she risks condemning the other to the domain of illusion and deception. From this comes a feminist critical practice that sees male authors as self-deluded and duped Narcissuses, their desire as illusory, and all male writing as directed towards the construction of a self-same subjectivity.

Yet we encounter texts written by male authors that deconstruct such narcissism, in which forces plough through such signifying binaries and categories as male/female, masculine/feminine, spirit/matter or even latent/manifest to deploy themselves at the surface. Feminism, it seems to me, has thus far been reluctant to understand these forces as desire. Irigaray's strong affirmation of the difference of the female body, and her unwillingness to push her critique of the representations to which the female body is subjected towards a questioning of the very categories of sex or bodies, has perhaps imprisoned feminist criticism in binaries and dualisms that lead to the despotism we witness in its readings of male-authored texts. Again, male writers are seen as duped Narcissuses suffering from an illusory desire that leads them to repress women in order to cover a lack and impossibility so that they may construct a subjectivity full and adequate in itself. Such a critique leaves in place a conception of desire as negation, as a negation of the other. The tendency to think within the terms of the dialectic or according to molar structures deflects feminist attention from the becomings at work in texts and causes it to ignore the workings of desire at the molecular level, where the real is perhaps produced with the greatest force. Feminist readings of male-authored texts tend not to acknowledge the becoming-woman, the becoming-feminine, that male authors are capable of charting in their writing. Or if they do perceive them, they are unwilling to impute to them any real desire or agency, choosing to see them as miraculous returns of a 'true' repressed within a fundamentally false and distorted desire, of a truer unconscious underneath a false one, rather than as real escapes and movements of an always real economy of desiring-production.

Sarrasine and *Le chef-d'oeuvre inconnu* show us that (great) writing is always able to free desire along the multiple lines of flight of a becoming-woman and a becoming-imperceptible. It is perhaps up to feminist thought to avoid calcifying itself within paranoid or despotic structures. It is in order to better articulate the need for an alternative politics of feminist thought that I turn to what follows in the next chapter.

5 Beyond the Dialectic of Self and Other: Towards a Thought of the Surface

The purpose of chapter 5 is twofold: to examine some of the inconsistencies that underlie psychoanalytical feminist theorizations of desire and to lay out the elements of a critique of affirmation that renounces the coordinates of depth and height in favour of a 'thought of the surface.' This chapter therefore attends to two moments of dialectical thought: the Platonic privileging of the idea over matter, and the Hegelian overcoming of difference (and matter) through the negating powers of self and spirit. Nietzsche's critique of dialectics will first help us to understand how the persistence of the above categories in feminist thought results in an inability to satisfactorily theorize the forces that exceed mythic structures in male-authored texts as forces of desire. We will then see how Deleuze's *The Logic of Sense* constructs an ontology that frees us from the dualisms of self and other, same and not-same, and allows us to conceive of desire as an affirmative force rather than as a denial of difference. Finally, we will evaluate the implications of a Deleuzian 'thought of the surface' for feminism, and the notions of sexuality, materiality, and corporeality in particular.

Nietzsche, Deleuze, and the Critique of Dialectics

In *Nietzsche and Philosophy*, Deleuze assesses the 'resolutely anti-dialectical' nature of Nietzschean thought. Nietzsche's genealogical method and his theory of forces go to the heart of his uncompromising refusal of the Hegelian dialectics of appropriation and negation. For Nietzsche, the essential relation of one force to another is determined not by the denial of difference, but by its affirmation. To the extent that it roots itself in the labour of the negative, the dialectic is a passive and reactive response to forces that dominate it. The dialectic denies life because it does not have the strength to affirm it. The labour of the negative is symptomatic of a slave morality characterized by reaction, revenge, and *ressentiment* rather than action, aggression, and affirmation of positive difference. But more important for Nietzsche, the dialectic is always the labour of the slave, a reflection of the slave's conception of history. Founded on the desire for the representation and recognition of power, the dialectic is always and already power as understood by the man of *ressentiment* and revenge, power as conceived of by the slave: 'Underneath the Hegelian image of the master we always find the slave.'[1] The master who wishes to assert his superiority through the denial of the 'other,' who wishes to have his power recognized at all costs is but a master understood as such by the slave. Representation is the domain of the relation of slave to slave; it has nothing to do with the will to power as the affirmation and enjoyment of a difference that does not need to negate in order to express itself. *Ressentiment* and revenge are negative forces because they deny the power of affirmation of life; they depreciate life forces by depriving them of what they can do. Nihilism and decadence stem from the disease of idealism; they are symptomatic of reactive and negative forces that seek to devalue life. Nietzsche's call for the reversal of Platonism is based on a refusal of the negative power of the Idea that takes away from life. The will to truth opposes superior values to life forces, or the abstraction of knowledge to the power of life. It is thus related to the will to treat the world as appearance, to the will to deny and annihilate life.

Not only is the dialectic based upon the denial of positive life forces, it can only function within a distorted image or fictive representation of their value. Its genealogy of morals (i.e., its ability to determine whether the differential element of a force is affirmation or negation) is already an inverted one. By positing negation as its a priori principle, it functions within an inverted image of the origin of values. The dialectic can only operate within the negative; it denies affirmation which it cannot understand for itself, or rather, the dialectic is able to envisage an affirmation solely within the terms of the negative and the reactive. Hegel's famous 'negation of negation' is nothing more than the positivity of the negative. Thus it is that the dialectic is led to take reactive forces for the positivity of action and transformation, slaves for masters.[2] The dialectic therefore, operates within an inverted image of forces. By postulating the positivity of the negative, the dialectic carries out the ultimate nihilistic act – it is an essentially reactive force that denies itself as force and operates within the mode of fiction. By enclosing itself within representation, by denying itself as a force, the dialectic is a false positive; it understands nothing of the will to nothingness that drives it.[3] Nietzsche proposes a different method of interpretation – a critique based not on the positivity of the negative but on the negativity of the positive. What Nietzsche understands by the negativity of the positive is the affirmation of a force that is able to refuse reactive values, to say 'no' to all that takes away from life.

Nietzsche's critique of the negativity of dialectic has many implications for feminism. As I will argue in the following pages, feminism offers a critique of the 'master' that remains bound within the terms of representation. It primarily understands desire as a force of denial of difference, i.e., in terms of the negative. It associates the 'master' with a sex or gender and links all desire to a desire for mastery as denial of difference. With this move, the ability of desire to escape its representations and fictions is denied. Or rather, these places of escape can never be theorized by feminism as real affirmations of positive difference, or even for that matter, as forces of real desire; they are only ever understood as irrecuperable excesses of negativity situated outside of any economy of desire. Feminism's critique of the master paradoxically continues to effectuate the dialectic's denial of forces of positivity and affirmation. Desire is doomed to the labour of the negative and enclosed within the slavish desire for mastery and sameness. Feminism's critique of 'masculine desire' operates within a distorted picture of desire that ignores the force of desire as affirmation. Its fidelity to the terms of the dialectic prevents it from seeing desire as an affirmation of difference. In other words, feminist critique remains an inverted critique of desire. What it requires perhaps is to wrest itself from the negative, to understand forces in terms other than those of the dialectic. Feminism, it seems to me, crucially needs to extend its critique of the dialectic in order to break apart the very terms within which it functions, and this, in order to affirm desire's possibility for difference and multiplicity. It is with a view to better articulate the urgency of this need that I wish to briefly focus my attention on the problems that psychoanalytical feminism's engagement with and indebtedness to dialectical thought leave largely unresolved.

Psychoanalytical Feminism and Dialectics

Irigaray and Cixous have together provided what is perhaps the most important feminist critique of the Platonic and Hegelian dialectic and its system of representation. The latter, they argue, is based on a denial of difference and a reduction of the other to the economy of the same. Both Irigaray and Cixous recognize that dialectics founds itself on a negation of feminine difference. The history of philosophy and litera- ture is one of reactive nihilism, wherein the positivity of the feminine is repressed and denied.[4] In short, both Cixous and Irigaray denounce the reactive forces of the dialectic and show us how from Plato to Hegel to Lacan, its movement imprisons desire within the mechanisms of repre- sentation.[5] In this sense, their thought allies itself with that of Nietzsche; they understand how the 'fiction' of dialectics operates, and how the his- tory of man is a history of the negative and the reactive.[6] Their project thus becomes an attempt to extricate the feminine from the denial of the dialectic, to free it from the binaries of opposition and contradiction, and to make of it a positive affirmation.

The move to rescue the feminine from the masculine economy of the self-same, however, paradoxically entrenches desire even more firmly within its fictions. With both Cixous and Irigaray, thought and desire can never be rescued from the binaries of the dialectic, and from its negative and reactive elements. The feminine always risks being expressed as opposition and contradiction and being reinscribed within its negating movement. Desire can never be freed from its conflictual oppositions, nor its plurality and power of affirmation be satisfactorily acknowledged.

By rooting the feminine in an anatomical difference and by locating sexual difference between two anatomically different sexes, Irigaray reverts to the duality of sex, to sexual difference as duality. She is unable (or rather unwilling) to theorize sexuality as a plural force, as a multiplic- ity that cannot be contained by the category of (a morphological) sex. Sexual difference is grounded on and within the materiality of a sexually marked body, but the integrity of that body or materiality is itself never questioned. In other words, Irigaray does not push her understanding of how both sex and bodies are produced as categories very far. She exposes the representations to which the female body is subjected, and seeks to recover its erased materiality, but her female body is always and already a body seized within the meaning of sexual difference, of sexual difference as meaning. Her call for the celebration of its forms, fluids, and flows, her elaboration of a feminine sexuality defined according to various morphological and anatomical parts, shapes, features, and markings of the female body risk reverting to a feminine essentialism. Bodies once again run the danger of being confined in despotic meanings and signi- fications. Naomi Schor's sympathetic reading of Irigaray has effectively demonstrated that Irigaray has the intelligence to not posit one essence for the feminine or provide a single, overarching definition of feminine sexuality.[7] Nevertheless, Irigaray's firm grounding of the feminine within the female sex and the female body, and her localizing of sexual differ- ence in the space between two distinct and mutually exclusive sexes pre- vents her from theorizing sexuality as multiplicity. Or rather, this multiplicity is severed between two anatomically distinct bodies. To each sex its multiplicity and ne'er the 'twain shall meet. Irigaray ignores the communication of multiplicities between the sexes, the multiplicity of sexuality within a sex, what each sex can contain of the other's multiplic- ity. Her multiplicity is thus an apportioned duality – the unicity and total- ity of one term opposed to the unicity and self-enclosed totality of the other. As a matter of fact, the multiplicity of sex is never really a question in *Speculum*: male sexuality is always isomorphic, female sexuality is always multiple. To the female her multiplicity, to the male, his isomor- phism. To the female sex its difference, to the male, its identity. So at best, we have the multiplicity of one sex opposed to the unicity of the other, a multiplicity that risks being brought back to the principle of opposition and contradiction. In other words, one has never really left the negativity of the dialectic. To be sure, in her later works, Irigaray does elaborate an ethics of sexual alterity,[8] but here too, sexual difference is a function of an anatomically different body. Sexual identity is distributed between two mutually exclusive series of terms – male/female or self/ other. In this respect, these works do little to extricate psychoanalytical feminism from the paradigmatic and negative reading practices permit- ted by the theses of *Speculum*. Desire in male-authored texts is impris- oned within oppositional and reactive fictional structures. Men are refused their becomings-woman, and the 'feminine' in these texts is sep- arated from all desire and agency on the part of their authors. Desire's ability to escape despotic fictions and representations is thus never understood as a positive force; it is separated from its powers of affirma- tion and is only ever configured within the relationship of reactive force to reactive force.

Careful to dissociate the terms 'masculine' and 'feminine' from 'male' and 'female,' Cixous avoids some of the extremities of Irigaray's thought. She is also able to theorize a multiplicity of sexuality that pre- vents her from succumbing to the facile conflation of male-narcissism- phallogocentrism; a set of terms that is then opposed to the cluster female-feminine-plural. 'The Laugh of the Medusa' does make an ardent and compelling plea for bisexuality, but it is a bisexuality that seems to be curiously subjected to the law of castration, a bisexuality that appears to accept this law and be valorized for this acceptance.[9] The underlying assumption is that the representational hierarchies and oppositions of the masculine order stem from an unacknowledged lack that is then projected onto the figure of the woman. To be sure, in 'First Names of No One,' Cixous does reject this reactive conception of desire, calling for (a more Deleuzian) one that would no longer be inscribed or directed by lack.[10] But this is a side of Cixous that is rarely enlisted in the feminist readings of male-authored texts. If anything, it is her outlining of two opposing economies of desire (the one masculine and appropriating, the other feminine and giving) in 'The Laugh of the Medusa' that continues to inform them.[11] They continue to think in paradigms that oppose male-lack-castration-fiction-negation to female-plenitude-truth-affirmation. An opposition is set up between two types of economies, which is then superposed on the opposition between two sexes. The presence of the 'feminine' in male/masculine texts is thereby lived as an impossible contradiction that cannot be understood or articulated as desire.

The deference paid in Cixous's thought to the tyranny of language (an inheritance of her engagement with Lacan and Derrida) plunges desire and sexuality into murkier waters. Language, the depository of the symbolic order, is seen as the regulating instance of sexuality. Sexual difference is a function of language; it is subjected to and determined by it. Complicit with the dominant phallogocentric order, language is an instrument of repression and oppression. Bodies, sexuality, identity, and desire are effects of language, reduced to the play of signifiers and signifieds. They are thus separated from their real and material forces, enclosed within a system of signs and signification, and placed under the yoke of the phallus. Language, subjectivity, and the lack that haunts them once again become the principal sources of torment and anguish. What is the place of the feminine subject? How is desire to be expressed within a phallogocentric symbolic order? Can it be expressed at all? Can one speak desire? How is the feminine body to be expressed in an oppressive male economy?[12] Lacan's valorization of the phallus as the ultimate signifying instance and Derrida's challenge to Lacan's phallogocentrism paradoxically have the same effect: materiality and agency become highly problematic within a discourse haunted by the absence, impossibility, and lack governing language.[13] The primacy and power accorded to (the lack of) language over bodies, sexuality, subjectivity, identity, and difference once again imprison desire within a reactive structure that separates it from its affirmative power. The presence of the feminine in male-authored texts is seen as a mere symptom of the failure of the signifying instance, as a linguistic effect severed from an affirmative force of desire.

To the extent that the Derridean critique of Platonism and the phallogocentrism of psychoanalysis remains a critique from within the negative, Cixous's and Irigaray's attempts, following Derrida's deconstructive lead, to stand dialectics on its head leave in place the negativity of desire. Their Derridean legacy results in a plea for a feminine difference that can only be articulated (if at all) within the mode of the negative. This difference is expressed as the negation of a negation, and inscribed as an absence, erasure, or trace within a dialectics of presence driven and undermined by lack. It is a reactive critique of representation that remains bound by its terms; the materiality of affirmative forces is condemned to the representation of lack and absence; the only possibility becomes that of the impossible. 'Feminine' difference can never be an affirmation. Both Irigaray and Cixous show that dialectics is founded upon a distortion of desire but they cannot free desire from the terms of the dialectic. Opposing a feminine desire and economy to a masculine symbolic, Cixous brings the unconscious back towards the Hegelian drama of contradiction and conflict. It is a house divided against itself, split between a manifest (surface) structure and a latent (deep) structure that a feminist critique must unearth.[14] Irigaray shows us how a male unconscious uses a fiction and an illusion to deny the operation of the feminine. Thus, she too pits a false unconscious against a truer feminine unconscious, an erroneous surface desire against a truer, deeper one. This move, it seems to me, calcifies desire even more solidly in its fictions and representations, because the deployment of the 'feminine' at the surface of 'male' texts is then seen as a return of the true repressed, as a symptom of a force that works against and despite itself, of a desire at odds with itself. In other words, we are led back to the Hegelian drama of conflict, opposition, and contradiction. The forces that escape the distortion of the dialectic can never be understood as affirmation. Irigaray's demystification of the dialectics of desire becomes a denial of desire's ability to resist its representations, its ability to escape, or even overcome its negations. She is led to deny the unconscious as a positive force; desire is enclosed within the negative and the reactive. Her attention to the negativity of the dialectic enables her to understand how desire denies difference, but prevents her from seeing how desire affirms difference. Ignoring the forces that escape it, Irigaray does not see how dialectics itself gives us a negative and distorted view of desire. She only understands desire as caught within its fictions, driven by a lack that it needs to overcome and negate. Once again, this results in a feminist reading practice in which 'male' desire is cut off from its agency and its power to affirm; it is severed from its affirmative element. Dialectics separates desire from what it can do because it represses desire as affirmation of positive difference. The dialectics of the master and the slave is thus a myth or fiction because it not only represses desire but also gives a distorted and skewed version of what is repressed. Psychoanalytical feminism believes it has done its work when it demonstrates that what is repressed is lack. But it ignores that it is the lack itself that is the repression, a repression of the multiplicity of desire, of desire as revolutionary force, of desire as the power to affirm difference. It is therefore not a question of revealing the truth of dialectics, but of showing how dialectics itself gives us a distorted and inverted image of forces of desire.[15]

Deleuze and Guattari's positing of desire as a continuum, as a single plane of desiring-production that oscillates between its reactionary, despotic pole of molar stratifications and its revolutionary, schizophrenic pole of molecular becomings does much to free desire from the Hegelian theatre of opposition, contradiction, and conflict.[16] Subjectivity is not the central stake in a drama played out between a self and an other; it is a multiplicity constructed in a field of nomadic and communicating singularities.[17] And as we have seen with *Sarrasine* and *Le chef-d'oeuvre inconnu*, art does not function as a specular space for the elaboration of a dialectics of identity and recognition. Nor does it permit an articulation of the self-same through the effacement of difference. Writing is neither a mirror for meaningful self-representation nor a surface for the reflection and recognition of a subjectivity identical to itself. Rather, as Maurice Blanchot argues, it is an encounter with the impersonal and the asubjective, the space of an alterity that exceeds the dialectic. Deleuze and Guattari, it seems to me, extend Blanchot's line of thought, albeit from a different philosophical vantage point – art and writing are multiplicities, machinic assemblages for the liberation of asignifying and asubjective flows of desire.[18] They are planes of composition for the unleashing of becomings, understood not as dialectical forces of appropriation, transformation, and negation, but as affirmations of multiplicity and difference. Art and writing, in other words, create new relations, connections, and syntheses between impersonal singularities and events.

Towards a Literature of Affirmation

The literary texts we have studied thus far have been analysed in the light of the relation between self and other. We have primarily understood sexual desire in terms of the dialectics of appropriation, negation, transformation, and overcoming of difference. Be it the Oedipal quest for truth in *Pierre et Jean*, the desire to overcome matter by subjecting it to the driving force of spirit in *Le chef-d'oeuvre inconnu*, or the desire to realize the perfect material incarnation of the idea in *Sarrasine*, the initial movement of sexual desire was seen as caught in a representation or abstraction that led to a denial of forces of difference. But we also saw how the will to truth and knowledge that impelled Pierre, Frenhofer, and Sarrasine could not carry itself beyond a certain point. Mme Roland resists appropriation, *La Belle Noiseuse* cannot be subjugated by the power of spirit, and la Zambinella escapes the despotism of the Idea. From one text to another, we witnessed the collapse of the dialectic into forces of becoming that were irreducible to it. In other words, in all three texts, we ran up against forces that escaped the negative trajectory of the dialectic. Difference could not be denied; there were spaces where desire was clearly something other than reactive. Using dialectical paradigms to understand the desiring-economy of literature, we encountered the limit of dialectics in forces that did not conform to its movement. But the paradigms we started out with risked inscribing these points of escape back within the negative terms of the dialectic. In other words, thinking within the framework of the latter led us to think of desire in terms of representation and fiction, and to thereby subject it once more to the categories of true/false, real/illusory, authentic/fictive. What is needed to break out of this circle is therefore an alternative practice of reading sexual difference, a critique of affirmation and not negation.

Deleuze and Guattari show us how subjecting desire to the 'will to truth' prevents us from dealing with desire as the real, as material force and production. By theorizing desire as a surface or continuum that moves between its paranoid or reactionary pole and its schizophrenic or revolutionary pole, they help us understand the unconscious not as a theatre of warring impulses or conflicting forces, but as a factory for the production of asignifying and ateleogical flows of desire. These forces can be captured and territorialized by signifying structures but cannot be contained by them. The unconscious is not a theatre of representation, of signs and their meanings; it is a theatre (as a machinic assemblage) of becomings and difference. Deleuze and Guattari thus make possible a critique of desire as the affirmation of a positive force rather than as a force of appropriation and negation. And they provide us with a means of reading literature not as an always oppressive machine of denial but as a desiring-machine for the liberation of becomings as affirmations of difference.

In what follows, we will trace the movement of thought and desire away from depth and height towards the plane of the surface. In order to do this, we will first study how Deleuze constructs a thought of the surface in *The Logic of Sense*. This will provide us with elements needed to rethink the relationship of subjectivity to language, identity, difference, and multiplicity. This will enable us to reformulate and recast the relationship between all of the above, and to construct a way of thinking difference and multiplicity other than in terms of the dialectical opposition between self and other, the same and not-same. The relationship between bodies, sexuality, and language will be reconfigured within the Deleuzian concepts of sense and event, and sexual difference displaced from the torments of height and depth towards the lightness and joy of the surface. This should then permit the articulation of a critique of affirmation and positive difference.

Towards a Thought of the Surface

In the *Logic of Sense*, Deleuze evaluates the revolution in philosophical thinking effectuated by the Stoics. The Stoics brought about a radical displacement of the causal relation by distinguishing between two kinds of things – bodies and states of affairs on the one hand, and their effects on the other. Bodies and states of affairs are characterized by their tensions, physical qualities and properties, actions, and passions. All bodies are causes, causes in relation to one another. That is, there are no effects among bodies. Bodies and states of affairs are causes for effects that differ in nature from them. These effects are not bodies or states of affairs, although they are caused by them. Rather, they are incorporeal entities or events. They are neither physical qualities nor properties, but attributes. They are not things or facts, but events. Bodies and states of affairs exist, but events subsist. They are not beings, but ways of beings. They are expressed not by adjectives or substantives, but by verbs, pure infinitives. They are not agents, but results of actions and passions.

The Stoics thus sever the cause-effect relation by referring causes (bodies, mixtures of bodies, and states of affairs) to themselves and effects (incorporeal events) to themselves.[19] Bodies, mixtures of bodies, and states of affairs have depth and thickness, whereas incorporeal events play themselves out at the surface as impassive results. The time of bodies and states of affairs is the living present, the time of fixed and limited qualities and measures. It is the all-encompassing present of Chronos. The time of events is that of the pure infinitive, the unlimited time of Aion, 'infinitely divisible into past and future,' and which always eludes the present.

How best to measure the revolutionary impact of Stoic thought? In Aristotle and Plato, idea, being, and substance have ontological priority. But for the Stoics, bodies, and states of affairs, their mixtures, qualities, and quantities are also part of substance. They are thus contrasted not with idea or being, but with an 'extra-Being,' or incorporeal events as non-existing entities. 'The highest term therefore is not being, but *Something (aliquid),* insofar as it subsumes being and non-being, existence and inherence.' The Stoics are therefore the first to reverse Platonism: 'For if bodies with their states, qualities, and quantities, assume all the characteristics of substance and cause, conversely, the characteristics of the Idea are relegated to the other side, that is to this impassive extra-Being which is sterile, inefficacious, and on the surface of things; *the ideational or the incorporeal can no longer be anything other than an "effect."*'[20]

Plato distinguishes between two dimensions. There is the dimension of limited and measured things, of qualities and quantities. Time is designated by pauses and rests, by presents which delimit subjects and assign identities. But there is also the domain of 'a becoming without measure,' which moves in two simultaneous directions, which eludes pauses and rests and the fixed moment of the present. As we saw earlier, this becoming is not the dualism between idea and matter or ideas and bodies. Rather, it is a dualism located in the very depths of bodies, a subterranean dualism hidden within the sensible and the material. It is the dualism between that which in the sensible and the material receives the action of the idea, and that which eludes it, or in other words, the difference between copies and simulacra. With Plato however, this is a conflict played out in the depth and thickness of the earth. The Stoic reversal is more profound: '*Everything now returns to the surface.*' Identity is divested of its causal and spiritual primacy. It is now a surface effect, an event. That which eludes the idea rises to the incorporeal limit of the surface. 'The most concealed becomes the most manifest.'[21] With the Stoics, the becoming of the depths comes to be the ideational and incorporeal effect of the surface.

But more important are the reversals between past and future, cause and effect, active and passive, and their consequences. To the extent that becoming reverses the relationship between past and future, cause and effect, more and less, moving in both directions at once, it is the paradox of infinite identity, a paradox essential to the event. The dualism between depth and height yields to a lateral sliding, to the width and flatness of the surface. And for Deleuze, it is Lewis Carroll who continues the exploration and conquest of the surface discovered by the Stoics; Alice discovers that the secret of events and things is not interred in the depths of bodies and their mixtures, nor to be excavated from a cavernous earth, but that it frolics on the lightness of the surface. Depth ceases to exist, it passes over to the other side of the surface, which is nothing other than the opposite direction. There is nothing to see behind the mirror, because everything plays itself out along its sides or edges, along the length of its surface. It is by staying on the surface that one reverses sides, by following one direction far enough to reverse onto the other:

> It is not therefore a question of *the adventures* of Alice, but of Alice's *adventure*: her climb to the surface, her disavowal of false depth and her discovery that everything happens at the border ... *It is by following the border, by skirting the surface, that one passes from bodies to the incorporeal.* Valéry had a profound idea; what is most deep is the skin. This is a Stoic discovery, which presupposes a great deal of wisdom and entails an entire ethic. It is the discovery of the little girl, who grows and diminishes only from the edges – a surface which reddens and becomes green. She knows that the more events traverse the entire, depthless extension, the more they affect bodies which they cut and bruise.[22]

Sense and Language

For Deleuze, there is an essential relationship between events-effects and language. Events are expressible; they have to be expressed in propositions. Since there are several relations within the proposition, one has to determine the one best suited for surface effects. In general, one recognizes three relations within the proposition: denotation, manifestation, and signification. Denotation refers to the relation of a proposition to an external state of affairs. Words are associated with images that represent bodies and states of affairs, their mixtures, qualities, and quantities. Denotation thus functions through association; it operates according to the criteria of true or false. Manifestation is the relation of the proposition with the person expressing himself or herself. It is the statement of desires and beliefs, which are causal inferences, not associations. It is important to note that it is manifestation (the personal 'I' functioning as a manifester) that founds denotation. Manifestation operates according to the logical values of veracity and illusion. Signification is the third dimension of the proposition. It is the relation of the word to universal or general concepts and to the implications of the concepts. The elements of the proposition signify implications that refer to other propositions. In signification, a proposition is the element of a demonstration – it is either a premise or a conclusion. Signification thus operates within the order of implication, i.e., the relationship between a premise and a conclusion. The signification of a proposition is located in its relation to other propositions from which it is inferred as a conclusion or which it renders possible as a premise. Signification functions as 'the condition of truth'; it refers to the conditions under which the proposition would be true.

The question then becomes: Which is the relation of the proposition that is primary? Which is the one that founds language and renders it possible? For Deleuze, it is sense, as the fourth dimension of the proposition, which makes language possible and which engenders the other three. But sense is that which merges neither with the object denoted, nor with the person who expresses himself/herself in the proposition, nor with the concepts signified. Sense is the *aliquid*, the expressed of the proposition as an incorporeal and impersonal entity that deploys itself at the surface. It does not exist outside of the proposition that expresses it, but neither does it merge with the expression. Rather, it is the expressed that inheres or subsists in the proposition. Sense is the fourth dimension of the proposition that founds the proposition and its three other dimensions while remaining irreducible to them. It is the extra-Being that founds language and renders it possible, and yet affirms its neutrality and impassibility in relation to it.

As we saw, sense can only be expressed in propositions, but does not resemble them. Sense is the attribute, but of bodies and states of affairs, not of the proposition. Sense affirms its independence from both bodies and states of affairs, as well as the proposition. Sense is the attribute of bodies and states of affairs that is irreducible to them, and the expressed of the proposition that is irreducible to it. It is the event that inheres at the boundary of things and propositions; sense is the event itself. In other words, sense is the event as it is expressed in the proposition. It is both the event as it happens to things and the event as it subsists in the proposition. It is simultaneously the incorporeal attribute at the surface of things and an incorporeal expressed that inheres in the proposition. Sense is the surface field that deploys itself at the frontier between words and things. Or rather, this frontier is constituted by sense itself. For Deleuze, in *The Logic of Sense*, this relation between sense, events, things, and propositions is not to be thought of as circular, but rather as 'the coexistence of two sides without thickness, such that we pass from one to the other by following their length' (22). In short:

> *Sense is both the expressible or the expressed of the proposition, and the attribute of the state of affairs.* It turns one side toward things and one side toward propositions. But it does not merge with the proposition which expresses it anymore than with the state of affairs or the quality which the proposition denotes. It is exactly the boundary between propositions and things. It is this *aliquid* at once extra-Being and inherence, that is, this minimum of being which befits inherences. It is in this sense that it is an "event": on the condition that the event is not confused with its spatio-temporal realization in a state of affairs. We will not ask therefore what is the sense of the event: the event is sense itself. (22)[23]

Sense, Nonsense, and the Causal Relation

Sense, as we saw thus far, has two sides or aspects. On the one hand, it insists in propositions, it is expressed by them, and yet is non-identical to them. On the other, it is the attribute of bodies and states of affairs, but differs in nature from them. It is the result of corporeal bodies and their mixtures, but is irreducible to them. Sense has both insistence and extra-being; it is impassible and neutral in relation to bodies, states of affairs, and propositions, yet is that which engenders them by ascribing to itself the power of the ideational. The sense/event affirms its independence from its corporeal cause by linking itself at the surface to other effects and events.

By referring causes to other causes (bodies and states of affairs), and effects to other effects (events), the Stoics subject the event to a double causality. The event is the result of bodies and states of affairs, but is connected at the surface to another incorporeal event as its quasi-cause. As a surface effect, sense refers itself to nonsense or paradox as its quasi-cause.[24] For Deleuze, sense is produced by the inherence, within sense, of the nonsensical element, as an excess of sense opposed to the absence of sense. It is this nonsensical or paradoxical element that enacts the donation of sense. It is in this respect that sense is an effect, a production.[25] For

Deleuze, paradoxes inhere and subsist in language and preside over the genesis of sense. Sense and nonsense are immanent to each other.[26] What assures sense its autonomy as an effect is both its difference in nature from its corporeal cause, and its relation to its quasi-cause:

> [A]s soon as sense is grasped, in its relation to the quasi-cause which pro-
> duces and distributes it at the surface, it inherits, participates in, and even
> envelopes and possesses the force of this ideational cause. We have seen
> that this cause is nothing outside of its effect, that it haunts this effect, and
> that it maintains with the effect an immanent relation which turns the prod-
> uct, the moment that it is produced, into something productive.[27]

Sense is thus both effect and quasi-cause, product and productive.

Sense and Genesis

We saw that the event preserves its impassibility and neutrality with respect to the bodies and states of affairs from which it results by aligning itself at the surface with another event as quasi-cause. How does sense/ event preside over the genesis of bodies and states of affairs? For Deleuze, the answer is not to be found in the transcendental field of either phenomenology or metaphysics, for both conceive of the condition in the image of the conditioned and the foundation by what is founded by imputing to the former a form of consciousness or a personal 'I.' In other words, the condition or foundation is conceived of in the form of a transcendental subject that retains the categories of person, personal consciousness, subjective identity, and individual. The transcendental field of sense as genesis must exclude forms of the personal, the general, the individual, and the particular. Deleuze postulates an impersonal, preindividual field of singularities and antigeneralities:

> We seek to determine an impersonal and pre-individual transcendental
> field, which does not resemble the corresponding empirical fields, and
> which nevertheless is not confused with an undifferentiated depth ... Singu-
> larities are the true transcendental events ... 'the fourth person singular.'
> Far from being individual or personal, singularities preside over the genesis
> of individuals and persons; they are distributed in a 'potential' which admits
> neither Self nor I, but which produces them by actualizing or realizing
> itself, although the figures of this actualization do not at all resemble the
> realized potential.[28]

To recapitulate, sense is the preindividual and impersonal surface field of singularities that assures the genesis of individuals, properties, states of affairs, and actions and passions, but remains neutral and impassible to them. In other words, it is the unconditioned condition of genesis that cannot be understood in terms of that which it conditions.

Sense and Time

What is the time in which events, sense, and becomings deploy themselves? As we saw, the Stoics proposed two simultaneous readings of time: one corresponding to bodies and states of affairs (Chronos) and one corresponding to events (Aion). The time of Chronos is the all-encompassing time of the present. Only the present exists in Chronos, because past and future are two dimensions of the present. They are oriented in such a manner that one always proceeds from the past to the future through a succession of interlocking presents. And past and future are in turn contracted within an ever larger cosmic and eternal present. Chronos is the time of depth, of the temporal realization and incorporation of events in bodies and states of affairs. It is the present of fixed qualities and measured quantities, of actions and passions.

The time of Aion is the time of the surface, and its characteristic is to elude the present. Only past and future inhere in the time of Aion to infinitely subdivide each instant. The present instant is thus constantly decomposed into past and future. The event escapes the present because it retreats simultaneously into the past and future, pulling in both directions at once. With Chronos, a succession of interlocking presents constantly absorbs past and future within itself, but in Aion, it is a past and future that divide each instant simultaneously into the two. It is an instant without depth or thickness, or rather, it is the instant itself which divides each present into past and future.[29]

What then is the relation between sense/events, time, and language? For Deleuze, it is the world of events, of incorporeal surface effects, that makes language possible:

> Pure events ground language because they wait for it as much as they wait for us, and have a pure, singular, impersonal, and pre-individual existence only inside the language which expresses them ... The most general operation of sense is this: it brings that which expresses it into existence; and from that point on, as pure inherence, it brings itself to exist within that which expresses it.[30]

And it is the line of Aion that traces the frontier between things and propositions; it organizes the surface of effects/events and sense and language.[31] Sense and event are deployed at this frontier, the event as the attribute of bodies and states of affairs, sense as the expressed of propositions.

Feminism and a Thought of the Surface

We are now in a better position to evaluate the contribution of the Stoics to the thought of the surface. The Stoics, as we saw, reverse Platonism by situating the ideational not in height, but at the surface. The primacy of the idea is challenged by a thought that turns its attention to bodies, their mixtures and states of affairs. Materiality is no longer repressed nor relegated to darkness, but it is freed from the weight of the idea. These bodies are dealt with not in their frightening or abominable depths (as with the pre-Socratics); instead, their materiality is brought to the surface as an incorporeal and independent effect. Essence is no longer an originary and directive cause, but an effect that is produced. It is the productivity of a displaced origin, the generativity and multiplicity of a surface event. Essence is not to be found in principles encrusted in the depth of bodies; it deploys itself as the lightness and possibility of the superficial. Essence is not the all-encompassing principle of the idea; it is the entire field of sense-events:

> This is a reorientation of all thought and of what it means to think: *there is no longer depth or height* ... The autonomy of the surface, independent of, and against depth and height; the discovery of incorporeal events, meanings or effects, which are irreducible to 'deep' bodies and to 'lofty' Ideas – these are the important Stoic discoveries against the pre-Socratics and Plato.[32]

What is the importance of a thought of the surface for feminism? As we saw in *Speculum*, Irigaray's project is to descend deep into the abyss of Plato's cave in order to bring to light the repressed materiality of philosophical thought. But it is an enterprise fraught with another peril, that of weighing down this materiality by means of a principle of sexual difference located deep within bodies. The articulation of sexuality and sexual difference as a surface effect of the order of the event, rather than its location in the depth of bodies, opens up a field of possibilities that a simple renunciation of height cannot. The surface saves bodies and materiality from the dual dangers of both the idealism of height and the essentialism of depth. The field of preindividual nomadic and impersonal singularities frees thought, desire, and subjectivity from the rigid self/other categories of dialectics. Or rather, the despotic categories of subjectivity and identity are displaced towards the multiplicities of becomings as events. Language is extricated from the tyranny of signification towards the freedom and independence of sense and expression. Its sexual specificity (or lack thereof) conceived in the image of the bodies it conditions becomes moot in the face of the possibility of the domain of sense and expression.[33] And the politics of literature is freed from the oppressive weight of history as the signifying regime of bodies and states of affairs as it moves towards the freedom and possibility of expression and event.[34] Literature is a desiring-machine of the possible, it is a desiring-machine that affirms. As such, it has little to do with a critique of *ressentiment* and revenge. It is with a view to exploring the 'surface politics' of literature that I would like to devote my attention to Gautier's *Mademoiselle de Maupin* in the chapter that follows.

6 'Une jouissance d'épiderme': From Platonic Height and Depth to the Deleuzian Surface in Gautier's *Mademoiselle de Maupin*

> It suffices that we dissipate ourselves a little, that we be able to be at the surface, that we stretch our skin like a drum, in order that the 'great politics' begin.
>
> Gilles Deleuze[1]

Théophile Gautier's *Mademoiselle de Maupin* constitutes the final male-authored text within the trajectory of the present study. The novel will be read in the light of the myth of androgyny, which, in the nineteenth century, functions as a nodal point for various aesthetic, social, and political discourses constructed upon the common denominator of sexual difference. Romanticism and Decadence, for instance, draw upon the figure of the androgyne to symbolize the aesthetic struggle between the ideal and the material as well as the conflict between essence and appearance. The androgyne also serves as an important trope in the (Hegelian) dialectic of historical progress and transformation, and as a symbol of the union between thought and nature. From a feminist perspective, the figure of the androgyne illustrates the aesthetic tension between the masculine and the feminine, the classic and the Romantic, the eternal and the transitory, with the first term of every binary being valorized in the hierarchy.

Beginning with an examination of the myth of the androgyne in nineteenth-century France, we will look at the intersection of the aesthetics of sexual difference with the discourses of historical progress and decadence elaborated during this time. We will see how the figure of the androgyne/hermaphrodite articulates Gautier's aesthetic tension between the classic and the Romantic, the eternal and the modern, the fixed and the immutable against the changing and the fugitive. Then we will study how *Mademoiselle de Maupin* moves beyond these dialectical oppositions towards an androgyny of difference and multiplicity in which the latent decadence and nihilism of Romanticism (epitomized in D'Albert) gives way to an aesthetics of affirmation and possibility.

As we saw in the literary texts studied thus far, sexual desire and difference was caught in a theatre of depth and height. It was a question of going beyond appearances, of lifting veils, of going from signifiers to their signifieds. The coordinates of depth and height informed the Platonic and Hegelian dialectic – one had to overcome and elevate matter towards spirit, body towards essence and truth. In the course of this chapter, I will show how Gautier's text moves away from the dialectics of negation in order to make way for difference as affirmation. Sexual difference is freed from the hierarchical dualities of opposition and contradiction towards the affirmation of multiplicity. The nihilism of Platonism is cast aside for the affirmation of difference in itself. Deploying the Deleuzian concepts of sense and event elaborated in the previous chapter, I will argue that it is in the topographic shift of thought, sexuality, and desire from the coordinates of height and depth towards the multiplicity and plurality of the surface that this affirmation is carried out.

Mademoiselle de Maupin and the Figure of the Androgyne

While the history of the myth of Hermaphroditus is a long and fascinating one,[2] in this chapter, we will focus specifically on the version of the myth provided by Ovid, and on Plato's account of dual-sexed beings in his *Symposium*. Ovid's *Metamorphoses* is an explicit reference in Gautier's novel, while Plato's account of love and desire informs not just psychoanalytical theory, but the blend of Neoplatonic cosmogony and Christian theology we find in the nineteenth-century mysticism that so informed the Romantic movement.[3]

In the *Symposium*, Aristophanes recounts a story in order to explain the origin of love and desire. Humanity's original nature, he explains, was androgynous. In the beginning were double beings, two bodies united in one, spherical in shape with four arms and four legs. They had differently sexed organs and two heads placed back to back on a common neck. There were three kinds of spherical beings, one formed by a male and female body, another with two male bodies, and the third with two female ones. Possessed of great strength and power, they had the temerity to challenge the might of the gods, thus incurring the wrath of Zeus. In order to punish them, Zeus split them in half, and ordered Apollo to turn their faces towards the cut in order that they never lose sight of their folly. It is from this lost unity that love and desire result, each sex seeking the other half that would restore humanity's original totality. Aristophanes thus accounts for both heterosexual and homosexual love. Love and desire are propelled by the nostalgia for a lost wholeness, and their movement placed within a dialectical tension – the division into two must be recuperated within the completeness of the one.

Ovid's recounting of the myth of Hermaphroditus casts bisexuality as a loss of power and virility, differing in this respect from legends that precede it.[4] In earlier versions, the dual sexual status of Hermaphroditus is present at his birth and does not represent a fall of any kind. With Ovid, it is the result of an aggression on the part of Salmacis, a nymph who falls in love with a beautiful boy and entwines him in an ardent embrace. The boy fights to free himself, but in vain. The gods grant Salmacis's prayer that the two never be separated. Thus, the union between Salmacis and Hermaphroditus is placed not under the sign of a harmonious melding of opposites, but under that of a rather violent struggle, with Hermaphroditus himself deriving little joy from this union. For Kari Weil, Ovid's myth represents the violence and conflict of the dialectics of sexual desire.[5]

In his remarkably comprehensive study of the figure of the androgyne in nineteenth-century France, A.J.L. Busst chooses not to separate the figure of the androgyne from that of the hermaphrodite. Instead, he treats the two synonymously as a constellation of varying aesthetic, political, religious, and social significations. The image of the androgyne/hermaphrodite is thus seen as an intersection of discourses built upon the common denominator of sexual difference. Busst distinguishes two tenors within these discourses. In the first half of the century, the androgyne functions as a symbol of political, historical, and social progress and unity. It functions as an important construct in the articulation of sexual and social inequality – it was through the emancipation of women that distinctions of class would be abolished. With Ballanche, the androgyne becomes an important trope within the framework of Saint-Simonism. Once again, the question of the emancipation of women is linked to the call for industrialization and material prosperity. By revalorizing the domain of the material and the sensual (associated with women), the Saint-Simonians sought to reunite thought and nature within a progressive movement of transformation and activity.[6] Later, the sexual harmony and unity that the androgyne represented came to be recuperated as a metaphor for man's religious and moral harmony with

God. In summary, the androgyne functioned as an important (and extremely optimistic) symbol of the progressivist discourses of the nineteenth century. Needless to say, man's androgynous nature constitutes an important trope with the English and German Romantics. In France, the works of mystics such as Boehme, Creuzer, and Swedenborg exerted a strong influence on its early Romanticism.

To the extent that the second half of the century breaks with the idealism of early Romanticism, for Busst, the figure of the androgyne becomes the expression of the disillusionment and scepticism of the Decadent movement. Aesthetically, this darker side of Romanticism manifests itself in the doctrine of *l'art pour l'art*, which already bears the seeds of the nihilism of the Decadents. It is the desire to divest oneself of the despairing ugliness of life that results in the privileging of art as the unique value. And for Busst, Gautier's *Mademoiselle de Maupin* marks this very disenchantment with and condemnation of Romantic idealism.[7] To the extent that the hermaphrodite as a mythic figure has no basis in reality, it represents the absolute power of art as the power of mind/spirit over disappointing matter.

According to Busst, the desire for an absolute ideal that reality cannot satisfy leads not so much to sexual abstinence as to what he terms 'cerebral lechery,' a perversion that Gautier embodies in *Mademoiselle de Maupin*. The voluptuousness that Gautier claims for art and the hermaphrodite is one divested of physical sensuality; it is the debauchery of a mind that the material can never satisfy. As the sexually uninitiated virgin, Mademoiselle de Maupin represents this cerebral perversity. The androgyne is now a figure of asexuality and disillusionment. With the Decadents, it becomes a figure of moral and sexual decay, a disturbing trope of incest, homosexuality, and sadomasochism, one might add, of unnatural unions and horrifying bodily mixtures. In this respect, the hermaphrodite symbolizes the confusion between good and evil; art now places itself beyond morality, beyond good and evil.[8]

In his introduction to *Mademoiselle de Maupin*, Michel Crouzet situates the novel within the problematic of artistic creation and of the artist as creator. *Mademoiselle de Maupin* is the Romantic 'Banquet'; it articulates the Platonic conflict between the ideal and the material, between essence and appearance, between the lofty sphere of the idea and the cavernous, labyrinthine depth of the world of shadows and appearances.[9] The androgyne/hermaphrodite is a symbol of the Romantic aesthetic, s/he embodies the conflict between the spirit and the flesh, the ideal and the real. The androgyne represents the duality of the artist

caught between opposing tendencies that he has to resolve. The artist/
hermaphrodite is a figure drawn into the trajectory of both the Platonic
and Hegelian dialectic – he has to impose the idea upon the chaos of
matter, he has to elevate matter towards spirit. He partakes of divine
power in his understanding of the idea, but as a man of flesh, has to
incarnate it within matter. The androgyne represents the resolution of
this conflict through the overcoming of contradiction and opposition. It
is a figure of unity, perfection, and harmony. To the extent that it is a
reminder of the fall from androgynous unity into the world of sexual
division, it is a figure that evokes the nostalgia for a lost perfection. But it
is a figure that symbolizes the recuperation of the lost totality through a
process of appropriation and assimilation. For the male artist, then, it is
a symbol of his creative power, of sexual unity, self-sufficiency, and auto-
genesis.

In his article 'Le mythe de l'androgyne dans "Mademoiselle de
Maupin,"' Pierre Albouy reads the novel in a similar light. The figure of
the androgyne/hermaphrodite is a figure of aesthetic and existential
reflection. It crystallizes the artist's thought on his condition as well as on
the nature of the beautiful. Albouy does make a distinction between the
androgyne and the hermaphrodite, but both are situated within the Platonic conflict between the ideal and the material. For Albouy, the
androgyne represents the plenitude and completeness of a totality; it is a
being of ascension, whereas the hermaphrodite is a being of lack, uncertainty, and incompleteness. Gautier's text is thus split between the dream
of unity and integration on the one hand, and haunted by lack, the
uncertainty of unresolved oppositions, and the blurring of boundaries
on the other. According to Albouy, Mademoiselle de Maupin, while in
reality a transvestite, participates in the ambiguity and uncertainty of the
hermaphrodite. And if, in Gautier's text, there is no final synthesis of
contradiction and opposition, but a celebration of metamorphosis and
change, this is a celebration restricted to the world of illusion and
appearance. In other words, attesting to the impossibility of resolving the
conflict between the superficial and the deep, the flesh and the soul,
realizing the impossibility of communicating, manifesting, and expressing the ideal towards which one aspires, Gautier settles for the comforting and compensatory illusions of art.[10]

In a similar vein, Kari Weil provides a feminist perspective that sees
Mademoiselle de Maupin as a play of veils set against the aesthetic tension
between the classical and the Romantic that runs through Gautier's
work.[11] The opposition between veils and nudity is centred on the figure

of woman, wherein the veil functions as a 'pure' sign emptied of all content, or in other words, as pure exteriority and artifice. But the veil that flaunts the absence of the signified paradoxically works to preserve the integrity of the Platonic ideal it shields from the gaze. So while the exterior clothes and ornaments of fashion may change with time, thereby assigning a historical present to beauty, they simultaneously preserve the fixity and durability of the classic. And for Weil, within the series of binary oppositions between masculine/feminine, classic/Romantic, and eternal/transitory, it is the masculine, classic ideal that is privileged over the feminine, Romantic term. The hierarchization of the interior over the exterior, beauty over veils, assures the mastery of the artist over the feminine.[12] Idealism is upheld through the suppression of feminine difference. As a hermaphroditic figure that blurs the opposition between masculine/feminine and classic/Romantic, Mademoiselle de Maupin, Weil admits, subverts the hierarchy of the text. But, she insists, such subversive play is at best, a defensive strategy on the part of Gautier, 'a means of retextualizing feminine desire so as to establish at least some form of intellectual mastery over its unknown power.'[13] It thus represents a final move towards dialectical appropriation and negation. In other words, as Naomi Schor reminds us, such a strategy could very well be the ultimate ruse of the master over the slave.

What is common to all of the above readings is that they circumscribe both the figure of the androgyne and its role in Gautier's text within the movements of the dialectic, be it the Hegelian dialectic of historical transformation (Busst), the conquering of chaotic depth through the ascension towards the Platonic idea (Crouzet), the tension between the ideal and the material (Albouy), or the erasure of sexual difference through the movement of self-appropriation and denial of otherness (Weil). I will argue that Mademoiselle de Maupin rejects the negativity inherent to all dialectic, and that Gautier's text succumbs to neither the Platonic valorization of the ideal, nor to its denial of the material. It refuses both the (false) positivity and progressivism of the historical movement of early Romanticism, as well as the nihilism and pessimism of Decadence. Mademoiselle de Maupin emerges as a different aesthetic, a new sensibility, which partakes of neither the utopic optimism of early Romanticism nor the despair of Decadence. Rather, it is an affirmation of joy and difference. A different feminine emerges, one that no longer expresses itself within the negative, one that does not content itself with a reversal of dialectical hierarchy or a reappropriation of power. The androgyne is thus not a figure of dialectical reversal or resolution; it is one opposed to all dialectic. Opposition and contradiction give way to an affirmation of difference as multiplicity. And this affirmation takes place not within the Platonic dualism of idea and matter, or in other words, between the dimensions of height and depth; rather, it deploys itself along the surface of sense-effects and events.

D'Albert's Romantic Agony

> [T]here are properly philosophical diseases. Idealism is the illness congenital to the Platonic philosophy and, with its litany of ascents and downfalls, it is even philosophy's manic-depressive form.
>
> Gilles Deleuze[14]

Gautier's D'Albert is the quintessential hero of Romanticism who manifests every symptom of the malady peculiar to it. He is driven by an unbounded desire for the absolute on the one hand, but confronted with the impossibility of satisfying or even articulating it on the other: 'Je ne désire rien, car je désire tout ... J'attends, – quoi? Je ne sais, mais j'attends.'[15] The torment of being unable to fix itself on an object causes desire to turn against itself and withdraw into the stasis of apathy:

> Par une disposition spéciale, je désire si frénétiquement ce que je désire, sans toutefois rien faire pour me le procurer, que si par hasard, ou autrement, j'arrive à l'objet de mon voeu, j'ai une courbature morale si forte, et suis tellement harassé, qu'il me prend des défaillances et que je n'ai plus de vigueur pour en jouir ... (78)

D'Albert is unable to define the object of his desire, knowing only that it is missing or lacking.[16] He decides finally that what he desires is something that will lead him out of the ordinary and the mediocre, that what he wants is a mistress who will put an end to the monotony of his life by satisfying his nostalgia for a lost ideal of beauty. His aesthetic sensibility gives him a privileged access to the knowledge and understanding of ideal love and beauty; as far he is concerned, it is mere matter of recognizing the former when it presents itself to him in its embodied form.[17] And he has no difficulty in identifying the type of beauty his mistress will exemplify; it will be 'un motif de Giorgione executé par Rubens' (84).

D'Albert's 'Romantic agony' stems from the impossibility of encountering the perfection of the ideal in the flesh, of finding the lost object that will satisfy his desire.[18] He is led to question and accuse art. Is not the beauty depicted in art a simulacrum, a falsehood, a poor copy of the idea? 'Que Platon avait raison de vouloir vous bannir de sa république, et quel mal vous nous avez fait, ô poètes!' (97). Not only does art provide us with a deceptive representation of the ideal, it makes life harder to bear because life can never satisfy the demand for truth that ideal beauty makes. The deception is double because art provides us with a false copy of the ideal, while life can satisfy neither the demand of art nor the truth of the ideal. It is a poor and inadequate rival of both, incommensurate with the purity of the ideal. Life and art are equally false, the one unable to measure up to the idea, the other incapable of even formulating it.[19]

D'Albert is then haunted by a feeling of unreality. The split he experiences between the ideal and the sensible, between ideas and 'facts' results in an inability to grasp the materiality of his experiences and world:

> Je suis très malheureux de ne pouvoir acquérir la certitude morale d'une chose dont j'ai la certitude physique. – C'est ordinairement l'inverse qui a lieu et c'est le fait qui prouve l'idée. Je voudrais me prouver le fait par l'idée; je ne le puis ... il s'agite autour de moi un pâle monde d'ombres et de semblants faux ou vrais qui bourdonnent sourdement, au milieu duquel je me trouve aussi parfaitement seul que possible, car aucun n'agit sur moi en bien ou en mal, et ils me paraissent d'une nature tout à fait différente. (123–4)

His need to assimilate another body to himself stems from a desire to experience its corporeality and materiality more intensely by subjecting it to the full force of idea and spirit. What D'Albert seeks is the experience that will unite body and idea to accede to the truth of a totality. D'Albert attempts to either subject bodies and their mixtures to the idea, or tries to locate the latter deep within mixtures of bodies. But he cannot do either:

> C'est surtout lorsque j'ai vécu avec une femme que j'ai le mieux senti combien ma nature repoussait invinciblement toute alliance et toute mixtion. Je suis comme une goutte d'huile dans un verre d'eau. Vous aurez beau tourner et remuer, jamais l'huile ne se pourra lier avec elle; elle se divisera en cent mille petits globules qui se réuniront et remonteront à la surface, au premier moment de calme: la goutte d'huile et le verre d'eau, voilà mon histoire. (125)

His soul prevents him from grasping the voluptuousness and materiality of earthly bodies, and this divisive dichotomy is responsible for his inability to experience life to the fullest: 'Cependant j'ai les sens très vifs; mais mon âme est pour mon corps une soeur ennemie, et le malheureux couple, comme tout couple possible, légal ou illégal, vit dans un état de guerre perpétuel' (125). His desire thus functions uniquely within the topography of depth and height; it moves to either elevate matter to the truth of spirit, or to fix the latter deep within the density and heaviness of bodily mixtures in order that they confer the positive weight of reality upon the insubstantial idea.[20] He rejects the surface because it seems to exclude the soul that cannot alight upon it to form a perfect unity between height and depth, idea and matter. D'Albert dismisses the lightness and inconsequentiality of a surface on which he cannot experience alterity as a deep mixture within bodies – he can neither assimilate nor be assimilated to the other:

> Après tout, *j'ai reconnu que cela ne passait pas la peau, et que je n'avais qu'une jouissance d'épiderme* à laquelle l'âme ne participait que par curiosité. J'ai du plaisir, parce que je suis jeune et ardent; mais ce plaisir me vient de moi et non d'un autre. La cause est dans moi-même plutôt que dans Rosette. (126; emphasis mine)

Unable to encounter difference and alterity, D'Albert is locked into his self from which there seems to be little hope of escape:

> J'ai beau faire, je n'ai pu sortir de moi une minute.
> – Je suis toujours ce que j'étais, c'est-à-dire quelque chose de très ennuyé et de très ennuyeux, qui me déplaît fort. Je n'ai pu venir à bout de faire entrer dans ma cervelle l'idée d'un autre, dans mon âme le sentiment d'un autre, dans mon corps la douleur ou la jouissance d'un autre. – Je suis prisonnier dans moi-même, et toute évasion est impossible ... – Ah! ne pouvoir s'augmenter d'une seule parcelle, d'un seul atome; ne pouvoir faire couler le sang des autres dans ses veines; voir toujours de ses yeux ... ne pouvoir s'en aller, se dérober à soi-même ... quel supplice, quel ennui! (126–7)[21]

He conceives of alterity in the mode of the dialectic of self and other; his desire for metamorphosis and change is thus linked to the desire to possess and appropriate the other: '[J]e n'ai jamais rien tant souhaité que de rencontrer sur la montagne, comme Tirésias le devin, ces serpents qui font changer de sexe; et ce que j'envie le plus aux dieux monstrueux et bizarres de l'Inde, ce sont leurs perpétuels *avatars* et leurs transformations innombrables' (127; emphasis in original).

D'Albert is driven by 'une fureur' to make the soul descend into the depths of bodies, to subject bodies and their mixtures to the idea:

Si tu savais tout ce que j'ai fait pour forcer mon âme à partager l'amour de mon corps! avec quelle furie j'ai plongé ma bouche dans sa bouche, trempé mes bras dans ses cheveux, et comme j'ai serré étroitement sa taille ronde et souple! Comme l'antique Salmacis, l'amoureuse du jeune Hermaphrodite, je tâchais de fondre son corps avec le mien; je buvais son haleine et les tièdes larmes que la volupté faisait déborder du calice trop plein de ses yeux. Plus nos corps s'entrelaçaient et plus nos étreintes étaient intimes, moins je l'aimais. (128)

And yet, he glimpses the multiplicity of the 'event' that is to be found on the surface, a multiplicity opened up by the 'baiser équestre' that goes beyond the terms of the dialectics of self and other: 'Ah! je t'assure que dans ce moment-là je ne songeais guère si j'étais moi ou un autre' (130).

[J]amais volupté pareille n'a passé sur ma tête: je me sentais réellement un autre. L'âme de Rosette était entrée tout entière dans mon corps. – Mon âme m'avait quitté et remplissait son coeur comme son âme à elle remplis-sait le mien. – Sans doute, elles s'étaient rencontrées au passage dans ce long baiser équestre ... et s'étaient traversées et confondues aussi intime-ment que le peuvent faire les âmes de deux créatures mortelles sur un grain de boue périssable.
    Les anges doivent assurément s'embrasser ainsi, et le vrai paradis n'est pas au ciel, mais sur la bouche d'une personne aimée. (132)

The Neoplatonic theme of the fusion of souls must not take away from the almost imperceptible shift effectuated in the above passage: where earlier nothing could take place within the dimension of depth ('avec quelle furie j'ai plongé ma bouche *dans* sa bouche' [emphasis mine]), now, hap-piness is a matter of a relocation to the surface ('le vrai paradis n'est pas au ciel, mais *sur* la bouche d'une personne aimée' [emphasis mine]).

We have discerned three moves thus far. In the first, D'Albert is plagued by the unreality of bodies that the idea can neither enter nor dominate. In a second, he tries to intermix with bodies in depth, but can-not. And in a third, he discovers the effect of a sensation that is to be found neither in height nor depth, but on the surface of sense and event. But he is unable to remain there; the conquering of the surface is yet to come.

Of Beauty and Decadence

'Pure personnification de Dieu' (167), beauty for D'Albert is the supreme and ultimate value.[22] 'La seule chose au monde que j'ai enviée avec quelque suite, c'est d'être beau' (170). D'Albert's desire for metamorphosis and transmutation is linked to a desire to possess beauty while being it, to animate statues through a transmigration of his soul into them. His frustration is compounded by the fact that the possession of beauty is a matter of chance, that both God and nature are less powerful than art in this respect.[23] The impossibility of incarnating or materializing it then becomes a source of despair.[24]

Why does D'Albert desire beauty above all else? What is the force that underlies the will to beauty? For D'Albert, beauty is a source of power that derives from its ability to put us beyond good and evil.[25] His love of beauty is thus linked to a puerile desire for power over others and to the thrill of a limitless, unbounded desire impelled towards the impossible.[26] This desire for the absolute is succeeded by the realization that nothing in this world can satisfy it, and leads to a disenchantment with and a denial of the possibility of life: '[C]'est une erreur de croire que la possession soit la seule route qui mène à la satiété ... Un désir tel que le mien est quelque chose d'autrement fatigant que la possession' (175).

Here we recognize the 'cerebral perversity' mentioned by Busst. D'Albert's demonic desire to be God ('Pourquoi donc ne suis-je pas Dieu, – puisque je ne puis être homme?') leads to an excess of nihilism – his heroes are Tiberius, Caligula, Nero, and Heliogabalus. D'Albert's thirst for the impossible leads to a negation of the possible; life is denied in favour of the ideal: '[J]e voudrais ce qui ne se peut pas et ce qui ne se pourra jamais' (217). Anger, rancour, and *ressentiment* become the defining elements of his relationship to the world, and he embarks upon a quest for the hateful, the monstrous, and the bizarre in a bid to rouse himself from his apathy. His decadence and 'moral depravity' stem from a desire for the ideal that results in (or from?) a will to nothingness, or a denial of all values.[27] 'Rien ne me touche, rien ne m'émeut,' he declares (214). 'J'ai perdu complètement la science du bien et du mal' (213). His nihilism is thus pushed to one more extreme; the will to nothingness leads to a nothingness of the will by means of which all values are denied. One progresses from a rejection of life in the name of higher ideals towards a detachment from and a denial of all values: 'Tout est indifférent à tout ... Oubli et néant, c'est tout l'homme' (233–4). Tormented by lack and impossibility, D'Albert is an *artiste manqué* alternately plunged into hate, resentment, indifference, and nihilism, a decadent 'champignon vénéneux.'

We saw that the split set up between the ideal and the material and the subsequent privileging of the idea leads to a denial of life and its possibilities. But we also see that this nostalgia is double, impelled towards the ideal on the one hand, and towards the materiality of bodies on the other. One the one hand, D'Albert seeks to subjugate matter to the idea, to make it receive the latter's action. But on the other, he is in search of the material fact that will substantiate the idea, rendering it as material and real rather than as an abstraction. He desires a material that will prove, measure, qualify, and quantify the idea for him. As he points out, he has a deeply sensual side, and he rejects the spiritualism of Christian idealism. 'La spiritualité n'est pas mon fait,' he says (226). Aesthetically, he prefers the pagan voluptuousness, sensuality, and virility of Antiquity to the ascetism of Christianity, Venus to the Virgin Mary, and the celebration of nude flesh to the veiling of Christian art.[28]

The more he delves into bodies, however, the more he sinks back into his depression and melancholy; he cannot grasp the materiality of bodies. Matter becomes oppressive; he fears his nightmarish plunge into its cavernous depths, where there is only stasis, fixity, and immobility:

> Peu à peu ce qu'il y avait d'incorporel s'est dégagé et s'est dissipé, et il n'est resté au fond de moi qu'une épaisse couche de grossier limon. Le rêve est devenu un cauchemar, et la chimère un succube ... tout se condense et se durcit autour de moi, rien ne flotte, rien ne vacille, il n'y a pas d'air ni de souffle; la matière me presse, m'envahit et m'écrase ... (234–5)

D'Albert's problem is thus twofold – the impossibility of spiritualizing matter and of materializing spirit. And his manic-depression is symptomatic of the ideal/material dichotomy that impels him first towards the truth of spirit, and then towards the desire to fix, quantify, and assign it an identity within the material. He wishes to crystallize the idea within bodies, but is then overcome by their monstrous mixes, by everything that evades the idea in depth.[29]

The Discovery of the Surface against the Despair of Depth

There is, however, a third avenue that is open to D'Albert, that of a healing surface. For a while, the theatre appears to offer him a possibility for the composition of such a surface. It is a theatre opposed to the comedy of manners, the drama, and tragedy; it is a theatre that is 'fantastique, extravagant, impossible.' In other words, a theatre of movement and becoming that dissolves fixed qualities and identities. It deals not with fixed meanings or significations that unfold according to the three temporal dimensions of Chronos (the past, present, and future of a linear plot structure), but with the simultaneity of sense-events freed from the heaviness of bodies on the lightness of the surface.

It is a world where identities and qualities are no longer static or immobile, and where the characters lack depth and consequence. This is no longer a world of conflict, or contradiction; its harmony comes from lightness and inconsequentiality, from a sliding of one quality or term into another:

> Les personnages ne sont d'aucun temps ni d'aucun pays; ils vont et viennent sans que l'on sache pourquoi ni comment ... C'est un goût qui n'est précisément ni anglais, ni allemand, ni français, ni turc, ni espagnol, ni tartare, quoiqu'il tienne un peu de tout cela ... Des acteurs ainsi habillés peuvent dire tout ce qu'ils veulent sans choquer la vraisemblance. La fantaisie peut courir de tous côtés ... Rien ne s'y oppose, ni les lieux, ni les noms, ni le costume. (272–3)

Words and actions are imponderous, insignificant, and inessential. Neither the characters nor the author need each other to speak or to act; they have no bearing upon one another. Language and gestures are freed from hierarchy and oppression, and expression becomes a matter of independence and impassibility:

> Ils parlent sans se presser, sans crier, comme des gens de bonne compagnie qui n'attachent pas grande importance à ce qu'ils font: l'amoureux fait à l'amoureuse sa déclaration de l'air le plus détaché du monde; tout en causant, il frappe sa cuisse du bout de son gant blanc, ou rajuste ses canons. La dame secoue nonchalamment la rosée de son bouquet, et fait des pointes avec sa suivante, l'amoureux se soucie très peu d'attendrir sa cruelle ... souvent même il s'efface tout à fait, et laisse l'auteur courtiser sa maîtresse pour lui ... Les yeux levés vers les bandes d'air et les frises du théâtre, il attend complaisamment que le poète ait achevé de dire ce qui lui passait par la fantaisie pour reprendre son rôle et se remettre à genoux. (274)

Chronology, temporality, and the causal relation are displaced; the dualities of before/after and cause/effect escape ordering and prioritization. This is a world of nonsense and paradox, of the slipping and sliding of words and actions into one another, rather than their anchoring within a well-ordered and linear chain of meaning and signification:

> Tout se noue et se dénoue avec une insouciance admirable: les effets n'ont point de cause et les causes n'ont point d'effet; le personnage le plus spirituel est celui qui dit le plus de sottises; le plus sot dit les choses les plus spirituelles; les jeunes filles tiennent des discours qui feraient rougir des courtisanes, les courtisanes débitent les maximes de morale. Les aventures les plus inouïes se succèdent coup sur coup sans qu'elles soient expliquées. (274)

The problem, however, is that D'Albert is unable to take the superficiality and frivolity of this theatre at face value, or in other words, to stay on the surface. D'Albert cannot keep it at the one-dimensional or skin-deep level; still tied to the categories of truth/illusion and essence/appearance, he views this theatre as yet another means of elevating oneself above the weight of reality and of attaining the idea. The *illusion comique* hides a more essential truth, and appearances conceal, but ultimately reveal, the poet's deepest dreams and ideals:

> Perdita, Rosalinde, Célie, Pandarus, Parolles, Silvio, Léandre et les autres, tous ces types charmants, si faux et si vrais, qui, sur les ailes bigarrées de la folie, s'élèvent au-dessus de la grossière réalité, et dans qui le poète personnifie sa joie, sa mélancolie, son amour et son rêve le plus intime sous les apparences les plus frivoles et les plus dégagées. (275)

D'Albert cannot avoid flying back up towards the ideal as a means of escape from the ordinary, the vulgar, and the banal of the living.[30] His flight towards the higher realm of beauty unfortunately plummets him back into the confusion of depth, and from there into the apathy of nihilism.[31] And with the descent into depth, D'Albert plunges back into a stasis that prevents him from reaching out to life.

He thus succumbs to the illness peculiar to an aesthetics of the idea – the mania of height or the depression of depth. But Gautier's last word is not to be found in the denial and despair of a thought and desire torn between these two coordinates. It lies rather with Mademoiselle de Maupin, the young woman who conquers the art of the surface in an aesthetics of the superficial and the one-dimensional, who discovers the world of sense-effects, who learns that sexuality is only skin-deep, and who affirms the joy and possibility of the weightless and the shallow.

Mademoiselle de Maupin: D'Albert's Mirror Image?

Mademoiselle de Maupin may be said to function as D'Albert's double: she is a Romantic figure subject to the same ennui and *mal du siècle*. She describes her life as a 'piétinement absurde et monotone' and manifests a similar, unbridled desire for the absolute: 'Les vrais, les seuls irrépara-blement malheureux sont ceux dont la folle étreinte embrasse l'univers entier, ceux qui veulent tout et ne veulent rien ... Il s'agite en moi beau-coup de désirs vagues qui se confondent ensemble, et en enfantent d'autres qui les dévorent ensuite. Mes désirs sont une nuée d'oiseaux qui tourbillonent et voltigent sans but ...' (195–6). Rosette, D'Albert's mis-tress, herself remarks on this resemblance;[32] like D'Albert, Mademoiselle de Maupin is given to a taste for the exotic, fantastic, and bizarre and this, despite a bucolic and pastoral childhood.[33] Like D'Albert, she too is on a quest for a soulmate who would be the model of love and perfec-tion. And like him, she is quickly disillusioned with the reality that can never correspond to the ideal to which she aspires; the very nature of men rendering it impossible.[34] Her lighthearted and satirical enumera-tion of their shortcomings at times hits a deeper and more discordant note: 'Plante de l'idéal, plus venimeuse que le mancenillier ou l'arbre upas, qu'il m'en coûte, malgré les fleurs trompeuses et le poison que l'on respire avec ton parfum, pour te déraciner de mon âme!' (262). The violence of desire coupled with the impossibility of satisfying it makes her prone to a lethargy from which she believes only the strange and unusual can arouse her. She then inclines towards the 'cerebral per-versity' and decadence that Busst mentions and which he associates with the figure of the androgyne.[35]

Madeleine de Maupin's quest is prompted not just by her longing for the ideal man, but also by a desire to break free of the ignorance in which her sex is held. The means to do this is to accede to the knowl-edge, power, and mastery that men detain, to infiltrate their world by piercing through their masks and layers of social conventions in order to get at the truth that lies behind or underneath them. In her bid to enter the secret world of men from which women are excluded, Madeleine de Maupin wishes to master their discourse and language. In this sense, hers is a thought and strategy of height and depth: it is to find the man who will correspond to her ideal by penetrating through masks and appearances in order to reach the truth that lies behind them. She thus seeks the true nature that lies behind the layer of convention; she wishes to discover the signified concealed by the signifier.

For Mademoiselle de Maupin, the power that men exercise over women derives from the depth and secrecy in which men clothe themselves, in contrast to the transparence of women's lives. The separation established between the two sexes preserves knowledge for men, but relegates women to ignorance, dependence, and weakness.[36] Roles allocated to women define their capacities for them and deprive them of (sexual) knowledge and speech. They are imprisoned within the limits that men lay down for both their minds and bodies. In this respect, Mademoiselle de Maupin offers a social critique very much like that of Mme de Merteuil in Laclos's *Les liasons dangereuses*.[37] And like Mme de Merteuil, she rebels against the role allotted for her sex and is consumed by a desire for the knowledge that is denied to her. She is determined to penetrate the barriers that men erect; she wishes to deploy the acuity of her look in order to dissect and study their hidden depths, and to master their discourse.[38] And after all this, she is disappointed by what lies behind the masks and appearance: 'Je le sais maintenant, et en vérité je suis fâchée de le savoir' (246). Where D'Albert falls into misogyny, Mademoiselle de Maupin succumbs to a hatred of men: '[J]'avais les hommes en horreur' (264). She dreams of giving herself up within an androgynous fusion, but is confronted with the impossibility of her dream.

Does Gautier's novel then content itself with a mere reversal of hierarchy in which Mademoiselle de Maupin learns to appropriate the discourse of men, to master the rules of their games, and to beat them at their sport, thereby satisfying her desire for power over them? Is Mademoiselle de Maupin content to limit herself to dialectical power games? I believe not. Mademoiselle de Maupin follows a different trajectory from the politics of revenge and *ressentiment* that Mme de Merteuil adopts. And her difference from D'Albert lies in her mastery of surface multiplicity, or rather, in her learning how to stay at the surface. Mademoiselle de Maupin acquires the freedom that comes from the discovery that there is no becoming-man or becoming-master, that there is no usurping their place. It lies in the possibility of difference, in a will to power that is not a desire *for* power, but a will to difference, an affirmation of difference.[39]

Depth, Surface, and Illusion in *Mademoiselle de Maupin*

As we noted earlier, scholarship on Gautier's aesthetics considers it principally in terms of a Platonic divide between being and appearance, truth and artifice, essence and illusion. But critics have also pointed to the manner in which his aesthetics problematizes or diverges from Platonism. Thus, Michel Brix argues that Gautier's work is not so much an unquestioning heritage of Platonism, as a conflictual dialogue with and critique of its precepts.[40] Similarly, Anne Bouchard, in her subtle analysis of *Mademoiselle de Maupin*, demonstrates how the metaphors of the mask and mirror dissolve the divide between appearance and reality by defining appearance as the real. '[Gautier] semble parfois suggérer que l'on était déjà ce que l'on choisit de paraître ... à moins que l'on ne devienne ce que l'on paraît.'[41] She follows this (very Nietzschean!) insight with a quote by Jean Rousset to conclude that representation in Gautier, far from constituting an empty or illusory play of appearances, is the expression of the reality of being: 'Chacun représente donc ce qu'il est.'[42]

Volker Kapp also interprets *Mademoiselle de Maupin* as a reversal of Platonic transcendence and a move away from metaphysics towards immanence, in a reorientation towards 'un plan purement horizontal.'[43] But Kapp's understanding of Gautier's aesthetics maintains art and desire within an unbreachable gulf between the ideal and the real.[44] In a view comparable to that of Kapp, Michelle Mielly proposes a feminist reading of *Mademoiselle de Maupin* that acknowledges Madeleine de Maupin's break with socio-sexual hierarchies and with temporality, but considers the androgynous figure she embodies as a narcissistic synthesis of Platonic opposites, and as such, a figure of the 'irréel.'[45]

What the convergences and divergences between some of the points of view enumerated above reveal is the difficulty of gauging the value of the play of appearances and illusion in *Mademoiselle de Maupin.* Sensing that Gautier's novel defies a simple reduction to the terms of Platonism, and that illusion in Gautier is invested with the power of the real, the critic seems forced to consider the play of appearance as either a fantasmatic experience of imaginary plenitude (Kapp), as a comforting fetishistic evasion from the truth of lack and emptiness (Albouy, Schnack), or even simply as the domain of the unreal (Mielly).

Following Bouchard, I would like to submit that surface illusion in Gautier harbours a positive and productive power, and that a different set of theoretical concepts may lead us to a better understanding of the value of the play of appearance in the novel. It is in order to better comprehend and evaluate this power that I would like to pause and follow the detour of a path laid out by Nietzsche (and Deleuze).

The Simulacrum, Difference, and Sense

In 'The Simulacrum and Ancient Philosophy,' Deleuze points out that the task of Platonism is to distinguish among pretenders to the truth by separating the authentic from the inauthentic, the pure from the impure, the true claimant from the false.[46] The Platonic authentification of the idea works in depth and height, in the selection of a lineage. It seeks 'to distinguish essence from appearance, intelligible from sensible, Idea from image, original from copy, and model from simulacrum'.[47] However, it is not a simple matter of establishing a difference between the idea and the image; it is also one of establishing a hierarchy of images. In short, Plato distinguishes between two kinds of images. First, there are the copies or icons, which are based on a well-founded resemblance to the idea. With copies/icons, the resemblance is internal and spiritual. Second, there are simulacra-phantasms, where resemblance is a superficial effect, based on dissimilarity, perversion, and deviation. The simulacrum is a perversion, because its effect of resemblance is external, it is produced by means different from those at work in the model. For Plato, the resemblance of the simulacrum is a non-productive effect obtained by ruse and subversion, by its power to evade the same. Generated by an internal difference or disparity, the simulacrum can no longer be defined in a relation of difference to a model, but points rather to the subversive power of a dissemblance, a 'becoming-mad' or a 'becoming-unlimited' that evades the same.[48] Platonism is thus motivated by a desire to limit the evasion of the simulacrum and to restrict its becoming.

In summary, the resemblance of the copy is internal and derived from the idea, but that of the simulacra is a false effect, a subversion which escapes the idea. There is thus an essential difference between the simulacrum and the copy: 'The copy is an image endowed with resemblance, the simulacrum is an image without resemblance.'[49] For Plato, the copy is productive because it is governed by relations and proportions constitutive of essence, whereas the simulacrum is non-productive because it evades essence.

Platonism establishes and operates within the domain of representation of icons that bear an intrinsic relationship to the model or foundation. The Platonic model is the same, the copy is the similar. The Nietzschean reversal of Platonism consists in the overturning of the Platonic motivation to the same and the similar, in overturning the hierarchy which places essence and truth at the top while relegating simulacra to the bottom of the cave. It consists therefore in affirming the difference of the simulacra, 'to make the simulacra rise and to affirm their rights among icons and copies.'[50] '[I]t has to do with undertaking the subversion of this world – the "twilight of the idols." The simulacrum is not a degraded copy, it harbors a positive power which denies *the original and the copy, the model and the reproduction.*'[51] In this reversal of Platonism, difference affirms itself for itself; it is not referred to a preexisting same or identity nor defined by their priority. With the simulacrum, identity is the product of disparity and resemblance is the product of an internal difference as an essence that is simulated or produced. There is no longer a hierarchy between model/copy, same/different; it is undone in favour of nomadic distributions and the simultaneity of events. The presupposed model or essence of truth and identity is destroyed, and, along with it, representation. The simulacrum is not an appearance or illusion determined by the overarching value of an essence or truth, nor is it a mere shadow relegated to the bottom of the cave. It is an effect of the surface, an event, a sign as 'the highest power of the false,' an effect of simulation as a 'Dionysian sense-producing machine.'

It is at the surface to which Nietzsche raises the simulacrum, as a surface effect that Deleuze recuperates it. What Deleuze sees in the simulacrum as event is the power of affirmation of the eternal return or the return of a difference that is produced by simulation and that reverses representation founded on the same and the similar: 'For all its long history, Platonism happened only once, and Socrates fell under the blade. For the Same and Similar become simple illusions when they cease to be simulated.'[52] What returns therefore is difference; an effect of the simulacrum as the affirmation of difference. What comes back is the positive power of difference, or difference as a positive power. We are now in a better position to evaluate the import of Mademoiselle de Maupin's difference from D'Albert.

The Hermaphrodite and the Will to Truth and Beauty

As we saw earlier, D'Albert is in search of the model that will embody the essence of beauty and that will authenticate and be authenticated by the idea. His inability to find ideal beauty in the flesh leads to an accusation of art. Art only offers us simulacra, pale shadows of the truth that bodies can never incarnate or represent.[53] When D'Albert meets Théodore, it seems to him that the idea has been authenticated and verified. But

Théodore's sex belies his claim to ideal beauty; the latter has been incarnated in a body that is dissimilar to it. Théodore is thus a false pretender, a simulacrum that subverts the ideal. Perfect feminine beauty has been substantiated in the body of a man. He is thus an aberration, as D'Albert believes his love for Théodore proves. D'Albert thus sets up an alternative between the world of the ideal and that of bodies: Théodore incarnates ideal perfection, but as an unnatural and demonic mixture. There is something in his body that goes against the ideal, and that leads D'Albert into the monstrous and perverse.[54] D'Albert's 'homosexual' attraction for Théodore results in an unsettling loss of self and identity; D'Albert is haunted by the possibility that behind the perfect body lies an aberrant and frightening mixture in depth. He thus calls into question an aesthetic that represents the ruse of the simulacrum, and that points to the terrifying depth from which it comes forth. His task then becomes to explain away this aesthetic of subversion and to account for a love he perceives as unnatural and abominable. The figure of the hermaphrodite becomes a justification for D'Albert's 'aberration': he points out that for the Greeks, the hermaphrodite represented aesthetic perfection and harmony, not violence and conflict:

Aussi l'hermaphrodite est-il une des chimères les plus ardemment caressées de l'antiquité idolâtre.
   C'est en effet une des plus suaves créations du génie païen que ce fils d'Hermès et d'Aphrodite. Il ne se peut rien imaginer de plus ravissant au monde que ces deux corps tous deux parfaits, harmonieusement fondus ensemble, que ces deux beautés si égales et si différentes qui n'en forment plus qu'une supérieure à toutes deux, parce ce qu'elles se tempèrent et se font valoir réciproquement ... (237)

The play D'Albert stages works to reintegrate the ambiguity of the hermaphrodite within the perfection of the whole. The harmony of the hermaphrodite is restored through an affirmation of the correspondance between the idea and the model, the model and the copy, between essence and appearance. D'Albert wishes to vanquish difference, to conquer the rebelliousness of depth in favour of the unity and cohesiveness of a totality. Sexual and aesthetic perversion must be explained away, the truth of sex and beauty revealed, and identity and harmony reestablished: 'J'éprouvais une sensation de bien-être énorme, comme si l'on m'eût ôté une montagne ou deux de dessus la poitrine. – Je sentis s'évanouir l'horreur que j'avais de moi-même, et je fus délivré de l'ennui de me regarder comme un monstre ... (car je ne veux plus me souvenir

que j'ai eu cette stupidité de la [Théodore] prendre pour un homme) ...'
(294). The play's hermaphroditic words and games of metamorphosis
will serve to uncover Théodore's true sex and restore normalcy to sexual
desire: '[I]l m'a semblé que Théodore s'était aperçu de mon amour ... et
qu'à travers le voile de ces expressions empruntées, sous ce masque de
théâtre, avec ses paroles hermaphrodites, il faisait allusion à son sexe réel
et à notre situation réciproque' (302). The play restores order and truth
to beauty, while fixing and stabilizing sexual identity:

> Mais vous êtes une femme, nous ne sommes plus au temps des métamor-
> phoses; – Adonis et Hermaphrodite sont morts – et ce n'est plus par un
> homme qu'un pareil degré de beauté pourrait être atteint; car, depuis que
> les héros et les dieux ne sont plus, vous seules conservez dans vos corps de
> marbre, comme dans un temple grec, le précieux don de la forme anathé-
> matisée par Christ ... vous représentez dignement la première divinité du
> monde, la plus pure symbolisation de l'essence éternelle – la beauté. (354)

However, as we shall see, sexuality and identity turn out to be slightly
more complicated affairs than what D'Albert imagines them to be.

Of Sense and Sexuality

Shakespeare's *As You Like It* provides for a role playing that blurs sexual
oppositions and gender roles. The play of disguises is rendered more
complex by the fact that one of its principal actors, Théodore, is already
a woman disguised as a man. So we have a situation in which a woman
playing the role of a man plays the role of a woman playing the role of a
man. In this doubling of roles, any original term of sexual opposition
becomes difficult to localize and identify. But even more than a deconstruction of the binaries man/woman and masculine/feminine, the play
within the novel becomes an undoing of the very opposition between sex
and gender, the natural and the artificial, the inner and the outer, the
actor and the role.

When Théodore/Madeleine appears on the scene as Rosalind, what
ought to be an unveiling of true and natural sex is placed under the sign
of a theatrical effect or performance: 'Mais on dirait qu'il n'a jamais
porté d'autre costume de sa vie! ... L'illusion est aussi complète que possible: on dirait presque qu'il a de la gorge, tant sa poitrine est grasse et
bien remplie' (296). And when Théodore/Madeleine/Rosalind appears
as Ganymede, femininity is once again inscribed as role play: '[I]l était

ajusté de manière à faire pressentir que ces habits virils avaient une doublure féminine; quelque chose de plus large dans les hanches et de plus
rempli à la poitrine, je ne sais quoi d'ondoyant que les étoffes ne présen-
tent pas sur le corps d'un homme ne laissaient que de faibles doutes sur
le sexe du personnage' (298–9). At the very moment when D'Albert
believes that the truth of a body and sex is being disclosed, these categories are shifted and displaced. The natural appears as artificial and vice-
versa: '[A]vec un art infini, il se donnait l'air aussi gêné dans un costume
qui lui était ordinaire qu'il avait eu l'air à son aise dans des vêtements qui
n'étaient pas les siens' (299).[55]

More important, however, the staging of As You Like It also dismantles
the binaries of signifier/signified, appearance/truth, and illusion/real-
ity. It is clearly not a matter of privileging the second term of each opposition over the first. But neither does the play make a simple move to
evacuate the second term in favour of the first. If the play within
Gautier's novel avoids the trap of fixing a stable signified, essence, truth
or nature, it also avoids indulging in an empty play of signifier over signified, appearance over reality, illusion over truth. Rather, the play itself
shifts from the domain of representation (from the dimensions of denotation and signification) to that of sense and expression. Sexuality and
identity are not played out in a battle between the signifier and the signified; they cease to be defined or understood as qualities or quantities of
bodies. Rather, they deploy themselves on the surface of sense-effects, as
simulacra or events, as incorporeal attributes that are irreducible to the
bodies that express them.

As mentioned earlier, in the situation of a woman disguised as a man
(Madeleine de Maupin disguised as Théodore de Sérannes) playing the
role of a woman disguised as a man (Rosalind playing Ganymede), the
original term becomes difficult to locate, since it generates several per-
mutations. One could have a woman playing a man (Madeleine playing
Théodore or Rosalind playing Ganymede), a woman playing a woman
(Madeleine playing Rosalind), a man playing a woman (Théodore playing Rosalind) or a man playing a man (Théodore playing Ganymede).
The terms spill over each other to such an extent that when D'Albert
remarks: '[I]l était ajusté de manière à faire pressentir que ces habits virils avaient une doublure féminine,' the pronoun 'il' could be occupied
by not just Théodore, but Ganymede, thereby extending into Rosalind
and even Madeleine. The priority of original over copy, actor over
role, undergoes a shift: Théodore could be playing both Rosalind and
Madeleine, or Ganymede could just as easily be playing Rosalind or

Madeleine de Maupin. Rosalind could be playing Madeleine, or Ganymede could even be playing Théodore. The relation between actor and role is subject to reversal, as is that between cause and effect, before and after, active and passive. A role is played as much as it plays, an actor acts as much as he is acted. There is no longer one sense or direction, or the good sense of a unique direction. What we have here is nonsense or paradox as that which defies (a) good sense and moves in both directions at once. And once again, the distinction between the original and the copy is displaced towards the simulacrum as that which evades both terms at once.

With Shakespeare's *As You Like It*, we leave the domain of fixed and assignable identities and qualities and shift towards the domain of sense, or what amounts to the same thing, that of nonsense and paradox. Nonsense and paradox move in either direction in a lateral sliding, in a becoming that is simultaneous and reversible. There is no true identity behind the mask, no truth of the actor behind the role, no true sex behind the clothes and costume. Sexuality and identity are productions; they are sense-effects irreducible to a signifier or a signified. They participate in nonsense or paradox as an excess of sense. Sexuality is not a quality or principle to be located in the body or idea; it is produced as a surface effect, an event or simulacrum. Femininity is the expressed or expressible of sense; it is neither the signified of a signifier, nor a signifier emptied of the signified. It is a *sign* in the Deleuzian sense of the term, as a paradoxical element that can be distributed along the series of signifier/signified, cause/effect, or even man/woman, but cannot be reducible to either. It is the paradoxical or nonsensical element that traverses both series, that operates at their boundary and assures communication between them. The sign-event is both sense and nonsense; it is the excess, not lack of sense. Bodies are capable of representation (of denoting and signifying), but they have an expressed which exceeds representation. Identity is an expression of difference; the constellation Théodore/ Madeleine/ Ganymede/ Rosalind is an incorporeal sense-event, a surface effect impassible to the body that expresses it. Representation thus differs in nature from the domain of expression. In playing a role, there is a representation that is effectuated, but this representation envelops a sense (or expression), which in turn cannot be reduced to either the representation or the body that expresses it.[56] Representation thus represents by means of the sense-event or expression that it envelops:

There is thus a 'use' of representation, without which representation would remain lifeless and senseless ... But such use is not defined through a function of representation in relation to the represented, nor even through representativeness as the form of possibility ... [U]se is in the relation between representation and something extra-representative, a nonrepresented and merely expressed entity. Representation envelops the event in another nature, it envelops it at its borders, it stretches until this point, and it brings about *this lining or hem* [emphasis mine]. This is the operation which defines living usage, to the extent that representation, when it does not reach this point, remains only a dead letter confronting that which it represents and stupid in its representativeness.[57]

D'Albert believes that he has succeeded in pinning down the sex and identity of Madeleine/Théodore through the characters of Rosalind/ Ganymede. But the role of Rosalind/Ganymede played by Madeleine/ Théodore has no final answer to offer regarding Madeleine's sexual identity, no ultimate sexual essence to capture. As we will see in a little more detail in the sections that follow, Madeleine's sexuality is of the order of multiplicity and plurality. Sexuality is an attribute that differs in nature from the body in which it is expressed; it is not a quality or an action but a neutral and impassible surface effect. The role playing of Madeleine/Théodore/Rosalind/Ganymede is of the order of a sense-event, irreducible to a one-to-one relation between signifier and signified. Sexuality is not a quality, category, or signified that lies behind clothes, waiting to be revealed. It is a lining of the clothes, coextensive with the surface, a 'doublure féminine'. Clothes are not signifiers that point to a signified that lies underneath. Rather, signifier and signified are flattened out in the domain of sense, which deploys itself on the line of the surface, in the continuity of the reversal of inside/out. It is no longer a problem of unveiling a 'true' body behind the clothes, a 'true' sex under the costume. Sexuality leaves the domain of truth and veracity to enter that of sense. It is a perversion at the surface, not a subversion in depth. It is not so much what in the depth of bodies flees the idea, as what in the incorporeal event is irreducible to the body. It is what affirms its difference from and impassibility to the body; it is what evades actualization in the present. Sexuality is thus a counter-actualization.[58] The theatre is more than a signifying or representational instance: it becomes a sense-producing machine, a Dionysian machine of the false, of the simulacrum as an effect of the surface.

D'Albert views the play within the terms of denotation, signification, and manifestation. *As You Like It* will serve to name Madeleine de Maupin as woman, it will unmask her real situation by means of an artifice, and will be the medium in which the actors can express their love for each other. Thus, the play and its roles are revelations of identity and representations of passions. The theatre is a device that enlists an illusion in the service of reality. The play *As You Like It* is a mirror image of the truth about Madeleine – a woman playing a man in the play reflects the truth about a woman playing a man in reality. By playing Orlando, D'Albert will manifest his true feelings for Théodore/Madeleine, while s/he will do the same by playing Rosalind/Ganymede. And in the final analysis, the staging of *As You Like It* is the actualization of the essence of beauty and truth in the figure of Mademoiselle de Maupin.

Once again, however, Mademoiselle de Maupin eludes capture within a fixed sex or sexuality, and her desire will not conform to the plot line of *As You Like It*. D'Albert invites her to inscribe herself within its structure: 'Rosalinde ... jouez votre rôle jusqu'au bout, jetez les habits du beau Ganymède, et tendez votre blanche main au plus jeune fils du chevalier Rowland des Bois' (359). D'Albert invites Mademoiselle de Maupin to finish out her role and carry it through to its preordained end. In other words, Shakespeare's play should be realized or actualized completely and perfectly in the story of his own adventure, 'l'histoire glorieuse et triomphante du chevalier d'Albert au pourchas de Daraïde, la plus belle princess du monde' (98–9).[59] But Mademoiselle de Maupin refuses this role and cannot be encompassed by it. She finally rejects the order of the dyadic heterosexual model that D'Albert holds out for her, and proclaims one of multiplicity and difference. While playing the role of Rosalind/Ganymede, she escapes its actualization as D'Albert envisages it. She does not merely incarnate the character or part of Rosalind. Rather, as an actor, she doubles as a quasi-cause of the event. In other words, the role itself cannot be simply or completely distributed within the categories of plot, meaning, qualities, and properties. Nor does it limit itself to a development within the past, present, and future of Chronos. The representation envelops an expression it cannot contain or limit within itself. Actor and role occupy the instant of a becoming, of the event.[60] Role and actor are both incorporeal effects, the actor doubling as a quasi-cause of the event (role). S/he is the paradoxical element that prevents identity and sexuality from being fixed within the thickness of a present. Through her role playing, Mademoiselle de Maupin places herself not in the deep present of Chronos, but on the fleeing instant of

Aion, on the line of a becoming:

> The role played is never that of a character; it is a theme (the complex theme or sense) constituted by the components of the event, that is, by the communicating singularities effectively liberated from the limits of individuals and persons ... The role has the same relation to the actor as the future and past have to the instantaneous present which corresponds to them on the line of the Aion. The actor thus actualizes the event, but in a way which is entirely different from the actualization of the event in the depth of things. Or rather, the actor redoubles this cosmic, or physical actualization, in his own way, which is singularly superficial – but because of it more distinct, trenchant and pure. Thus, the actor delimits the original, disengages from it an abstract line, and keeps from the event only its contour and its splendor, becoming thereby the actor of one's own events – *a counter-actualization*.[61]

The present of the actor or the instant of Aion is different from the vast and deep present of Chronos. It is not the present of the incorporation or actualization of the event in bodies and their mixtures. Nor is it a present buried still deeper in bodies that subverts or eludes Chronos. Rather, it is the instant that prevents the incorporation of the event from being confused with its counter-actualization. It is the moment of perversion at the surface, not that of a subversion in depth. It is the fleeting instant 'which comes to duplicate the lining (*redoubler la doublure*).'[62]

D'Albert invites Madeleine de Maupin/Rosalind to doff her masculine attire and to assume her female identity. Mademoiselle de Maupin realizes that the clothes one wears have an important influence on one's sexual identity: by donning a man's garments, she is taken up with a desire to become a man. She sharpens the use of her wit and sword, she perfects her horsemanship and jousting skills, she masters the courting game. Clothes change the perspective she has on her sex – she recognizes that men rightly ascribe certain faults to women, but she also develops a greater appreciation of feminine beauty. Wearing masculine garments causes her to forget her sex, and even call into question the naturalness of a body's sex.[63] But if Madeleine learns that it is not one's body that makes a sex, she also discovers that one's clothes do not either. Sexual identity is not a simple function of one's outer clothing. It is something that cannot be ultimately located in either term of the oppositions inner and outer, body and garments, nature and culture. (Dressed) as a woman, Madeleine was already a man.[64] She is both man and woman in her relationship with Rosette, and the young girl Ninon dressed as a pageboy would still play the part of her mistress.[65] D'Albert loves her dressed as a man and a woman, and loves both the man and the woman in her.[66] And Mademoiselle de Maupin herself can find pleasure as (and with) both sexes.

Mademoiselle de Maupin refuses the alternative of either/or; she heralds a sexuality that would not content itself with one exclusive term, but would participate in both. She rejects the limits (and limitations) of two sexes to proclaim a third sex that cannot be explained by the configurations of height and depth: '[J]e suis d'un troisième sexe à part qui n'a pas encore de nom: *au-dessus ou au-dessous*, plus défectueux ou supérieur: j'ai le corps et l'âme d'une femme, l'esprit et la force d'un homme, et j'ai trop ou pas assez de l'un et de l'autre pour pouvoir m'accoupler avec l'un d'eux' (393–4; emphasis mine). She renounces the alternatives of height and depth to move towards the surface, and this in order to affirm difference and possibility: 'Ma nature se produirait ainsi tout entière au jour, et je serais parfaitement heureuse, car le vrai bonheur est de se pouvoir développer librement en tous sens et d'être tout ce qu'on peut être' (394).

Mademoiselle de Maupin refuses to operate within the terms of the dialectic. She does not content herself with a mere reversal or hierarchy of power. She rejects a femininity that would still inscribe itself within the reactive and the negative by reverting to strategies of power and domination. Not for her the position of the master who denies and negates. She moves outside of the opposition and conflict that characterize the binaries man/woman, masculine/feminine. She refuses the negativity that founds and results from sexual hierarchization: 'En vérité, ni l'un ni l'autre de ces deux sexes n'est le mien; je n'ai ni la soumission imbécile, ni la timidité, ni les petitesses de la femme; je n'ai pas les vices des hommes, leur dégoûtante crapule et leurs penchants brutaux' (393). Madeleine affirms the plurality of the third sex. She avoids the nihilism and decadence of D'Albert and rejects a femininity that would be dominated by revenge and *ressentiment*. What she understands at the end of her adventures is that it is not a question of seizing power and of occupying the place of the unseated master. The secret of things was not to be sought in the depths of the hidden world of men, nor was it to be sought in the height of the ideal. When she cannot find her real life ideal, it is the ideal itself that she rejects, not life. Happiness and possibility are matters of the surface, and are to be affirmed in a 'will to power' of the surface. She discovers that there is no becoming-man, that there is only the lightness and joy of a becoming-woman, of a becoming-multiple. Thus, she is not so much in dialectical opposition to D'Albert, as opposed to all dialectic. She heralds a new power of metamorphosis, one that is different from D'Albert's 'transmigration' or the movement of the same essence or soul across different bodies. Hers is a metamorphosis that celebrates not the return of the same through different corporeal actualizations, but the return of difference as counter-actualization. Hers is the power not of transmigration, but of transmutation. Sexuality is an expressed multiplicity irreducible to the body that expresses, an incorporeal sense-event impassible and neutral to the bodies in which it is effectuated. She is not so much the harmonious resolution of a dialectical opposition between two mutually exclusive sexes, as a paradoxical element that traverses two divergent series and ensures communication between them, an excess of sense that assures the production of sense: 'Aimez-vous tous deux en souvenir de moi, que vous avez aimée l'un et l'autre, et dites-vous quelquefois mon nom dans un baiser' (416).

An Aesthetics of Sense or the Sensibility of the Surface

With Mademoiselle de Maupin, a new aesthetic figure emerges, one who wrests the power and movement of life away from the denial of truth and ideal. Théodore/Madeleine wields the art of affirmation, s/he affirms the productivity and multiplicity of the false. S/he is not an androgynous figure of dialectical appropriation, but of communication (as production of multiplicity) of the sexes. She is neither the hermaphroditic figure that symbolizes the violent effacement of difference, nor does she stand for the harmonious reunion of two halves of a severed totality. Rather, she represents the play of difference of a healing surface. She does not represent lack or incompleteness; she expresses the plenitude and immanence of the most thin and one-dimensional plane of desire. Her androgyny or bisexuality does not derive from the Platonic duality established between the depth of the material and the height of the spiritual and ideal; it is an androgyny of the superficial, of the simulacrum. D'Albert seeks in Madeleine de Maupin the incorporation of ideal beauty, the actualization of a superior essence in the depth of a body. He wishes to have it realized and captured in the thick, eternal present of Chronos. Madeleine de Maupin performs a counter-actualization of this essence; she crystallizes it in the most fleeting and instantaneous of moments. The profoundest essence is to found at the thinnest, most insubstantial of surfaces and becomings. The ideational returns as the most shallow and frivolous of simulacra. It refuses to be weighted down by Platonic truth and essence. It returns as the power and joy of the false.[67]

Mademoiselle de Maupin does not represent the eternal, immutable, and unchanging ideal of classic beauty. Neither is her beauty something that can be fixed in the all-encompassing present of Chronos. It is not a quality that develops in a temporality. Hers is neither the eternal beauty of the classical nor the movement and transformation of the modern. Both of these situate themselves within a present that is either overarching in its eternity or defined in terms of a chronology determined by the past and oriented towards the future. Mademoiselle de Maupin expresses the fugitive beauty of a becoming that situates itself on the axe of Aion; it eludes the present, it is simultaneously past and future. Or rather, she occupies the fleeting instant that is constantly subdivided by the past and future. Hers is a beauty that escapes the fixity of the Platonic essence and eludes the sameness of the model. It returns as the power of difference, as the power of the simulacrum that is neither cause nor principle, but is something that is produced as an effect. It is the movement, force, and transmutation of sense and becoming.[68] Gautier's aesthetics moves away from the Hegelian dialectic of beauty as the adequation of spirit to itself through transformation and negation of weighty matter.[69] Mademoiselle de Maupin effectuates a counter-actualization of beauty in the most fugitive and untimely of instants. Beauty is the affirmation of the active force of transmutation.

Opposed to the negativity of dialectic, and rejecting the politics of revenge and *ressentiment*, Mademoiselle de Maupin affirms an aesthetics (and ethics) of the superficial and the one-dimensional as an expression of joy and multiplicity. With *Mademoiselle de Maupin* then, Gautier lays out an aesthetics of sense and in so doing, affirms an aesthetics of the possibility of difference, of difference as possibility. What are the implications of an aesthetics of sense for a politics of sense? Or to ask what is perhaps the same question, what politics of the possible will allow for an aesthetics of the possible? It is to Virginia Woolf that we must turn as our present study draws towards its conclusion.

Conclusion

> To write is also to become something other than a writer. To those who ask what literature is, Virginia Woolf responds: To whom are you speaking of writing? The writer does not speak about it, but is concerned with something else.
>
> Gilles Deleuze[1]

We embarked upon this study with a simple suspicion – that literature expresses forces that cannot be explained away by representational paradigms. Writing is expressive of a desire that is irreducible to the dimension of representation, and that exceeds the categories of a macropolitics. An interpretive method that functions solely within the terms of signification and representation, that proceeds by way of the oppositional categories of signifier and signified or self and other is inadequate to the multiplicity of sense produced by writing. In other words, a macropolitics of reading is unequal to the micropolitics of literature. Literature, in blatant defiance of every historical common sense, insists upon practising a politics of sense.

Each text studied thus presents feminism with an exigency: it demands a politics of reading that would not blind itself to the difference and multiplicity it is capable of affirming. Literature calls for a different ethics of interpretation, for a critique that would both affirm its possibility and make possible its affirmation. What it demands, in other words, is a (very materialist) thought that would be worthy of the freedom and possibility of the event.

Interestingly, Elizabeth Grosz articulates the need for such an (untimely) feminist thought in her most recent book, *Time Travels: Femi-*

nism, Nature and Power, in which she envisions feminist theory as a play of impersonal and inhuman forces, and advocates a feminist politics of imperceptibility rather than identity.[2] Grosz's compelling arguments for a new future of sexual difference must here be counterbalanced by Braidotti's defence of what she terms the 'historical and epistemological specificity of the female condition.'[3] In a sense, the philosophical differences between Grosz and Braidotti raise the very literary and political questions that have occupied the centre of feminist dialogue over the past three decades (indeed, questions that are of necessity implicated within an inquiry into the value of the feminine in male-authored texts): Can writing by women escape structures of repression, and how? Is there a writing that is specifically female or feminine? Do men belong in feminism? Can the artistic production of men be qualified as feminist? Does the embracing of sexual multiplicity carry with it the danger of yet another erasure of women's history and materiality? Does it preempt the possibility of writing for women? And how do we read and understand the politics of literature?[4] Remembering these seemingly simple questions that feminists have never stopped asking themselves reminds us of the stakes and implications of the feminist politics and ethics that we choose to practise. And here too, it is literature that provides the most forceful thinking through of the consequences that a politics of sense might have for feminism, and one writer in particular, whose work has served as such a powerful fulcrum for feminist thinkers of the past century and the present.

There is no feminist writer I believe, who articulates and practises a politics of sense in a more compelling fashion than Virginia Woolf. While recognizing the negating force of historical oppression brought to bear against one sex by another, *Orlando* and *A Room of One's Own* place writing in a mode removed from it. *Orlando* understands that history can (and does) exert a negative force upon writing, but it also grasps writing as an event that is not of the same order as that history. It cannot be fully explained by the latter, nor reduced to its reckonings and accountings. Both *Orlando* and *A Room of One's Own* understand writing as a becoming that can always fall back into history, but which is not of it and does not come from it. Woolf's rewriting of literary history in these texts is not so much an attempt to overcome one version by another, as an attempt to trace the lines of affirmation that escape every negative historical force; it is an attempt to chart the lines of a literature that is of the (untimely) order of events and becomings. Orlando realizes that becoming a writer is a delicate matter of negotiating with the spirits of different ages in

order to obtain either their recognition or their approval. There can be
no doubt that it is the spirit of an age that will determine whether it will
allow a writer to write, and there is no question that the spirits of different ages have been singularly ill-disposed towards women. Orlando will
be accorded fame, recognition, seven editions, a prize, and photographs
in the evening papers only in the twentieth century. But Orlando also
understands writing as an event that was always and already taking place,
as something that could always happen and that was always and already
happening:

> What has praise and fame to do with poetry? What has seven editions ... got
> to do with the value of it? Was not writing poetry a secret transaction, a voice
> answering a voice? So that all this chatter, and praise, and blame and meet-
> ing people who admired one and meeting people who did not admire one
> was as ill suited as could be to the thing itself – a voice answering a voice.
> What could have been more secret, she thought, more slow, and like the
> intercourse of lovers, than the stammering answer she had made all these
> years to the old crooning song of the woods, and the farms and the brown
> horses standing at the gate, neck to neck, and the smithy and the kitchen
> and the fields, so laboriously bearing wheat, turnips, grass, and the gardens
> blowing irises and fritillaries?[5]

And in *A Room of One's Own*, Woolf is adamant about the following: literature is not a matter of writing a self and its history, nor one of carving
out a space for the self within a history. It is neither the celebration of an
Edenic sexual specificity, nor an adding up of a long line of political and
historical grievances. Instead, writing must disengage itself both from
the onerous weight of history, as well as the despotism of an 'I' to move
towards the possibility and multiplicity of an intense lived.[6]

'[F]iction,' writes Woolf, 'is like a spider's web, attached ever so lightly
perhaps, but still attached to life at all four corners ... [W]hen the web is
pulled askew, hooked up at the edge, torn in the middle, one remem-
bers that these webs are not spun in mid-air by incorporeal creatures,
but are the work of suffering human beings, and are attached to grossly
material things, like health and money and the houses we live in.'[7] *A
Room of One's Own* begins with a simple thesis – that women need money
and a room of their own if they are to write fiction. And thereby begins a
very materialist feminist inquiry into the reasons for the marked
absence of women writers from the great works of literature. Why is it,

asks Woolf, that women are everywhere represented in literature, but do not themselves write? But more important, what is the reason for the misogyny perpetrated by men of erudition? Why are the professors angry at women?

A Room of One's Own starts out as a strong attempt to rewrite literary tradition by denouncing its history of sexual oppression and exclusion. The difference in access to wealth and opportunity is responsible for women's inability to write great works of literature. 'England,' Woolf concludes, 'is under the rule of patriarchy.' It was the male professor who wielded money, power, and influence. 'Yet he was angry.' What is the reason for this anger, Woolf wonders, and how is one to understand the misogyny that drives it? Her response is clear – it is the desire for power that leads men to assert their superiority through the presumed inferiority of women. The patriarch conquers and rules by positing the inferiority of another. The need to maintain the power to believe in themselves causes men to relegate women to a lower status.[8] Their resentment against women stems from their desire to have their power recognized in every aspect of life: '[M]irrors are essential to all violent and heroic action' (36).

Unwilling to confine her critique to the dialectics of recognition, Woolf seeks to rescue sexual politics, thought, and writing from the motivations of anger and resentment. Her own anger towards men is checked by the simple matter of a legacy worth five hundred pounds a year. But money brings more than the economic security that will ensure the exercise of writing as a profession. With money (and even more so than the vote) comes 'the greatest release of all,' which is the 'freedom to think things in themselves.' Money causes the hatred, bitterness, and fear of the opposite sex to dissipate, opening one up to the possibility of a writing freed from the pressures of a personal and identitarian politics. '[M]y aunt's legacy unveiled the sky to me, and substituted for the large and imposing figure of a gentleman ... a view of the open sky' (39).

For Woolf then, writing cannot take place in the face of an oppressive sexual politics. Shakespeare's sister could not have written great literature because her time would not have permitted it. But, had she written, her work would nevertheless have been deformed or flawed; her mind would have suffered the consequences of the sexual politics brought to bear against her. Rancour and resentment (both on the part of men against her, and on her part against men) would have interfered with her ability to create.[9] Woolf is thus led to what is perhaps the most important question of *A Room of One's Own*, one that bears upon men and women alike: 'But what is the state of mind that is most propitious to the act of creation, I asked' (51). And here too, Woolf's response is clear – it is the liberation from a self, from its self-consciousness, self-reflexivity, and self-absorption; it is the move away from its grievances and grudges that makes literature possible. '[B]ecause the mind of an artist, in order to achieve the prodigious effort of freeing whole and entire the work that is in him, must be incandescent ... There must be no obstacle in it, no foreign matter unconsumed' (56). Shakespeare's sister may have never been allowed to write as Shakespeare was, but what made Shakespeare a great writer was not a simple matter of a history that happened to be on his side. His genius and merit lay elsewhere – in his ability to free himself from the politics of a self and subjecthood:

> For though we say that we know nothing about Shakespeare's state of mind, even as we say that, we are saying something about Shakespeare's state of mind. The reason perhaps why we know so little of Shakespeare – compared with Donne or Ben Jonson or Milton – is that his grudges and spites and antipathies are hidden from us. We are not held up by some 'revelation' which reminds us of the writer. All desire to protest, to preach, to proclaim an injury, to pay off a score, to make the world the witness of some hardship or grievance was fired out of him and consumed. Therefore his poetry flows from him free and unimpeded ... If ever a mind was incandescent, unimpeded, I thought ... it was Shakespeare's mind. (56–7)

Not for Woolf then, a writing racked by a feminist politics of 'opposing factions.'[10] An exacerbated consciousness of sex, self, and person interferes with the integrity of writing, whence the flaw in the work of Charlotte Brontë, 'a writer at war with her lot,' 'who will write of herself where she should write of her characters' (69–70). Her writing will be marred to the extent that it can only express itself as a defensive reaction to a negative critical force.[11] Woolf admires Jane Austen for the same reason she admires Shakespeare – there is no anger, no despotic 'I' or self to make its presence felt; only the humble anonymity of an incandescent mind:

> Here was a woman about the year 1800 writing without hate, without bitterness, without fear, without protest, without preaching. That was how Shakespeare wrote, I thought, looking at *Antony and Cleopatra*; and when people compare Shakespeare and Jane Austen, they may mean that the minds of both had consumed all impediments; and for that reason we do not know

Jane Austen and we do not know Shakespeare, *and for that reason Jane Austen pervades every word that she wrote, and so does Shakespeare.* (68; emphasis mine)

It is by becoming imperceptible and indiscernible that they suffuse their writing with the greatest force. Where Charlotte Brontë remained imprisoned within the power politics of tradition, Jane Austen and Emily Brontë were able to affirm difference by practising a writing that was able to free itself from the terms of historical oppression, and this, by devising sentences for their own use, without resorting to hate: 'They wrote as women write, not as men write' (74–5).[12] And to write as a woman, for Woolf, is to write 'as a woman who has forgotten that she is a woman' (93). Writing can come about only when the category of sex is renounced or forgotten to make room for a sensibility that responds to the imperceptible, the small, the unknown, and the unrecorded.[13] One writes through a *becoming-woman* in which writing is filled with a 'curious sexual quality which comes only when sex is unconscious of itself' (93).

Does Woolf's call for the disappearance of sexual consciousness imply an effacement of difference? In order to respond to this question, one must necessarily consider another that Woolf ponders – what is it that the male sex obtains from its alliance with the female? The need for narcissistic self-valorization is rejected as a hypothesis – if great thinkers and writers have sought the companionship of women, they have done so for other reasons. The answer lies perhaps in a desire for an encounter with the creative and productive difference of another world.[14] The sexual consciousness that Woolf rejects is one that would imprison each sex within a binary structure that would exclude the one from the other, and in which sex would only be seen in relation to its opposing term.[15] If *A Room of One's Own* is an earnest plea for a space for women, it is an equally impassioned one against the compartmentalization and isolation of the sexes. '[A]nd I thought how unpleasant it is to be locked out; and I thought how it is worse perhaps to be locked in' (24). Sex is no dualistic categorization; it is an opening on to a multiplicity that exceeds binary logic.[16] The room that Woolf seeks for women is not one that is intended to shut men out; it is one that generates a complexity that is poorly served by the sole and unique category of sex:

One goes into the room – but the resources of the English language would be much put to the stretch, and whole flights of words would need to wing their way illegitimately into existence before a woman could say what happens when she goes into a room. The rooms differ so completely; they are calm or thunderous; open on to the sea, or, on the contrary, give on to a prison yard; are hung with washing; or alive with opals and silks; are hard as horsehair or soft as feathers – one has only to go into any room in any street for the whole of that extremely complex force of femininity to fly in one's face. How should it be otherwise? For women have sat indoors all these millions of years, so that by this time the very walls are permeated by their creative force, which has, indeed, so overcharged the capacity of bricks and mortar that it must needs harness itself to pens and brushes and business and politics. (87)

The communication between the sexes must extend on to a 'view of the open sky.' It is neither a question of becoming like the other sex, nor of shutting it out. Instead, it is a matter of affirming the difference and multiplicity of the real. And reality for Woolf is whatever leads us out of the drama of the human and the personal 'I'; it is that which is in touch with the common life, rather than the neatly separated lives of individuals.[17] *A Room of One's Own* does not seek to box women further into their individual cells; it encourages them to connect with the impersonal multiplicity and intensity of life:

> What is meant by 'reality'? It would seem to be something very erratic, very undependable – now to be found in a dusty road, now in a scrap of newspaper in the street, now in a daffodil in the sun. It lights up a group in a room and stamps some casual saying. It overwhelms one walking home beneath the stars and makes the silent world more real than the world of speech – and then there it is again in an omnibus in the uproar of Piccadilly ... Now the writer, as I think, has the chance to live more than other people in the presence of this reality ... So at least I infer from reading *Lear* or *Emma* or *La Recherche du Temps Perdu*. For the reading of these books seems to perform a curious couching operation on the senses; one sees more intensely afterwards; the world seems bared of its covering and given an intenser life. Those are the enviable people who live at enmity with unreality ... *So that when I ask you to earn money and have a room of your own, I am asking you to live in the presence of reality.* (110; emphasis mine)

To live in the presence of reality is to leave the narrow framework of human sexual relations; it is to create and make entire worlds communicate.

Why her adamant refusal of sexual divisions? Because they interfere with the unity of the mind, a point that a simple scene on a London street, the sight of a man and a woman getting into a taxi-cab, helps bring home. This unity of mind has less to do with a harmonious fusion of two symmetrically opposed halves, and everything to do with a state of being freed from the strain of severances and oppositions, from whatever represses its flows:

> What does one mean by 'the unity of the mind,' I pondered, for clearly the mind ... seems to have no single state of being ... But some of these states of mind seem, even if adopted spontaneously, to be less comfortable than others. In order to keep oneself continuing in them one is unconsciously holding something back, and gradually the repression becomes an effort. But there may be some state of mind in which one could continue without effort because nothing is required to be held back. And this perhaps, I thought, coming in from the window, is one of them. (97)

Woolf here makes a plea for an androgyny as a mode of being that would renounce the rigidity of sexual categories in favour of the freedom of creative and productive flows: 'Coleridge perhaps meant this when he said that a great mind is androgynous. It is when this fusion takes place that the mind is fully fertilised and uses all its faculties. Perhaps a mind that is purely masculine cannot create, any more than a mind that is purely feminine' (98). This is an androgyny that has little to with a sexual politics; it is an expression of a state of mind (a plane of immanence?), one and multiple at the same time:

> Coleridge certainly did not mean, when he said that a great mind is androgynous, that it is a mind that has any special sympathy with women; a mind that takes up their cause or devotes itself to their interpretation. Perhaps the androgynous mind is less apt to make these distinctions than the single-sexed mind. He meant, perhaps, that the androgynous mind is resonant and porous; that it transmits emotion without impediment; that it is naturally creative, incandescent and undivided. (98)

Shakespeare's was an androgynous mind precisely because it would be impossible to say what he thought of women, as 'it is one of the tokens of the fully developed mind that it does not think specially or separately of sex.' An exaggerated sense of sexual distinctiveness works hand in glove with the despotism of a self and subject; it imprisons the vastness of a landscape within the narrow and 'straight dark bar' of an 'I.' It casts an arid shadow within which nothing can grow. The emphasis on a self and its sex restricts and confines the flows of creative energy, 'but when one takes a sentence of Coleridge into the mind, it explodes and gives birth to all kinds of other ideas, and that is the only sort of writing of which one can say that it has the secret of perpetual life' (101). A writing that cannot free itself from the tyranny of the categories of an 'I,' a self, and a sex cannot sustain itself for long:

> [I]t is fatal for any one who writes to think of their sex. It is fatal to be a man or woman pure and simple; one must be woman-manly or man-womanly. It is fatal for a woman ... in anyway to speak consciously as a woman. And fatal is no figure of speech; for anything written with that conscious bias is doomed to death. It ceases to be fertilised ... [I]t cannot grow in the minds of others ... The whole of the mind must lie wide open if we are to get the sense that the writer is communicating his experience with perfect fullness. There must be freedom and there must be peace. (104)[18]

Against the 'I' that obliterates all within its shadow, against the category of the human, against the divisions of sex, against the sitting-room dramas of human relations, Woolf chooses the view of the open sky and the trees, the plenitude of life and reality.[19] The fulness and unity of which Woolf speaks is not an all-encompassing whole that would subsume all of life under its law and principle; it is itself a small fragment of a teeming, impersonal, and multiple flow of the real: 'And I saw again the current which took the boat and the undergraduate and the dead leaves; and the taxi took the man and the woman, I thought, seeing them come together across the street, and the current swept them away, I thought, hearing far off the roar of London's traffic, into that tremendous stream' (104–5).

This then is the final word of *A Room of One's Own*: it exhorts the writer towards a celebration of (asubjective) life, rather than a self-absorbed mourning for the death, loss, or absence of a self. Writing (indeed, sexuality itself) is a force that ought to keep us in touch with the intensity of life forces, rather than limiting itself to the drama of human selfhood and subjectivity. *Orlando* is a novel that conceives of writing in the same manner. It could be read as the journey of a (to be) writer in search of the essence of literature, a quest that risks failure and disappointment: 'She [Orlando] had thought of literature all these years ... as something wild as the wind, hot as fire, swift as lightning; something errant, incalculable, abrupt, and behold, literature was an elderly gentleman in a grey suit talking about duchesses' (160). But Orlando is saved by the discovery that literature *is* something as errant and wild as the wind; it is about mapping the affects, percepts, and intensities of the lived; it is about laying out and exploring different modes of being:

> 'A toy boat, a toy boat, a toy boat,' she repeated, thus enforcing upon herself the fact that it is not articles by Nick Greene on John Donne nor eight hour bills nor covenants nor factory acts that matter; it's something useless, sudden, violent; something that costs a life; red, blue, purple; a spirt; a splash; like those hyacinths (she was passing a fine bed of them); free from taint, dependence, soilure of humanity or care for one's kind; something rash, ridiculous, 'like my hyacinth, husband I mean, Bonthrop: that's what it is – a toy boat on the Serpentine, it's ecstasy – ecstasy.' (164)

Against the strident and clamorous claims to representation of an 'I,' Woolf opts for the ethics of a literature that seeks to envelop itself in and be enveloped by the obscurity and anonymity of life: 'the delight of having no name, but being like a wave which returns to the deep body of the sea ... which must have been the way of all great poets, he supposed ... for, he thought, Shakespeare must have written like that' (*Orlando*, 61).

Could this be the ethics that will save feminism as thought? If one of feminism's greatest contributions as a politics has been to denounce the despotic systems of representation in which literature may be imprisoned, might not its greatest contribution as an ethics of thought lie in its affirmation of the possibility of literature to create new and multiple modes of being, in the infinity of worlds it promises to bring into existence? Could not this ethical thought lie in following the abstract lines of flight of writing, in the affects and percepts, in the events and becomings that writers are able to produce on their myriad planes of composition? 'What expert judgement, in art, could ever bear on the work to come?'[20] Opening one's mind to the difference that literature is capable of producing does not imply a renunciation of one's critical faculty, or a suspension of all politics. Rather, such moments of interpretive receptivity might well be the best means whereby sites of effective thought and political action are created for the present and preserved for the future.

Notes

1 Deleuze, *Essays Critical and Clinical*, lv.
2 Marguerite Duras, *New French Feminisms*, ed. Marks and de Courtivron, 174.
3 See Millet, *Sexual Politics*.
4 I have found the following formulation by Judith Butler of the relationship between politics and representation to be a very useful starting point: 'On the one hand, *representation* serves as the operative term within a political process that seeks to extend visibility and legitimacy to women as political subjects; on the other hand, representation is the normative function of a language which is said either to reveal or to distort what is assumed to be true about the category of women. For feminist theory, the development of a language that fully or adequately represents women has seemed necessary to foster the political visibility of women. This has seemed obviously important considering the pervasive cultural condition in which women's lives were either misrepresented or not represented at all' (*Gender Trouble*, 1). Also, the following understanding of feminist theory articulated by Rosi Braidotti will guide my use of the terms 'feminist theory' and 'feminism' during the course of this study: 'It refers both to a political practice and a discursive field marked by a specific set of methodological and epistemological premises, which I would call the political practice of sexual difference. This practice is the claim to material and symbolic recognition on the part of politically motivated women: "the female feminist subject" is a new epistemological and political entity to be defined and affirmed by women in the confrontation of their multiple differences, of class, race, sexual preference.' ('Towards a New Nomadism: Feminist Deleuzian Tracks; or Metaphysics and Metabolism,' in *Gilles Deleuze and the Theater of Philosophy*, ed. Boundas and Olkowski, 159.)
5 For an overview of the above, see Eagleton, *Feminist Literary Theory*; Warhol

and Herndl, *Feminisms*; and Evans, *Feminism*. See also Suleiman, *The Female Body in Western Culture*; and Conboy, Medina, and Stanbury, *Writing on the Body*. For feminist film theory, see De Lauretis, *Alice Doesn't*, and *Technologies of Gender*. See also Mulvey, *Visual and Other Pleasures*; Rose, *Sexuality in the Field of Vision*; and Silverman, *The Acoustic Mirror*.

6 See Miller, *The Heroine's Text*, and *French Dressing*; Schor, *Breaking the Chain*; Segal, *Narcissus and Echo*; Apter, *Feminizing the Fetish*; Waller, *The Male Malady*; Beizer, *Ventriloquized Bodies*; Cohen and Prendergast, *Spectacles of Realism*; Frank, *The Mechanical Song*; Ender, *Sexing the Mind*; Buchet Rogers, *Fictions du scandale*; and Hinton, *The Perverse Gaze of Sympathy*. Kelly, *Fictional Genders*, offers a more subtle and nuanced analysis of the representation of femininity in nineteenth-century French literature, a feminist critical strategy not unlike the one psychoanalytic feminist critic Shoshana Felman employs. Reading for the feminine, Felman seeks out sites of disruptive excess in male-authored texts that reveal the presence of feminine otherness. However, this emergence of the feminine is recuperated as a sign attesting to the blindness and self-deception of desire: 'Ultimately, femininity itself becomes a euphemism, a euphemism at once for difference and for its repression, at once for sexuality and for its blindness to itself; a euphemism for the sexuality of speaking bodies and their delusions and their dreams, determined by a signifier fraught with their castration and their death' ('Rereading Femininity,' 44). See also Felman, *What Does Woman Want?* This is a presupposition that I will contest in the course of this study. While my work is deeply indebted to her insights (a debt that is apparent in my first chapter), it veers away from hers in its call to understand the disruptive textual spaces of feminine difference not just as products of a feminist reading strategy, but also as expressions of the positivity of (male) authorial desire. Similarly, while the present study continues Kelly's exploration of feminine difference in male-authored texts, it argues for the need to abandon the theoretical framework that supports her analyses, in particular the psychoanalytical notions of the fetish and castration. In a sense, my book may also be seen as a response to the challenge that Kelly opens up for future feminist scholars at the end of *Fictional Genders*: 'If ... the real woman cannot appear on the stage of this theater of phallic representation in the nineteenth century except in the aporetic and paralyzing moments of the text, she perhaps remains to be written (or to write) in our modernity *when a different perspective on difference can allow her to emerge. Perhaps a study of the linguistic detours, those involved in the creation of the fetish and of those aporetic moments which contradict the realist project, may lead to a new understanding of gender*' (*Fictional Genders*, 179; emphasis mine).

7 One could also include race, nationality, and class among the latter, although they fall outside the scope of the present study.
8 While his thought will not constitute the focal point of this study, these are some of the theses developed by Jacques Rancière in his study of the relationship between the aesthetical and the political; see his *Le partage du sensible*; *Aux bords du politique*, *La parole muette*, and most recently, *Politique de la littérature*.

1 *Pierre et Jean,* or the Erring of Oedipus

1 Goux, *Oedipus, Philosopher,* 24.
2 Irigaray, *Speculum de l'autre femme.* See also Goux, *Oedipus, Philosopher,* 115. For a more recent study along similar lines, see Griselda Pollock, 'Beyond Oedipus: Feminist Thought, Psychoanalysis, and Mythical Figurations of the Feminine,' in *Laughing with Medusa,* ed. Zajko and Leonard, 67–117.
3 Barthes, *Le plaisir du texte,* 75–6.
4 Ibid., 20; emphasis in original.
5 Ibid.
6 See Schor, *Breaking the Chain,* 167.
7 De Lauretis, *Alice Doesn't,* 121.
8 Freud, 'Instincts and Their Vicissitudes,' in *The Standard Edition of the Complete Works of Sigmund Freud,* 14:109–40.
9 Mulvey, 'Visual Pleasure and Narrative Cinema.'
10 De Lauretis, *Alice Doesn't,* 156.
11 Ibid., 157.
12 Cited in Buisiné, 'Je suis avant tout un regardeur,' 31.
13 Maupassant, *Pierre et Jean* (Paris: Gallimard, 1982), 58. All future references will be to this edition.
14 Uwe Dethloff, 'Patriarcalisme et féminisme dans l'oeuvre romanesque de Maupassant,' *Maupassant et l'écriture,* ed. Forestier, 117–26.
15 Jennings, 'La dualité de Maupassant.'
16 Mary Donaldson-Evans, 'La femme (r)enfermée chez Maupassant,' in *Maupassant et l'écriture,* ed. Forestier, 66–9.
17 Guy de Maupassant, cited in Donaldson-Evans, 'La femme,' 72.
18 Donaldson-Evans, 'La femme,' 74.
19 Ibid.
20 See Jaap Lintvelt's excellent article, 'La polyphonie de l'encadrement dans les contes de Maupassant,' in *Maupassant et l'écriture,* ed Forestier, 173–85.
21 Mulvey, 'Visual Pleasure and Narrative Cinema,' 14.
22 Ibid.

23 Interestingly, Mary Donaldson-Evans does offer a more nuanced reading of Maupassant's doctor-narrator in an article entitled 'Maupassant and the Physician-Narrator,' wherein she recognizes an ironic undermining of the scientific objectivity and neutrality of the doctor's voice, which she considers as a strategy that questions the authority and credibility of the narrative voice. However, this challenge to narrative authority is not linked to any particular feminist sensibility on Maupassant's part. See Mary Donaldson-Evans, 'Maupassant and the Physician-Narrator,' in *Maupassant conteur et romancier*, ed. Lloyd and Lethbridge, 97–110.

24 Todorov, 'Typologie du roman policier,' 7.

25 Ibid., 6.

26 Todorov, cited in Eisenzweig, *Le récit impossible*, 54.

27 Eisenzweig, *Le récit impossible*, 6.

28 For a reading of *Pierre et Jean* that considers it as a drama of self-knowledge and ignorance, see Sachs, 'The Meaning of "Pierre et Jean."'

29 Eisenzweig, *Le récit impossible*, 102–4.

30 See Felman, 'Beyond Oedipus.'

31 Ibid.

32 Sophocles, *Oedipus Rex*, in *Three Theban Plays*, 182.

33 As Goux notes, Oedipus claims to have solved the Sphinx's riddle 'with no help from the birds.'

34 Goux, *Oedipus, Philosopher*, 115

35 'For him [Oedipus], man's viewpoint is the unique center of perspective: the "I" that reflects consciousness of self, is the only source capable of shedding light and clarity on all things. From his answer to the Sphinx, which offends the obscurity of the sacred and denies the signs of the gods in making man the measure of all things, up to the inquiry designed to shed all possible light on the self, Oedipus is the one who inflects the injunction to "know thyself" toward total mastery of the ego, toward an autoreflective consciousness, without any transindividual alterity' (Goux, *Oedipus, Philosopher*, 134).

36 Goux's formulations provide an interesting (and strong) echo to the theses put forth by feminist philosopher Luce Irigaray in her *Speculum de l'autre femme*. *Speculum* is a work that seeks to undo the self-sufficiency of philosophical (and psychoanalytical) discourse through an unworking of the mastery of its (Oedipal) vision. For Irigaray, the history of philosophy from Plato to Freud and Lacan is founded on a visual metaphor that is blind to female difference. Western philosophy privileges a single model of subjectivity, the masculine. The repression of feminine difference is the gesture that permits and ensures the functioning of its narcissistic economy. The radical alterity of the feminine is what is written out of the masculine 'dream of

symmetry.' These elaborations will be studied in greater detail in the following chapter.

37 While it would be too tedious for the reader to give a comprehensive account of each of these occasions, the following quotes might help make the point: 'Elle hésita une seconde ou deux; *ou du moins il se figura qu'elle hésitait*' (138); 'Elle *aurait pu* encore répondre plus vite' (138); 'Elle y jeta un regard rapide, vite détourné, qui *semblait* craintif' (147); 'Pierre comprit, *ou crut comprendre* sa terreur et son angoisse' (148; emphasis mine).

38 See *Pierre et Jean*, 85, 86–7, and 115.

39 See Culler, 'Story and Discourse in the Analysis of Narrative,' in *The Pursuit of Signs*, 169–87.

40 'L'amour de l'homme et de la femme est un pacte volontaire où celui qui faiblit n'est coupable que de perfidie; mais quand la femme est devenue mère, son devoir a grandi puisque la nature lui confie une race. Si elle succombe alors, elle est lâche, indigne et infâme' (145).

41 'Sophocles' play portrays Oedipus as the one person in history *without* an Oedipus complex in the conventional sense: he has murdered his father and married his mother in an appreciation of expediency rather than in the satisfaction of a desire. The one person who actually enacts patricide and incest completely misses the experience – until after the fact' (Chase, 'Oedipal Textuality,' 58; emphasis in original).

42 Compare the following: 'Les femmes, se disait-il, doivent nous apparaître dans un rêve ou dans une auréole de luxe qui poétise leur vulgarité' (103). 'Un flot d'amour et d'attendrissement, de repentir, de prière et de désolation noya son coeur ... La [Mme Roland] connaissant comme il la connaissait, comment avait-il pu la suspecter? Est-ce que l'âme, est-ce que la vie de cette femme simple, chaste et loyale n'étaient pas plus claires que l'eau? Quand on l'avait vue et connue, comment ne pas la juger insoupçonnable? Et c'était lui, le fils, qui avait douté d'elle! Oh! S'il avait pu la prendre en ses bras à ce moment, comme il l'eût embrassée, caressée, comme il se fût agenouillé pour demander grâce!' (128).

43 See the preface to *Pierre et Jean* by Bernard Pingaud, 7–41.

44 Ibid. See also Danger, 'Le père défait.'

45 Pierre is equally 'privé de la mer par la présence de son frère' (90). Once again, the play on the words *mer/mère* is not fortuitous; the novel will bear out the premonition contained in this sentence.

46 See Brooks, 'Freud's Masterplot.'

47 Goux identifies the regular and fundamental narrative structure of Western myth through an analysis of the myths of Jason, Perseus, and Bellerophon, which he then compares with that of Oedipus. The following are the ele-

ments he extracts and condenses: '(1) A king fears that a younger man, or one not yet born, will take his place, as an oracle has predicted. He then uses all available means to try and prevent the child's birth, or to get rid of the presumed intruder. (2) The future hero escapes from the king's murderous intentions. Nevertheless, much later, he finds himself in a situation in which a different king attempts to do away with him. But the second king cannot bring himself to commit the crime with his own hands, so he assigns a perilous task in which the future hero is expected to lose his life. (3) The trial takes the form of a fight with a monster. The hero succeeds in defeating the monster, not on his own, but with the help of a god, a wise man, or a future bride. (4) Finally, the hero's triumph over the monster allows him to marry the daughter of a king' (Goux, *Oedipus, Philosopher,* 6).

48 Perseus confronts the Gorgon, while Bellerophon battles the Chimaera. The monster that Jason kills (the Colchis dragon) is of an indeterminate sex. The Sphinx that Oedipus conquers is female.

49 'The myth of Oedipus is an anomaly. Matricide, not patricide is at the heart of the heroic myth in its typical and universal form. The hero who is to become king is the hero who kills the female dragon, the female serpent, the female monstrosity, in bloody combat. By murdering a dangerous, dark, feminine force, the hero liberates the bride. Compared to this widely attested prototype, which I shall call the "monomyth," the Oedipus story is an aberrant myth, obtained by a disruption of the initial narrative form' (Goux, *Oedipus, Philosopher,* 2–3).

50 Ibid., 28.

51 For Goux, incest requires no paternal mediation because 'incestuous desire is intrinsically agonizing; no conventional interdiction makes it so. It is the young man's desire itself that creates, out of its own inclinations, a horrible, anguish-generating monster' (ibid., 36).

52 Again, a thesis that echoes the argument of Irigaray's *Speculum de l'autre femme.* For Irigaray, philosophy sets up the category of the human subject at the expense of the feminine. In other words, the neutrality of the universal human subject posited by Western philosophy is based upon a repression of female difference.

53 Goux here is faithful to the Lacanian formulation of castration or lack as 'symbolic lack' or the absence of the true object of desire.

54 Goux, *Oedipus, Philosopher,* 202.

55 Barthes, *S/Z,* 47.

56 Lacan, 'Le séminaire sur la lettre volée,' in *Écrits,* 1:48.

57 Gallop, *The Daughter's Seduction,* 48; emphasis in original.

58 My reading *of Pierre et Jean* thus differs from that of Naomi Schor, who views

the novel as an illustration of the (masculine) authorial appropriation of the mother's text: 'We might say, in somewhat schematic terms, that what authorizes the son's text is the pulverization, the dispersion of a maternal *Ur-text*' (Schor, *Breaking the Chain*, 69). Contrary to Schor, I see *Pierre et Jean* as a story of feminine repossession, not dispossession.

59 For more on Mme Rosémilly's ability to subvert the homosocial space of patriarchy, see Patrick, 'Maupassant's *Pierre et Jean*,' 5–8.

60 See Irigaray, 'Le marché des femmes,' in *Ce sexe qui n'en est pas un.*

61 Ibid., 172, 179–80.

62 Irigaray, 'Des marchandises entre elles,' in *Ce sexe qui n'en est pas un*, 193; emphasis in original.

63 'Le portrait, portrait d'ami, portrait d'amant, était resté dans le salon bien en vue, jusqu'au jour où la femme, où la mère s'était aperçue, la première, avant tout le monde, que ce portrait ressemblait à son fils. Sans doute, depuis longtemps, elle épiait cette ressemblance; puis, l'ayant découverte, l'ayant vue naître et comprenant que chacun pourrait, un jour ou l'autre, l'apercevoir aussi, elle avait enlevé, un soir, la petite peinture redoutable et l'avait cachée, n'osant pas la détruire' (139).

64 See Lacan, 'Le séminaire sur la lettre volée,' in *Erits*, 1:19–75. For such a Lacanian analysis of *Pierre et Jean*, see Engel, 'Qui voit quoi?' My reading diverges from Engel's in the importance it pays to the role of Mme Roland in the chain of signification, a role that Engel ignores by attributing a power to M. Roland that is belied by the novel.

65 Lacan, 'Le séminaire sur la lettre volée,' in *Erits*, 1:45.

66 Ibid., 1:41.

67 Ibid., 1:53.

68 Derrida, 'Le facteur de la vérité,' 113.

69 Ibid., 110; emphasis in original.

70 Ibid., 113; emphasis in original.

71 Lacan 'Le séminaire sur la lettre volée,' in *Erits*, 1:42. 'Ce que le conte de Poe démontre par mes soins, c'est que l'effet de sujétion du signifiant, de la lettre volée en l'occasion, porte avant tout sur son détenteur d'après-vol, et qu'à mesure de son parcours, ce qu'il véhicule, c'est cette Fémininité même qu'il aurait prise en son ombre ...' Lacan, cited in Derrida, 'Le facteur de la vérité,' 113.

72 Lacan, 'Le séminaire sur la lettre volée,' in *Erits*, 1:38.

73 Ibid., 1:42.

74 See Goux, *Symbolic Economies after Marx and Freud.*

75 Such a break in the linearity of the chain of desire echoes the very feminist strategy that Schor calls for in her *Breaking the Chain*. This 'rupture' also

offers a compelling counterpoint to Charles Stivale's thesis that narrative
desire in Maupassant displays an art of rupture that seeks to break the chain
that women wield over men, while maintaining that of men over women. See
Stivale, *The Art of Rupture.*

76 Derrida, 'Le facteur de la vérité,' 96; emphasis in original.

77 See Brooks, 'Fictions of the Wolfman,' 74.

78 Freud, *The Interpretation of Dreams*, 295.

79 'There is at least one spot in every dream at which it is unplumbable – a
navel, as it were, that is its point of contact with the unknown.' Freud, *The
Standard Edition of the Complete Works*, 4:111.

80 Felman, 'Beyond Oedipus.'

2 The Error of Narissus

1 Woolf, *A Room of One's Own*, 35.

2 Irigaray, *Speculum de l'autre femme*, 168.

3 Irigaray, *Ce sexe qui n'en est pas un*, 72.

4 Irigaray, *Speculum de l'autre femme*, 21.

5 Ibid., 224.

6 Irigaray, *Ce sexe qui n'en est pas un*, 72–3.

7 Ibid., 74; emphasis in original.

8 Ibid., 76.

9 Irigaray, *Speculum de l'autre femme*, 178–9; emphasis in original.

10 Ovid, 'Narcissus and Echo,' in *Metamorphoses*, 95. All future references will be
to this edition.

11 See Vinge, *The Narcissus Theme*. Her monumental work has done much to
confirm my intuitions. What follows in this section is a (rather sketchy) summary of her research.

12 Ibid., 76.

13 Plotinus, cited in ibid., 37; emphasis in original.

14 Ficino, cited in ibid., 125–6; emphasis in original.

15 Guy Michaud, cited in ibid., 330.

16 Brooks, *Body Work*, 3.

17 Barthes, *S/Z*, 220.

18 Brooks, *Body Work*, 7.

19 Jean-Paul Sartre, cited in ibid., 96.

20 Barthes, *Le plaisir du texte*, 20.

21 '[P]laisir oedipéen (dénuder, savoir, connaître l'origine et la fin), s'il est vrai
que tout récit (tout dévoilement de la vérité) est une mise en scène du Père
(absent, caché ou hypostasié)' (ibid., 20).

22 Barthes, *S/Z*, 69.

23 Brooks, *Body Work*, 22, 25.

24 See Schor, *Breaking the Chain*, xi.

25 Ovid, *Metamorphoses*, 335.

26 Brooks, *Body Work*, 25.

27 Plotinus, *Enneads*, 201–9. This section of the *Enneads* forms the basis of Irigaray's critique in *Speculum*.

28 Ibid.

29 Ovid, *Metamorphoses*, 93.

30 Irigaray, *Ce sexe qui n'en est pas un*, 147; emphasis in original.

31 Ovid, *Metamorphoses*, 94.

32 I am grateful to Louise Vinge for this insight.

33 Balzac, quoted in Brooks, *Body Work*, 84.

34 See Nochlin, *Women, Art, and Power: And Other Essays*: '[R]epresentations of
women in art are founded upon and serve to reproduce indisputably
accepted assumptions held by society in general, artists in particular, and
some artists more than others about men's power over, superiority to, difference from, and necessary control of women ... This complex of beliefs
involving male power, naked models, and the creation of art receives its
most perfect rationalization in the ever-popular nineteenth-century representation of the Pygmalion myth: stone beauty made flesh by the warming
glow of masculine desire ... One might add that the passivity implicit to
the imagery of the naked woman in Western art is a function not merely
of the attitude of the owner spectator, but that of the artist-creator himself: indeed the myth of Pygmalion, revived in the nineteenth century,
admirably embodies the notion of the artist as sexually dominant creator;
man – the artist – fashioning from inert matter an ideal erotic object for
himself, a woman cut to the very pattern of his desires' (1–2, 19, and
143).

35 See J. Hillis Miller in *Versions of Pygmalion*: 'Pygmalion has made himself
Galatea. She is the mirror image of his desire ... Here Narcissus' vain desire
seems fulfilled ... For Galatea to see at all is to see Pygmalion and to be subject to him. It is as if Narcissus' reflection in the pool had come alive and
could return his love' (4–5).

36 Irigaray, *Ce sexe qui n'en est pas un*, 129–30; emphasis in original.

37 Balzac, 'Des artistes,' in *Le chef-d'oeuvre inconnu* (Paris: Garnier Flammarion,
1981), 278. All future references will be to this edition.

38 When Frenhofer is first presented in the narrative, we read: 'Imaginez un
front chauve, bombé, proéminent, retombant en saillie sur un petit nez
écrasé, retroussé du bout comme celui de *Rabelais ou de Socrate ...*' (Balzac,
Le chef-d'oeuvre inconnu, 44; emphasis mine).

39 For Balzac, 'Forme' here refers not to the essential, organizing principle

prior and exterior to matter, but to matter itself, to the world of appearance and effect. See the notes to *Le chef-d'oeuvre inconnu*, 245.

40 Balzac, 'Des artistes,' in *Le chef-d'oeuvre inconnu*, 282; emphasis mine.

41 For interpretations of the short story in this vein, see Bernard, 'La problématique de "l'échange" dans *Le chef-d'oeuvre inconnu* d'Honoré de Balzac'; Paulson, 'Pour une analyse dynamique de la variation textuelle'; Lathers, 'Modesty and the Artist's Model in *Le chef-d'œuvre inconnu*'; and Bresnick, 'Absolute Fetishism.'

42 For an overview of such readings, see Peter Whyte, '*Le chef-d'oeuvre inconnu* de Balzac: esthétique et image,' in Hutton, *Text(e)/Image*.

43 Goux, 'The Unrepresentable,' in *Symbolic Economies*, 172–3; emphasis in original.

44 Hegel, cited in ibid., 178.

45 Ibid.

46 Ibid., 178.

47 Balzac, *Le chef-d'oeuvre inconnu*, 70–1.

48 Kandinsky, cited in Goux, *Symbolic Economies*, 181.

49 Ibid., 182.

50 Ibid., 182–3.

51 Ibid., 187.

52 Ibid., 190.

53 Ibid., 196; emphasis in original.

54 See for instance Nathalie Heinich, '*Le chef-d'oeuvre inconnu*, ou l'artiste investi,' in École nationale supérieure des arts décoratifs (France), *Autour du Chef-d'œuvre inconnu de Balzac*, 75–83.

55 Irigaray, *Ce sexe qui n'en est pas un*, 76.

56 Goux, *Symbolic Economies*, 189.

57 Goux here recalls Lenin's remark that 'it is when Hegel is the most idealist that he is also the most materialist.' See 'The Unrepresentable,' in *Symbolic Economies*, 193.

58 Ibid.

59 Blanchot, *The Space of Literature*, 23.

60 Balzac, 'Des artistes,' in *Le chef-d'oeuvre inconnu*, 285–6.

61 See the introduction to *Le chef-d'oeuvre inconnu* by René Guise, 23–4.

62 Balzac, 'Des artistes,' in *Le chef-d'oeuvre inconnu*, 278.

63 Goux, *Symbolic Economies*, 189.

64 Balzac, 'Des artistes,' in *Le chef-d'oeuvre inconnu*, 282–3.

65 It is important to note that according to Goux, the epigenetic mode is characteristic of societies that have attained a certain level of technical and scientific capacity for self-transformation and self-invention. In these societies, the

power to create (poiesis and demiurgy) ceases to be localized in a transcendence, and is absorbed into the process of an atheological society. See 'The Unrepresentable,' 195. Interestingly, in an earlier version of the same essay, Goux situates the leap towards the operable within a social will to production: 'Dans le champ spécifique de la production esthétique, l'art abstrait (et ce qui suit) a un statut sémiotique qui correspond à une socialité *constructiviste* ... L'art abstrait, comme symptôme, marque le moment où quelque chose change dans les schèmes de la productivité sociale. Sans même que l'on doive dire que l'abstraction est contemporaine de la naissance de sciences nouvelles (ce qui est aussi à considérer), elle est d'abord congruente à un nouveau statut social en partie anticipé, imaginé, de la science. *L'ingénuosité pure*, le jeu logique et mathématique ne sont plus des pratiques détachées, sans lien avec la réalité, ou ne donnant accès qu'à un ciel d'opérations idéales; ils constituent le détour préalable nécessaire pour une prise directe sur l'étoffe du réel. Dès lors, ces "combines" axiomatiques de la pensée deviennent source de manipulation effective de la matière.' See Goux, *Les iconoclastes*, 139; emphasis in original. Goux is still Hegelian.

66 Blanchot, *The Space of Literature*, 215.
67 Ibid., 218.
68 Ibid.
69 Ibid., 219.
70 Hegel, quoted in ibid., 214.
71 Blanchot, *The Space of Literature*, 228.
72 Ibid., 232.
73 Ibid., 228.
74 See 'Orpheus' Gaze,' in *The Space of Literature*, 171–6.
75 For an excellent study on Blanchot's reflection on the relationship between poetry and philosophy, see Bruns, *Maurice Blanchot*.
76 Blanchot's concept of art as excess and Adorno's contention that 'art negates the conceptualization foisted upon the real world' converge with Irigaray's articulation of the feminine as an irrecuperable excess that 'fait exploser, toute forme, figure, idée, concept, solidement établis.' No less a striking parallel is the feminine that Cixous and Kristeva have recognized in the modernity of Joyce, Genet, and Céline.
77 Blanchot, *The Work of Fire*, 328; emphasis in original. See also Bruns, *Maurice Blanchot*.

3 The Three Virtues of Imperceptibility, Indiscernibity, and Impersonality

1 Blanchot, *The Writing of the Disaster*, 135.

2 Ovid, 'Narcissus and Echo,' in *Metamorphoses*, 96.

3 Ibid.

4 Blanchot, *The Writing of the Disaster*, 125.

5 Ibid., 125, 127.

6 Ibid., 126, 134.

7 Blanchot, *The Space of Literature*, 33.

8 Ibid.

9 'The third person substituting for the "I": such is the solitude that comes to the writer on account of the work. It does not denote objective disinterestedness, creative detachment. It does not glorify consciousness in someone other than myself or the evolution of a human vitality which, in the imaginary space of the work of art, would retain the freedom to say "I". The third person is myself become no one, my interlocutor turned alien; it is my no longer being able, where I am, to address myself and the inability of whoever addresses me to say "I"; it is his not being himself' (ibid., 28).

10 Blanchot, *The Writing of the Disaster*, 135.

11 Ibid., 126.

12 See Irigaray, *Ce sexe qui n'en est pas un*, 88.

13 See ibid., 122–4.

14 See Deleuze and Guattari, *Anti-Oedipus*.

15 For a more detailed consideration, see Grosz, *Volatile Bodies*.

16 Deleuze and Guattari, *Anti-Oedipus*, 24.

17 Ibid., 77–8.

18 'Molar' and 'molecular' refer to types of organization or segmentation of desiring-flows. The term molar refers to large statistical categories or aggregates organized according to binary oppositions and dualisms. This is a segmentation that distributes differences according to social classes, sexes, fixed and rigid identities. Molecular workings refer to the supple and imperceptible movements of desire that escape the organizing categories of the molar. The molar constitutes a macropolitics of the masses, while the molecular constitutes a micropolitics of molar decomposition. See Deleuze and Guattari, *A Thousand Plateaus*, 213. Hereafter referred to as *A Thousand Plateaus*. It is important to note here that the molar and molecular are not so much two opposing terms as two poles of a continuum of flows. They are coextensive and interpenetrating multiplicities or assemblages. See *A Thousand Plateaus*, 34–5.

19 Deleuze and Guattari, *Anti-Oedipus*, 96.

20 See Goodchild, *Gilles Deleuze and the Question of Philosophy*, 48.

21 Deleuze and Guattari, *A Thousand Plateaus*, 254.

22 In *What Is Philosophy*, Deleuze and Guattari refer to the plane of consistency or immanence as 'a powerful Whole, that, while remaining open, is not frag-

mented: an unlimited One-All, an "Omnitudo"' (35). The plane of immanence is immanent only to itself, and not to a one or an other. They mark
their difference from Plato, for whom this immanence is related to a 'dative,'
that is, to either matter or mind (44).

23 See Goodchild, *Gilles Deleuze and the Question of Philosophy*, 71.

24 *A Thousand Plateaus*, 270.

25 Goodchild, *Gilles Deleuze and the Question of Philosophy*, 71.

26 *A Thousand Plateaus*, 270.

27 See *A Thousand Plateaus*, 237.

28 Ibid., 238.

29 Ibid., 272–3; emphasis in original. 'An example: Do not imitate a dog, but
make your organism enter into composition with *something else* in such a way
that the particles emitted from the aggregate thus composed will be canine
as a function of the relation of movement and rest, or of molecular proximity, into which they enter (emphasis in original) ... That is the essential
point for us: you become-animal only if, by whatever means or elements,
you emit corpuscles that enter the relation of movement and rest of the
animal particles, or what amounts to the same thing, that enter the zone of
proximity of the animal molecule. *You become animal only molecularly. You do
not become a barking molar dog, but by barking, if it is done with enough feeling,
with enough necessity and composition, you emit a molecular dog,*' 274–5; emphasis mine).

30 Ibid., 280.

31 'Dismantling the organism has never meant killing yourself, but rather opening the body to connections that presuppose an entire assemblage, circuits,
conjunctions, levels and thresholds, passages and distributions of intensity,
and territories and deterritorializations measured with the craft of a sur-
veyor' (ibid., 160).

32 Ibid., 165.

33 As we saw thus far with Irigaray, metaphysics (and consequently, feminist ethics) constructs itself on the question of the body, as that which must be
negated or repressed in order to make for the emergence of thought. Thus,
a transcendental condition that enables subjectivity is posited as prior to the
given. Deleuzian feminist Claire Colebrook calls for a feminist ethics that
would ask a different set of questions: '[N]ot "what does this body mean –
what is its intent, condition or genesis?" but "how does this body work?"' In
other words, she asks for a move towards thinking of the body, not as a condition for thought and subjectivity, but as a form of positive difference. See
Colebrook, 'Is Sexual Difference a Problem?' in *Deleuze and Feminist Theory*,
ed. Buchanan and Colebrook, 124. For more on the pertinence of Deleuze
and Guattari for feminism, see also Tamsin E. Lorraine, 'Becoming-Imper-

ceptible as a Mode of Self-Presentation: A Feminist Model Drawn from a
Deleuzian Line of Flight,' in *Resistance, Flight, Creation*, ed. Olkowski, 179–94;
Moira Gatens, 'Through a Spinozist Lens: Ethology, Difference, Power,' in
Deleuze: A Critical Reader, ed. Patton, 162–87; Rosi Braidotti, 'Towards a New
Nomadism: Feminist Deleuzian Tracks; or, Metaphysics and Metabolism,' in
Boundas and Olkowski, *Gilles Deleuze and the Theater of Philosophy*, 159–86; and
Elizabeth Grosz, 'A Thousand Tiny Sexes: Feminism and Rhizomatics,' ibid.,
187–210.

The relevance of Deleuze and Guattari for feminism is not without debate
and controversy. For a largely negative appraisal of their value for feminists,
see Jardine, 'Becoming a Body without Organs: Gilles Deleuze and His
Brothers,' in *Gynesis*, 1985, 208–23; Rosi Braidotti, 'Of Bugs and Women:
Irigaray and Deleuze on the Becoming-Woman,' in *Engaging with Irigaray*, ed.
Burke, Schor, and Whitford, 111–37; and Braidotti, *Nomadic Subjects*. For a
refutation of Jardine's and Braidotti's arguments, see Goulimari, 'A Minoritarian Feminism?'

While Elizabeth Grosz recognizes the contribution that Deleuze and
Guattari can make to the theorization of feminine materiality *pace* an ontology that avoids the dualism of mind and body, transcendence and immanence (see in this regard her *Volatile Bodies*), and takes Rosi Braidotti to task
for the notion of the 'real woman' in whose defence the latter objects to
Deleuze and Guattari (See Elizabeth Grosz, 'Sexual Difference and the Problem of Essentialism,' in *The Essential Difference*, ed. Schor and Weed, 82–97),
she does caution against the use of Deleuze on the grounds that his thought
effaces sexual specificity for women. Taking care to state that sexual difference is neither ontological, originary, nor constitutive, and never natural or
biological, but always cultural and historical, she nonetheless fails to adequately articulate the theoretical ground for the (female) sexual specificity
she wishes to defend against Deleuze. Her appeal (following Irigaray) to fluids, forms, and flows runs perilously close to an understanding of materiality
as biology. See, for instance, her article 'Ontology and Equivocation: Derrida's Politics of Sexual Difference,' in *Feminist Interpretations of Derrida*, ed.
Holland, 73–101, in which she reveals an understanding of the female body
in biological terms (see especially pages 94, 95, and 97). In addition, she
does not satisfactorily push her deconstruction of the sex/gender divide
towards an awareness of the materiality of sex as a discursive production (in
this regard, see Judith Butler, 'Bodies that Matter,' in *Engaging with Irigaray*,
ed. Burke, Schor, and Whitford, 141–73). In *Volatile Bodies*, Grosz refers to
Deleuze's concept of becoming-woman as 'an acidic dissolution of the body'
(179), ignoring Deleuze and Guattari's nuanced understanding of the body

as force and movement. Furthermore, their call for the destruction of the molar understanding of the body is not unlike that of Monique Wittig for the destruction of the category of sex (see *The Straight Mind*).

To be fair to Grosz, her work constitutes an extremely important investigation into the future of sexual difference, and in all three of her texts mentioned above, she reiterates the need to conceive of sexuality outside of structural binaries and dualisms. But Deleuze's *The Logic of Sense* already enables such a conceptualization of sexual difference, through the laying out of an ontological field that cannot be understood in terms of the bodies to which it gives rise. Thus, for Deleuze, sexual difference cannot be constructed in the image of the bodies that it conditions. By locating sexual difference in the domain of sense and becoming, Deleuze and Guattari offer a way out of the feminist double bind, and save materiality by postulating the immanence of mind and body. While I will postpone a detailed discussion of *The Logic of Sense* to chapter 4, at this moment, I would simply like to observe that Grosz's call in *Volatile Bodies* for a 'disappearing horizon' of sexual difference (209) is not as far removed from Deleuze's becoming-imperceptible as one might think. It is also interesting to note that in her most recent work, *Time Travels*, she does enlist Deleuze and Guattari to propose an alternative model of feminine difference, arguing very clearly and convincingly for their relevance to feminism. Rosi Braidotti appears to reveal a similar renunciation of her earlier misgivings towards Deleuze. See her *Metamorphoses*.

4 Becoming-flower, Becoming-imperceptible

1 Deleuze and Guattari, *A Thousand Plateaus*, 187; emphasis in original.
2 Balzac, *Sarrasine. Gambara. Massimila Doni* (Paris: Gallimard, 1995), 56. All future references will be to this edition.
3 Borowitz, *The Impact of Art*, 119.
4 'Croyez-vous que l'Allemagne ait seule le privilège d'être absurde et fantastique?'
5 Charles de Bernard du Grail had noted the ressemblance of Balzac's *La peau de chagrin* to Hoffman's works.
6 Ficino establishes a hierarchy of the senses in which reason, sight, and hearing lead to the higher realm of the soul, while smell, taste, and touch belong to the inferior realm of the body.
7 Borowitz, *The Impact of Art*, 119–24.
8 Barbara Johnson remarks that 'the castrato's reality ... is a mere play of signifiers, emptied of any ultimate signified.' See her article 'The Critical Difference,' 9. While her reading provides an invaluable corrective to that of

Barthes, it runs the danger of a complete evacuation of content and materiality. Ross Chambers also reads *Sarrasine* as a narrative about the deception and disillusionment with the 'emptiness of artistic signs.' The statue of la Zambinella is an illusory object of desire that attests to the manipulative power of signs 'divorced from substance,' which claim to embody an 'unreal referent.' While his interpretation of *Sarrasine* does seek to contend with the materiality of art, ultimately, for Chambers, Balzac's story articulates the recognition that art must be separated from life, desire, and reality in order to be 'true.' My reading opposes this view of art in *Sarrasine* as 'a flight from its insertion into the real.' See Chambers, '*Sarrasine* and the Impact of Art.' Similarly, Thomas Pavel interprets the novella as an illustration of the dangers of confounding imaginary and real desire, which results in an evacuation of vital energy or life forces. Following Chambers, he too regards the figure of la Zambinella as an incarnation of 'pure absence,' as a creature that signifies artifice and death. See his 'Énergie et Illusion. I will return to these points a little later in the chapter.

9 Deleuze, *The Logic of Sense*, 2.
10 Ibid.; emphasis in original.
11 For Barthes, of course, the body of la Zambinella is primarily a linguistic signifier. He does read it as a body that jams the duplicative chain of bodies in *Sarrasine*, but in his view, it does so as a 'code,' a 'replica.' In other words, the only bodily materiality to which Barthes gives any serious consideration is that of the linguistic and discursive. See Barthes, *S/Z*, 198–9 and 114–15.
12 Deleuze, *Logique de la sensation*, 1:10.
13 Deleuze and Guattari, *Anti-Oedipus*, 39.
14 See Deleuze, *Logique de la sensation*. For Deleuze, the Figure is that which in figuration, is the expression of force and movement that cannot be fixed or contained within representation. A little later, Deleuze will refer to the Figure as sensation. See *Logique de la sensation*, 27.
15 Deleuze, *Logique de la sensation*, 9–14. It is in this sense that Deleuze opposes 'le figural' to 'le figuratif.' The figurative relates to the domain of representation, narration, and signification. The figural expresses the domain of an incorporeal movement or becoming that cannot be illustrated fully by the figurative.
16 See Deleuze and Guattari, '1730: Becoming-Intense, Becoming-Animal, Becoming-Imperceptible ...' in *A Thousand Plateaus*, 238–9.
17 *A Thousand Plateaus*, 25.
18 See Deleuze and Guattari, 'November 28, 1947: How Do You Make Yourself a Body without Organs?' in *A Thousand Plateaus*, 149–66. Deleuze and Guattari conceive of writing in the same manner: 'A book is an assemblage of this

kind ... One side of a machinic assemblage faces the strata, which doubtless make it a kind of organism, or signifying totality, or determination attributable to a subject; it also has a side facing a *body without organs*, which is continually dismantling the organism, causing asignifying particles or pure intensities to pass or to circulate, and attributing to itself subjects that it leaves with nothing more than a name as the trace of an intensity.' See 'Introduction: Rhizome,' in *A Thousand Plateaus*, 4; emphasis in original.

19 Deleuze and Guattari, *A Thousand Plateaus*, 159.
20 Ibid.
21 Ibid., 163.
22 For such a reading of *Sarrasine*, see Harkness, 'Resisting Realist Petrification.'
23 See Barthes, *S/Z*.
24 See Deleuze and Guattari, 'Year Zero: Faciality' in *A Thousand Plateaus*, 167–8.
25 Ibid., 177.
26 Ibid., 178. By the same token, the narrator's rather condescending dismissal of the wild tales surrounding Zambinella, his designation of the creature at the ball as just an old man, and the subsequent anatomization of Zambinella he offers are just as despotic as the manoeuvers of those who brand him as a vampire, ghoul, criminal, or assassin.
27 Deleuze and Guattari, 'Year Zero: Faciality,' 181.
28 'Affects are becomings. Spinoza asks: What can a body do? ... We know nothing about a body until we know what it can do, in other words, what its affects are, how they can or cannot enter into composition with other affects, with the affects of another body, either to destroy that body or to be destroyed by it, either to exchange actions and passions with it or to join with it in composing a more powerful body.' Deleuze and Guattari, '1730: Becoming-Intense, Becoming-Animal, Becoming-Imperceptible ...,' in *A Thousand Plateaus*, 256–7.
29 Ibid., 261.
30 In this respect, he is very much like Zambinella, a creature who, we are told, only appears at equinoxes and solstices.
31 Deleuze and Guattari, *A Thousand Plateaus*, 262–3.
32 The hermaphroditic figure that surges before the narrator is not just the fusion of a male Zambinella and a female Mme de Rochefide, but also an incorporation of an animal composite (the chimera) and the vegetal (the garlands of flowers).
33 Deleuze and Guattari, *A Thousand Plateaus*, 241–2.
34 Barthes essentially does this. See *S/Z*, 81–3. However, Eric Bordas and Michel Serres stress the productive power of the voice and music in *Sarrasine*. See Bordas, '*Sarrasine* de Balzac,' 45, and Serres, *L'hermaphrodite*.

35 For readings that emphasize the positive and productive power of desire in Sarrasine, see Bordas and Serres above (note 34). See also Vernier, 'Le corps créateur ou L'artiste contre la nature.'

36 See *S/Z*, 108.

37 Deleuze and Guattari, *A Thousand Plateaus*, 264.

38 Ibid., 162.

39 Ibid., 154.

40 Ibid., 155.

41 Ibid., 156.

42 To reiterate a point made earlier, my reading of desire in *Sarrasine* rejects the dichotomy established between imaginary and real desire by Ross Chambers and Thomas Pavel (see note 8).

43 See, for example, Katherine Kolb, who argues that the success of narrative in *Sarrasine* depends on maintaining the Oedipal structure of opera ('The Tenor of *Sarrasine*,' 1568). See also Diana Knight, who views both *Sarrasine* and *Le chef-d'oeuvre inconnu* as 'ambitious rendering[s] of the aesthetic of burial, endoscopic analysis and excavation so powerfully elaborated in *S/Z*' ('From Painting to Sculpture,' 92).

44 'It [the novella] evolves in the element of "what happened" because it places us in a relation with something unknowable and imperceptible (and not the other way around: it is not because it speaks of a past about which it can no longer provide us knowledge)' (Deleuze and Guattari, *A Thousand Plateaus*, 193).

45 Ibid., 286.

46 Ibid., 288; emphasis in original.

47 'We can say, in summary fashion, that psychoanalysis has gone from a hysterical to an increasingly paranoid conception of the secret. Interminable analysis: the Unconscious has been assigned the increasingly difficult task of itself being the infinite form of secrecy, instead of a simple box containing secrets. You will tell all, but in saying everything you will say nothing because all the "art" of psychoanalysis is required to measure your contents against the pure form' (ibid., 289).

48 Ibid.

49 Ibid., 290.

50 'En nul pays peut-être l'axiome de Vespasien n'est mieux compris. Là, les écus même tâchés de sang ou de boue ne trahissent rien et représentent tout.' *Sarrasine*, 39.

51 Michel Serres, for example, assigns a positive meaning to castration in *Sarrasine*. 'Exclure l'exclusion ou éradiquer la dominante loi phallique, voilà le sens le plus profond de la castration.' In his view, Balzac's novella consti-

tutes a decrial against judgment and exclusion, and a valorization of positive difference and alterity (*L'hermaphrodite*, 81–2). Dorothy Kelly attributes a similar positive value to castration in *Sarrasine*. See her *Fictional Genders*, 114–15.

52 Deleuze and Guattari, *A Thousand Plateaus*, 197.

53 Ibid.

54 Ibid., 290; emphasis in original.

55 See Deleuze, *Logique de la sensation*, 9–14, 65–71, 87–9, and 99–103.

56 My understanding of the foot as an expression of difference diverges from interpretations that essentially view it as a fetish or a symbol of castration, even if to affirm its productive power. See in this light Kelly, *Fictional Genders*, 172–8. Marie Lathers, for instance, calls for a reading of the foot that would allow readers to inscribe the participation of feminine life forces in the painting ('Modesty and the Artist's Model,' 69). See also Didi-Huberman, *La peinture incarnée*. His brilliant study of *Le chef-d'œuvre inconnu* considers the foot as an expression of difference, but retains its signification as a fetish. In addition, for Didi-Huberman, the foot ensures the visibility of the destruction of woman. In other words, it works to preserve the disappearance or the rendering invisible of woman, whereas I see in it the appearance of a becoming-woman. While both of our readings highlight the rendering visible of a becoming-imperceptible, the value attached to this becoming-invisible is not the same. Didi-Huberman's analysis of the foot is guided by a 'sémiosis de l'évanouissement [et] de la disparition,' which understands the female body as absence, immobility, and death. Mine favours the emergence of life and movement. See his *La peinture incarnée*, 113–16. For further scholarship that views Frenhofer's painting not as a failure, but as an expression of productive forces, see Filoche, '"Le chef-d'oeuvre inconnu"'; Hatem, 'L'anticipation de l'abstrait'; and Bongiorni, 'Balzac, Frenhofer, *Le chef-d'oeuvre inconnu*.' See especially Serres, *Genèse*. For Serres, the chaos of colours points to the multiplicity of the possible, while the foot opposes its *ichnography* (or difference) to the *scenography* of a subject, an insight that offers a valuable counterpoint to Irigaray's formulations in *Speculum*.

57 False as in life forces that refuse to submit to the dialectics of truth and idea.

58 I will elaborate some of the above terms and concepts a little later with respect to Gautier's *Mademoiselle de Maupin*.

5 Beyond the Dialectic of Self and Other: Towards a Thought of the Surface

1 Deleuze, *Nietzsche and Philosophy*, 10.

2 Ibid., 61.

3 Ibid., 196.

4 See Cixous and Clément, *Newly Born Woman*, 63–4.

5 See Irigaray, *Speculum de l'autre femme*; and Cixous and Clément, *Newly Born Woman*.

6 Cixous and Clément, *Newly Born Woman*, 79–80.

7 Schor, 'This Essentialism Which Is Not One: Coming to Grips with Irigaray' in *Bad Objects*, 44–60.

8 See Irigaray, *Je, tu, nous*, *Thinking the Difference*, and *Être deux*.

9 Cixous and Clément. 'The Laugh of the Medusa,' in *Newly Born Woman*, 84–5.

10 See Cixous, 'First Names of No One,' in *The Hélène Cixous Reader*, ed. Sellers, 27–8.

11 See, for instance, Segal, *Narcissus and Echo*; Beizer, *Ventriloquized Bodies*; and Ender, *Sexing the Mind*.

12 See 'Angst' in *The Hélène Cixous Reader*, ed. Sellers, 71–9.

13 See Lacan, 'Le séminaire sur la lettre volée,' in *Écrits*, 1:11–41; and Derrida, 'Le facteur de la vérité.'

14 Cixous and Clément, *Newly Born Woman*, 65.

15 While I am deeply appreciative of the intellectual creativity that fuels attempts to bring together Irigaray and Deleuze (particularly by Tamsin Lorraine, Rosi Braidotti, and Elizabeth Grosz), I believe that they do so at the expense of ignoring the crucial difference in philosophical grounding that separates the two thinkers. On the one hand, Irigary is committed to the Hegelian dialectic and to a fundamental dualism which it prioritizes over the multiple; on the other, Deleuze proposes a philosophy that derives from Spinozist monism and which privileges multiplicity. On the one hand, we have a philosophy that claims the primacy of sexual difference over all other differences, and that locates sexual difference first between the sexes and only then within each sex; on the other, we have a transcendental ground that does not establish a hierarchy among differences. When thought through to their consequences, the divergences between Deleuze and Irigaray lead to mutually untenable conclusions with respect to the location and production of sexual difference. As a case in point, Braidotti's engagement with Deleuze leads her to claim the positivity of becoming-woman uniquely for women. Deleuze is not spared a stinging reproach for ignoring the sexual specificity and dissymmetry of women, and his concept of becoming-woman is qualified as an act of masculine appropriation. An understanding of sexual difference that leads one to view the becomings-woman of men as colonizations of feminine space and to reserve becomings for the exclusive use of one sex carries a risk of essentialism that may be too burdensome for feminism to bear. See Braidotti, *Nomadic Subjects*, chapters 5, 7, 8, and 9. Similarly,

attempts to draw parallels and correspondences between the feminisms elaborated by Kristeva and Cixous and Deleuze's notion of becoming must also confront the implications of the differences in philosophical grounding between each of these thinkers (Kristeva's unswerving loyalty to the psychoanalytical model of the unconscious, for example). In other words, the productive will to becoming that we witness in contemporary feminist thought, while invaluable and commendable, must acknowledge its necessary betrayal or departure from the concepts and tenets that have given rise to it, especially from the will to save the priority of sexual difference and the category of 'women' over all others. I am thinking here of Claire Colebrook's fine and beautifully articulated appeal for a move in feminist thinking away from the (Irigarayan) condition of thought, from metaphysics as the horizon of all thought, towards a (Deleuzian) view of philosophy as 'not an enquiry into the conditions of difference but as the challenge to think difference in the absence of conditions for difference.' Colebrook's bringing together of Irigaray, Derrida, and Deleuze recognizes that in this encounter, an Irigarayan ethics of sexual difference (of sexual difference as an originary difference that founds the ethical subject) will have to be renounced in favour of a thought where sexual difference is but one among many problems that call for 'the task of thinking differently,' and which demand the construction of a different plane of thought, or a redefinition of what it means to think. See Colebrook, 'Is Sexual Difference a Problem?' in *Deleuze and Feminist Theory*, ed. Buchanan and Colebrook, 124–5. To cite another example, Elizabeth Grosz's recent call to garner inhuman and impersonal forces in the service of a feminist politics necessarily preempts the ontological priority of a specifically female sexual difference or body. See her *Time Travels*, 185–95.

16 For Deleuze and Guattari's more rigorous engagement with the relationship of the one and the multiple, see *A Thousand Plateaus*, 248–52 and 265–72, and *What is Philosophy*, 35–51.

17 See Deleuze, *The Logic of Sense*. I will elaborate this point in the section that follows on *The Logic of Sense*.

18 In *Essays Critical and Clinical*, 3, Deleuze writes: '[L]iterature begins only when a third person is born in us that strips us of the power to say "I" (Blanchot's "neuter").'

19 Deleuze, *The Logic of Sense*, 5.

20 Ibid., 7; emphasis in original.

21 Ibid., 7, 8; emphasis in original.

22 Ibid., 9–10; emphasis in original.

23 'The event occurring in a state of affairs and the sense inhering in the proposition are the same entity' (ibid., 182; emphasis in original).

24 Ibid., 95.

25 See ibid., 70, 80.

26 See 'Eighth Series of Structure' and 'Eleventh Series of Nonsense' in Deleuze, *The Logic of Sense*, 48–51 and 66–73. It is important to note that for Deleuze, sense is neither originary, nor a predicate. Sense and nonsense are not in a simple opposition to each other, but are copresent to each other.

27 Deleuze, *The Logic of Sense*, 95.

28 Ibid., 102–3.

29 We saw that in *A Thousand Plateaus*, Deleuze and Guattari distinguish between two modes of individuation, that of persons, subjects, things, and substances, and that of haecceities. Haecceities are becomings, multiplicities, and assemblages of the order of the event. The plane of consistency on which haecceities are deployed could thus be understood as the surface or plane of sense-effects. The plane of organization or stratification could be understood as the plane of bodies and states of affairs, of forms and structures. And each unfurls within a different mode of temporality: '[T]he individuation of a life is not the same as the individuation of a subject that leads it or serves as its support. It is not the same Plane: in the first case, it is the plane of consistency or of compositions of haecceities, which knows only speeds and affects; and in the second case, it is the altogether different plane of forms, substances and subjects. And it is not in the same time, the same temporality. *Aeon*: the indefinite time of the event, the floating line that knows only speeds and continually divides that which transpires into an already-there that is at the same time not-yet-here, a simultaneous too-late and too-early, a something that is both going to happen and has just happened. *Chronos*: the time of measure that situates things and persons, develops a form, and determines a subject' (261–2). But it is important to note that here too, it is a new topography of thought that is being constructed. It is not a matter of opposing two types of planes, a plane of height and a plane of depth. Nor is it a matter of composing a plane in height and a plane in depth. Depth and height now take on a different orientation; they are lines of molar stratification or lines of flight of molecular becomings charted along a surface continuum. The other side is the other direction, the other pole of the surface: 'It is as though an immense plane of consistency of variable speed were forever sweeping up forms and functions, forms and subjects, extracting from them particles and affects. A clock keeping a whole assortment of times' (271).

30 Deleuze, *The Logic of Sense*, 166.

31 For a more detailed discussion on how the line of Aion organizes the surface

of language, see *The Logic of Sense*, 166–7. Essentially, the line of Aion organizes the surface of sense to the extent that it is traversed by the paradoxical
element of nonsense, which is the instance that traverses the series that it
separates. To the extent that the paradoxical element is copresent to sense, it
bestows sense upon the terms of each series. '*Sense is always an effect produced
in the series by the instance which traverses them.* This is why sense, such as it is
gathered over the line of Aion, has two sides which correspond to the dissym-
metrical sides of the paradoxical element: one tending toward the series
determined as signifying, the other tending toward the series determined as
signified. Sense insists in one of the the the series (propositions): it is that which
can be expressed by propositions, but does not merge with the propositions
which express it. Sense crops up suddenly in the other series (states of
affairs): it is the attribute of states of affairs, but does not merge with the
states of affairs to which it is attributed, or with the things and qualities
which realize it' (81; emphasis mine).

32 Ibid., 130–2; emphasis in original.
33 To go back to Claire Colebrook, this allows feminist thought to veer away
from transcendence as the origin of a given or as 'the genesis of the meaning
of the given.' See 'Is Sexual Difference a Problem?' 113.
34 As mentioned earlier, Elizabeth Grosz also calls for such an ontology and history of the event in her latest book, *Time Travels*. I will take up this point in
greater detail in my conclusion.

6 'Une jouissance d'épiderme': From Platonic Height and Depth to the Deleuzian Surface in Gautier's *Mademoiselle de Maupin*

1 Deleuze, *The Logic of Sense*, 72.
2 See Delcourt, *Hermaphrodite*.
3 Busst, 'The Image of the Androgyne in the Nineteenth Century.'
4 Delcourt, *Hermaphrodite*, 54.
5 Weil, *Androgyny and the Denial of Difference*, 19–20.
6 Busst, 'The Image of the Androgyne in the Nineteenth Century,' 25.
7 Ibid., 41.
8 Ibid., 39–76.
9 Michel Crouzet, introduction to Gautier, *Mademoiselle de Maupin*, 9–28.
10 Albouy, 'Le mythe de l'androgyne dans "Mademoiselle de Maupin."'
Frédéric Monneyron points to a similar split that the androgyne symbolizes
between the unity and harmony of the ideal and the impossibility of its actualization in the real in *Mademoiselle de Maupin*, although he concludes that

the androgyne holds out a possible solution to Gautier's dilemma at the end of the novel. The answer, according to him, lies in a Platonic fusion of two beings in an act of love. See his *L'androgyne romantique*, 129.

11 Weil, 'An Obscure Object of Aesthetic Desire: Gautier's Androgyne/Hermaphrodite,' in *Androgyny and the Denial of Difference*, 113–42.

12 Ibid., 119. 'If the modern world can only conceive of art or beauty in feminine terms, this is because the role of both is ultimately subservient to the artist-lover who is brought to his fullest potential, not in fusion with the woman, but in the absorption and mastery of the "feminine." Gautier often describes the artist as a "microcosm," one who bears within himself (I use the masculine deliberately) the image of beauty he will transfer to the page. Like others of the Petit Cénacle, Gautier lavished as much attention on details of clothes and ornaments in himself as he did in his writing. A Baudelarian dandy *avant la lettre*, his self-conscious will to embellish reads not merely as the desire to create beauty everywhere but also as the desire to be, himself, an object of beauty. The figure of the hermaphrodite responds to this narcissistic desire to be both subject and object, lover and beloved, artist and work of art. As a microcosm, the artist is self-sufficient, dedicated to art and to beauty as feminine, mirror images of the masculine, artist self. The idealism of Gautier's critical writings is dependent upon this suppression of sexual and textual difference' (ibid., 121–2).

13 Ibid., 142.

14 Deleuze, *Logic of Sense*, 127–8.

15 Théophile Gautier, *Mademoiselle de Maupin* (Paris: Garnier, 1973), 75. All subsequent references will be to this edition, hereafter referred to as *Maupin*.

16 *Maupin*, 74–5.

17 Ibid., 83–4.

18 Ibid., 92–3.

19 'Poètes, peintres, sculpteurs, musiciens, pourquoi nous avez-vous menti? ... – Soyez maudits, imposteurs! ...' (ibid., 98)

20 See in this regard Schnack's, 'Surface et profondeur dans "Mademoiselle de Maupin."' Schnack also reads *Mademoiselle de Maupin* as a text that explores the tension between depth and surface. Schnack is, to my knowledge, the only critic to draw serious attention to the importance of depth in the novel, thus offering an important corrective to the critical tendency to view *Mademoiselle de Maupin* as a text that is uniquely concerned with surface appearances. Where my reading differs from Schnack's is in the attention it draws to the manner in which the figure of Mademoiselle de Maupin offers a way out of the dualism that plagues D'Albert. I will return to this point a little later in the chapter.

21 For more on the narcissism that overtakes the textual space of the novel, see Vincent Vivès, 'Le narcissisme dans la poétique de l'Art pour l'Art.' According-ing to Vivès, *Mademoiselle de Maupin* is structured by the phantasy of the one and the same, and driven by the desire to neutralize sexual and 'generic' dif-ference.

22 'J'adore sur toutes choses la beauté de la forme; – la beauté pour moi, c'est la Divinité visible, c'est le bonheur palpable, c'est le ciel descendu sur la terre' (*Maupin*, 167).

23 Ibid., 171–2.

24 Ibid., 224.

25 Ibid., 173.

26 Ibid., 173–4.

27 Ibid., 213–17.

28 Ibid., 169. See also 227–9.

29 Ibid., 277–8. See also Schnack, 'Surface et profondeur dans "Mademoiselle de Maupin."'

30 *Maupin*, 277.

31 See ibid., 278–9. 'Redoutez tout: l'herbe, le fruit, l'eau, l'air, l'ombre, le soleil, tout est mortel' (*Maupin*, 280).

32 'Vous avez avec D'Albert beaucoup de points de ressemblance, et, quand vous parlez, il me semble quelquefois que ce soit lui qui parle' (*Maupin*, 196).

33 Ibid., 320.

34 Ibid., 377–9.

35 '[J]e suis possédée des plus violents désirs, - et je languis et je meurs de volupté ... une idée de plaisir qui ne se réalise jamais flotte vaguement dans ma tête, et ce rêve plat et sans couleur me fatigue et m'ennuie ... par un con-traste assez bouffon, je reste chaste et vierge comme la froide Diane elle-même, au sein de la dissipation la plus éparpillée et entourée des plus grands débauchés du siècle. Cette ignorance du corps que n'accompagne pas l'ignorance de l'esprit est la plus misérable chose qui soit. Pour que ma chair n'ait pas à faire la fière devant mon âme, je veux la souiller égale-ment ...' (*Maupin*, 398).

36 'C'est une chose effrayante à penser et à laquelle on ne pense pas, combien nous ignorons profondément la vie et la conduite de ceux qui paraissent nous aimer et que nous épouserons ... Nous autres, notre vie est claire et se peut pénétrer d'un regard ... [C]e que nous faisons n'est un mystère pour personne ... Nous sommes bien et dûment cousues à la jupe de nos mères, et, à neuf ou dix heures au plus, nous rentrons dans nos petits lits tout blancs, au fond de nos cellules proprettes et discrètes, où nous sommes ver-

tucuscment verrouillées et cadenassées jusqu'au lendemain matin ... Le cristal le plus limpide n'a pas la transparence d'une pareille vie' (*Maupin*, 247–8).

37 See ibid., 248–9.

38 '[J]e voulais étudier l'homme à fond, l'anatomiser fibre par fibre avec un scalpel inexorable et le tenir tout vif et tout palpitant sur ma table de dissection ...' (*Maupin*, 247). '[U]ne chose m'inquiétait principalement, c'était de savoir ce que les hommes se disaient entre eux et ce qu'ils faisaient lorsqu'ils étaient sortis des salons et des théâtres ... j'écoutais, je regardais; mes yeux étaient baissés cependant, et je voyais tout à droite, à gauche, devant et derrière moi: - comme les yeux fabuleux du lynx, mes yeux perçaient les murailles, et j'aurais dit ce qui se passait dans la pièce à côté' (ibid., 244–5). In this respect, Madeleine de Maupin's attempts are not unlike those of D'Albert, who seeks to pierce the secrets and masks of women in order to master the game of *libertinage*. See ibid., 101–11.

39 Rosemary Lloyd proposes a reading of *Mademoiselle de Maupin* that is sympathetic to Gautier's sexual politics in her article 'Rereading *Mademoiselle de Maupin*.'

40 Michel Brix, 'Gautier, Nerval et le platonisme,' in *Relire Théophile Gautier*, ed. Henry, 172.

41 Bouchard, 'Le masque et le miroir dans "Mademoiselle de Maupin,"' 593.

42 Ibid., 599.

43 Kapp, 'Le bonheur de l'instant dans *Mademoiselle de Maupin*,' 96.

44 Ibid., 97.

45 Mielly, 'Madeleine séductrice/Théodore séducteur,' 58. Natalie David-Weill offers a similar feminist analysis of Gautier in which she notes that 'la femme est inexistante, vide et artificielle, elle n'est que l'apparence d'elle-même ... La femme est fétichisée ...' (*Rêve de pierre*, 127).

46 Deleuze, *Logic of Sense*, 253–79.

47 Ibid., 256.

48 Ibid., 258.

49 Ibid., 257.

50 Ibid., 262.

51 Ibid.; emphasis in original.

52 Ibid., 265.

53 *Maupin*, 97–8.

54 Ibid., 216–17 and 218–20.

55 Up to this point, my ideas echo those put forth by Weil in *Androgyny and the Denial of Difference*. I mark my differences from her interpretation in what follows.

56 See Deleuze, *Logic of Sense*, 145.

57 Ibid., 146.

58 Ibid., 150–2.

59 See also *Maupin*, 83–7.

60 Deleuze, *The Logic of Sense*, 147.

61 Ibid., 150; emphasis in original.

62 Ibid., 168; emphasis in original.

63 'A force d'entendre tout le monde m'appeler monsieur, et de me voir traiter comme si j'étais un homme, j'oubliais insensiblement que j'étais femme; – mon déguisement me semblait mon habit naturel, et il ne me souvenait pas d'en avoir jamais porté d'autre' (*Maupin*, 327). 'S'il me reprend jamais fantaisie d'aller chercher mes jupes dans le tiroir où je les ai laissées, ce dont je doute fort ... au lieu d'une femme déguisée en homme, j'aurai l'air d'un homme déguisé en femme' (ibid., 393).

64 '[L]a jupe est sur mes hanches et non dans mon esprit. Il arrive souvent que le sexe de l'âme ne soit point pareil à celui du corps, et c'est une contradiction qui ne peut manquer de produire beaucoup de désordre' (ibid., 327).

65 'Et réellement, il y avait entre elle [Ninon] et moi la même différence qu'il y a entre moi et les hommes ... elle est une femme même pour moi qui suis femme ...' (ibid., 391–2).

66 'Je me suis épris d'une beauté en pourpoint et en bottes, d'une fière Bradamante qui dédaigne les habits de son sexe, et qui vous laisse par moments flotter dans les plus inquiétantes perplexités; – ses traits et son corps sont bien des traits et un corps de femme, mais son esprit est incontestablement celui d'un homme' (ibid., 304–5). 'Si je venais à savoir avec certitude que Théodore n'est pas une femme, hélas! je ne sais point si je ne l'aimerais pas encore' (ibid., 241).

67 While I am happy to note some convergences between my study of *Mademoiselle de Maupin* and that in a recent book published by Marlène Barsoum (Gautier's critique of misogyny, Madeleine de Maupin as an active rather than a reactive force, androgyny as a counter-actualization rather than a materialization), my analysis differs in the power of expression ascribed to language. In my view, Gautier's androgyny is an immanence expressible in language, whereas for Barsoum, it is a sign of transcendence that attests to 'the irremediable limitations of language.' Her reading is guided by Lyotard's concept of the unrepresentable, mine by the Deleuzian notion of sense. See Barsoum, 'Théophile Gautier's Mademoiselle de Maupin,' ix.

68 My reading of the beauty expressed by the androgynous figure in *Mademoiselle de Maupin* is opposed to that of Natalie David-Weill, for whom '[l]e monde imaginaire de Gautier tend vers la stabilité de la beauté, l'immobilité

du temps, la permanence des clichés ...' (*Rêve de pierre*, 73).

69 Any attempt to fence Gautier's aesthetic theory within a cohesive and unify-
ing discourse can only set up the flimsiest of defences against the complex,
contradictory, and paradoxical nature of his thought. He was a firm believer
in the eternal perfection of Greek art, yet was an ardent champion of the
Romantic modernity of a Delacroix. Like Baudelaire, he never ceases to
espouse a fixed and eternal ideal of beauty, but is also attracted by the fleeting and transitory. But one thing is certain: for Gautier, art is not subject to
the laws of historical progress or perfectibility. Neither does he believe in an
aesthetic history of progressive movements, transformations, and evolutions.
Rather, he adheres to a history of art as the untimeliness of the event. For a
consideration of the above, see Spencer, *The Art Criticism of Théophile Gautier*;
Marcel Voisin, 'La pensée de Théophile Gautier,' in *Relire Théophile Gautier*,
ed. Henry, 73–89; Michel Brix, 'Gautier, Nerval et le platonisme,' in *Relire
Théophile Gautier*, ed. Henry, 165–78; Book, 'Théophile Gautier et la notion
de progrès'; James Kearns, 'On his knees to the past? Gautier, Ingres and
Forms of Modern Art,' in *Impressions of French Modernity*, ed. Hobbs, 58–75;
and in particular, Hartman, 'Théophile Gautier on Progress in the Arts.'

Conclusion

1 Deleuze, 'Literature and Life,' in *Essays Critical and Clinical*, 6.
2 Grosz, *Time Travels*, 193–5.
3 Braidotti in *Engaging with Irigaray*, ed. Burke, Schor, and Whitford, 118.
4 I am thinking here especially of the debates that have opposed feminists
such as Elaine Showalter, Toril Moi, Nancy Miller, and Peggy Kamuf in the
past.
5 Woolf, *Orlando*, 185.
6 While I believe that *Orlando* prepares the way for much of Woolf's thought in
A Room of One's Own, for reasons of brevity and conciseness, I will (regret-
fully) sacrifice a closer reading of the novel and focus primarily on *A Room of
One's Own* in the conclusion.
7 Woolf, *A Room of One's Own*, 41–2.
8 Ibid., 35.
9 See ibid., 50–3.
10 See ibid., 59–63.
11 'One has only to skim those old forgotten novels and listen to the tone of
voice in which they are written to divine that the writer was meeting criticism; she was saying this by way of aggression, or that by way of conciliation.
She was admitting that she was "only a woman," or protesting that she was "as

good as a man" ... Down comes her book upon our heads. There was a flaw in the centre of it. And I thought of all the women's novels that lie scattered, like small pock-marked apples in an orchard, about the second-hand book shops of London. It was the flaw in the center [*sic*] that had rotted them. She had altered her values in deference to the opinion of others' (ibid., 74).

12 See ibid., 76–7.

13 See ibid., 92.

14 See ibid., 86–7.

15 '[I]f an explorer should come back and bring word of other sexes looking through the branches of other trees at other skies, nothing would be of greater service to humanity' (ibid., 88).

16 See ibid., 82–3.

17 Ibid., 113.

18 One could certainly make the point that Woolf's androgyny is no different from the visions of harmonic sexual fusion that have been with us since Plato and even earlier. But *Orlando* lays these objections to rest – Orlando and Marmaduke Bonthrop Shelmerdine compose blocks of man-womanly and woman-manly becomings, creating zones of indiscernibility that render each term more fluid. Together, they produce assemblages in which the self/ other divide becomes irrelevant – the construction of a plane of consistency for the creation of affects and percepts. See *Orlando*, 142–9.

19 Woolf, *A Room*, 113–14.

20 Deleuze, 'To Have Done with Judgement,' in *Essays Critical and Clinical*, 135. While my conclusions regarding the importance of Deleuze's thought for an ethics of literature were reached independently, I am very grateful for the echo-chamber they have found in Daniel W. Smith's wonderfully clear and concise introduction to *Essays Critical and Clinical* entitled 'A Life of Pure Immanence: Deleuze's "Critique et Clinique" Project.' See *Essays Critical and Clinical*, xi–liii.

Bibliography

Albouy, Pierre. 'Le mythe de l'androgyne dans "Mademoiselle de Maupin."' *Revue d'histoire littéraire de la France* 72 (1972): 600–8.

Apter, Emily. *Feminizing the Fetish: Psychoanalysis and Narrative Obsession in Turn-of-the-century France.* Ithaca, NY: Cornell University Press, 1991.

Balzac, Honoré de. *Le chef-d'oeuvre inconnu.* Paris: Garnier Flammarion, 1981.

– *Sarrasine. Gambara. Massimila Doni.* Paris: Gallimard, 1995.

Barsoum, Marlène. *Théophile Gautier's Mademoiselle de Maupin: Towards a Definition of Androgynous Discourse.* New York: Peter Lang, 2001.

Barthes, Roland. *Le plaisir du texte.* Paris: Éditions du Seuil, 1970.

– *S/Z.* Paris: Éditions du Seuil, 1970.

Beauvoir, Simone de. *The Second Sex.* Trans. and ed. H.M. Parshley. New York: Alfred A. Knopf, 1993.

Beizer, Janet. *Ventriloquized Bodies: Narratives of Hysteria in Nineteenth-Century France.* Ithaca, NY: Cornell University Press, 1994.

Bernard, Claude E. 'La problématique de l'échange dans *Le chef-d'oeuvre inconnu* d'Honoré de Balzac.' *L'Année Balzacienne* 4 (1984): 201–13.

Blanchot, Maurice. *The Space of Literature.* Trans. Ann Smock. Lincoln: University of Nebraska Press, 1982.

– *The Work of Fire.* Trans. Charlotte Mandell. Stanford, CA: Stanford University Press, 1995.

– *The Writing of the Disaster.* Trans. Anne Smock. Lincoln: University of Nebraska Press, 1986.

Bongiorni, Kevin. 'Balzac, Frenhofer, *Le chef-d'œuvre inconnu: Ut Poesis Pictura.' Mosaic* 33.2 (June 2000): 87–99.

Book, Claude-Marie. 'Théophile Gautier et la notion de progrès.' *Revue des sciences humaines* 128 (1967): 545–57.

Bordas, Éric. '*Sarrasine* de Balzac: une poétique du contresens.' *Nineteenth-Century French Studies* 31.1–2 (fall 2002–winter 2003): 41–52.

Borowitz, Helen. *The Impact of Art on French Literature from de Scudéry to Proust.* Newark: University of Delaware Press, 1985.

Bouchard, Anne. 'Le masque et le miroir dans "Mademoiselle de Maupin."' *Revue d'histoire littéraire de la France* (1972): 583–99.

Boundas, Constantin V., and Dorothea Olkowski, eds. *Gilles Deleuze and the Theater of Philosophy.* London: Routledge, 1994.

Braidotti, Rosi. *Nomadic Subjects: Embodiment and Sexual Difference in Contemporary Feminist Theory.* New York: Columbia University Press, 1994.

– *Metamorphoses: Towards a Materialist Theory of Becoming.* Cambridge: Polity, 2002.

Bresnick, Adam. 'Absolute Fetishism: Genius and Identification in Balzac's "Unknown Masterpiece."' *Paragraph* 17.2 (July 1994): 134–52.

Brooks, Peter. *Body Work: Objects of Desire in Modern Narrative.* Cambridge, MA: Harvard University Press, 1993.

– 'Fictions of the Wolfman: Freud and Narrative Understanding.' *Diacritics* 9.1 (spring 1979): 71–81.

– 'Freud's Masterplot: Questions of Narrative.' In *Literature and Psychoanalysis: The Question of Reading: Otherwise*, ed. Shoshana Felman, 280–300, Baltimore, MD: Johns Hopkins University Press, 1982.

Bruns, Gerald L. *Maurice Blanchot: The Refusal of Philosophy.* Baltimore, MD: Johns Hopkins University Press, 1997.

Buchanan, Ian, and Claire Colebrook, eds. *Deleuze and Feminist Theory.* Edinburgh: Edinburgh University Press, 2000.

Buchet Rogers, Nathalie. *Fictions du scandale: corps féminin et réalisme romanesque au dix-neuvième siècle.* West Lafayette, IN: Purdue University Press, 1998.

Buisiné, Alain. 'Je suis avant tout un regardeur.' *Magazine littéraire* 310 (May 1993): 31–3.

Burke, Carolyn, Naomi Schor, and Margaret Whitford, eds. *Engaging with Irigaray: Feminist Philosophy and Modern European Thought.* New York: Columbia University Press, 1994.

Busst, A.J.L. 'The Image of the Androgyne in the Nineteenth Century.' In *Romantic Mythologies*, ed. Ian Fletcher, 1–95. New York: Barnes and Noble, 1967.

Butler, Judith. *Gender Trouble: Feminism and the Subversion of Identity.* London: Routledge, 1990.

Chambers, Ross. '*Sarrasine* and the Impact of Art.' *French Forum* 5 (1980): 218–38.

Chase, Cynthia. 'Oedipal Textuality: Reading Freud's Reading of Oedipus.' *Diacritics* 9.1 (spring 1979): 54–68.

Cixous, Hélène, and Catherine Clément. *The Newly Born Woman*. Trans. Betsy Wing. Minneapolis: University of Minnesota Press, 1993.

Cohen, Margaret, and Christopher Prendergast, eds. *Spectacles of Realism*. Minneapolis: University of Minnesota Press, 1995.

Conboy, Katie, Nadia Medina, and Sarah Stanbury, eds. *Writing on the Body*. New York: Columbia University Press, 1997.

Culler, Jonathan. *The Pursuit of Signs: Semiotics, Literature, Deconstruction*. Ithaca, NY: Cornell University Press, 1981.

Danger, Pierre. 'Le père défait.' *Magazine littéraire* 310 (May 1993): 54–7.

David-Weill, Natalie. *Rêve de pierre: la quête de la femme chez Théophile Gautier*. Geneva: Droz, 1989.

De Lauretis, Teresa. *Alice Doesn't: Feminism, Semiotics, Cinema*. Bloomington: Indiana University Press, 1984.

– *Technologies of Gender: Essays on Theory, Film and Seduction*. Bloomington: Indiana University Press, 1987.

Delcourt Marie. *Hermaphrodite: Myths and Rites of the Bisexual Figure in Classical Antiquity*. Trans. Jennifer Nicholson. London: Studio Books, 1961.

Deleuze, Gilles. *Difference and Repetition*. Trans. Paul Patton. New York: Columbia University Press, 1994.

– *Essays Critical and Clinical*. Trans. Daniel W. Smith and Michael A. Greco. Minneapolis: University of Minnesota Press, 1997.

– *Francis Bacon: Logique de la sensation*. Paris: La vue le texte, Éditions de la différence, 1981.

– *The Logic of Sense*. Trans. Mark Lester and Charles Stivale. Ed. Constantin V. Boundas. New York: Columbia University Press, 1990.

– *Nietzsche and Philosophy*. Trans. Hugh Tomlinson. New York: Columbia University Press, 1983.

– *Proust and Signs*. Trans. Richard Howard. New York: G. Braziller, 1972.

Deleuze, Gilles, and Félix Guattari. *Anti-Oedipus: Capitalism and Schizophrenia*. Trans. Robert Hurley, Mark Seem, and Helen R. Lane. Minneapolis: University of Minnesota Press, 1983.

– *Kafka: Towards a Minor Literature*. Trans. Dana Polan. Minneapolis: University of Minnesota Press, 1986.

– *A Thousand Plateaus: Capitalism and Schizophrenia*. Trans. Brian Massumi. Minneapolis: University of Minnesota Press, 1987.

– *What Is Philosophy?* Trans. Hugh Tomlinson and Graham Burchell. New York: Columbia University Press, 1994.

Derrida, Jacques. 'Le facteur de la vérité.' *Poétique* 21 (1975): 98–146.

Didi-Huberman, Georges. *La peinture incarnée*. Paris: Éditions de Minuit, 1985.

Eagleton, Mary, ed. *Feminist Literary Theory*. Oxford: Blackwell, 1996.

École nationale supérieure des arts décoratifs, France. *Autour du chef-d'œuvre inconnu de Balzac*. Paris: École nationale supérieure des arts décoratifs, 1985.

Eisenzweig, Uri. *Le récit impossible: forme et sens du roman policier*. Paris: C. Bourgois, 1986.

Ender, Evelyne. *Sexing the Mind: Nineteenth-Century Fictions of Hysteria*. Ithaca, NY: Cornell University Press, 1995.

Engel, Vincent. '"Qui voit quoi?" Lecture de *Pierre et Jean* de Maupassant.' *Les Lettres Romanes* 48.3–4 (Aug.–Nov. 1994): 237–57.

Evans, Mary, ed. *Feminism: Critical Concepts in Literary and Cultural Studies*. 4 vols. London: Routledge, 2001.

Felman, Shoshana. 'Beyond Oedipus: The Specimen Story of Psychoanalysis.' *MLN* 98.5 (December 1983): 1021–53.

– ed. *Literature and Psychoanalysis: The Question of Reading: Otherwise*. Baltimore, MD: Johns Hopkins University Press, 1982.

– 'Rereading Femininity.' *Yale French Studies* 62 (1981): 19–44.

– *What Does Woman Want? Reading and Sexual Difference*. Baltimore, MD: Johns Hopkins University Press, 1993.

Filoche, Jean-Luc. '"Le chef-d'oeuvre inconnu": peinture et connaissance.' *Acta Baltica* 1 (1980): 47–59.

Forestier, Louis, ed. *Maupassant et l'écriture: Actes du colloque de Fécamp 21-22-23-May 1993*. Paris: Nathan, 1993.

Frank, Felicia Miller. *The Mechanical Song: Women, Voices and the Artificial in Nineteenth-Century French Narrative*. Stanford, CA: Stanford, University Press, 1995.

Freud, Sigmund. *The Interpretation of Dreams*. Trans. and ed. James Strachey. New York: Avon, 1965.

– *The Standard Edition of the Complete Works of Sigmund Freud*. 24 vols. Trans. and ed. James Strachey. London: Hogarth Press, 1966.

Gallop, Jane. *The Daughter's Seduction: Feminism and Psychoanalysis*. Ithaca, NY: Cornell University Press, 1982.

Gautier, Théophile. *Mademoiselle de Maupin*. Paris: Gallimard, 1973.

Goodchild, Philip. *Gilles Deleuze and the Question of Philosophy*. London: Associated University Presses, 1996.

Goulimari, Pelagia. 'A Minoritarian Feminism? Things to Do with Deleuze and Guattari.' *Hypatia* 14.2 (spring 1999): 97–120.

Goux, Jean-Joseph. *Les iconoclastes*. Paris: Éditions du Seuil, 1978.

– *Oedipus, Philosopher*. Trans. Catherine Porter. Stanford, CA: Stanford University Press, 1993.

– *Symbolic Economies: After Marx and Freud*. Trans. Jennifer Curtiss Gage. Ithaca, NY: Cornell University Press, 1993.

Grosz, Elizabeth. *Time Travels: Feminism, Nature, Power.* Durham, NC: Duke University Press, 2005.

– *Volatile Bodies: Towards a Corporeal Feminism.* Bloomington: Indiana University Press, 1994.

Harkness, Nigel. 'Resisting Realist Petrification in George Sand's *Lélia* and Balzac's *Sarrasine*.' *French Studies* 59.2 (April 2005): 159–72.

Hartman, Elwood. 'Théophile Gautier on Progress in the Arts.' *Studies in Romanticism* 12 (1973): 530–50.

Hatem, Jad. 'L'anticipation de l'abstrait: lecture du *Chef-d'oeuvre inconnu* de Balzac.' *Études classiques* 67.1 (1999): 57–61.

Henry, Freeman G., ed. *Relire Théophile Gautier: le plaisir du texte.* Amsterdam: Rodopi, 1998.

Hinton, Laura. *The Perverse Gaze of Sympathy: Sadomasochistic Sentiments from Clarissa to Rescue 911.* Albany: State University of New York Press, 1999.

Hobbs, Richard, ed. *Impressions of French Modernity: Art and Literature in France 1850–1900.* Manchester: Manchester University Press, 1998.

Holland, Nancy J., ed. *Feminist Interpretations of Derrida.* University Park: Pennsylvania State University Press, 1997.

Hutton, Margaret-Anne, ed. *Text(e)/Image.* Durham, UK: University of Durham, 1999.

Irigaray, Luce. *Ce sexe qui n'en est pas un.* Paris: Éditions de Minuit, 1977.

– *Ethique de la différence sexuelle.* Paris: Éditions de Minuit, 1984.

– *Être Deux.* Paris: Grasset, 1997.

– *Je, tu, nous: Towards a Culture of Difference.* Trans. Alison Martin. London: Routledge, 1993.

– *Speculum de l'autre femme.* Paris: Éditions de Minuit, 1974.

– *Thinking the Difference: For a Peaceful Revolution.* Trans. Karin Montin. London: Routledge, 1994.

Jardine, Alice. *Gynesis: Configurations of Woman and Modernity.* Ithaca, NY: Cornell University Press, 1985.

Jennings, Chantal. 'La dualité de Maupassant: son attitude envers la femme.' *Revue des sciences humaines* 140.35 (Oct.–Déc. 1970) 559–78.

Johnson, Barbara. 'The Critical Difference.' *Diacritics* 8.2 (June 1978): 2–9.

Kapp, Volker. 'Le bonheur de l'instant dans *Mademoiselle de Maupin*.' *Les Lettres Romanes* 38.1–2 (Feb.–May 1984): 77–97.

Kelly, Dorothy. *Fictional Genders: Role and Representation in Nineteenth-Century French Narrative.* Lincoln: University of Nebraska Press, 1989.

Knight, Diana. 'From Painting to Sculpture: Balzac, Pygmalion and the Secret of Relief in *Sarrasine* and *The Unknown Masterpiece*.' *Paragraph* 27.1 (March 2004): 79–95.

Kolb, Katherine. 'The Tenor of "Sarrasine."' *PMLA* 120.5 (October 2005): 1560–75.

Lacan, Jacques. *Écrits*. 2 vols. Paris: Éditions du Seuil, 1966.

Lathers, Marie. 'Modesty and the Artist's Model in *Le chef-d'œuvre inconnu*.' *Symposium* 46.1 (spring 1992): 49–71.

Lesser, Wendy. *His Other Half: Men Looking at Women through Art*. Cambridge, MA: Harvard University Press, 1991.

Lloyd, Christopher, and Robert Lethbridge, eds. *Maupassant conteur et romancier*. Durham, UK: University of Durham, 1994.

Lloyd, Rosemary. 'Rereading *Mademoiselle de Maupin*.' *Orbis Litterarum* 41.1 (1986): 19–32.

Lorraine, Tamsin E. *Irigaray and Deleuze: Experiments in Visceral Philosophy*. Ithaca, NY: Cornell University Press, 1999.

Marks, Elaine, and Isabelle de Courtivron, eds. *New French Feminisms: An Anthology*. Amherst: University of Massachusetts Press, 1980.

Maupassant, Guy de. *Pierre et Jean*. Paris: Gallimard, 1982.

Mielly, Michelle. 'Madeleine séductrice/Théodore séducteur: rupture et réconciliation dans *Mademoiselle de Maupin*.' *Nineteenth-Century French Studies* 25.1–2 (fall 1996 – winter 1997): 50–9.

Miller, J. Hillis. *Versions of Pygmalion*. Cambridge, MA: Harvard University Press, 1990.

Miller, Nancy K. *French Dressing: Women, Men and Ancien Régime Fiction*. New York: Routledge, 1995.

– *The Heroine's Text: Readings in the French and English Novel*. New York: Columbia University Press, 1980.

Millet, Kate. *Sexual Politics*. New York: Doubleday, 1969.

Monneyron, Frédéric. *L'androgyne romantique: du mythe au mythe littéraire*. Grenoble: ELLUG, 1994.

Mulvey, Laura. *Visual and Other Pleasures*. Bloomington: Indiana University Press, 1989.

– 'Visual Pleasure and Narrative Cinema.' *Screen* 16.3 (1975): 6–18.

Nochlin, Linda. *The Politics of Vision: Essays on Nineteenth-Century Art and Society*. New York: Harper and Row, 1989.

– *Women, Art, and Power: And Other Essays*. New York: Harper and Row, 1988.

Olkowski, Dorothea, ed. *Resistance, Flight, Creation: Feminist Enactments of French Philosophy*. Ithaca, NY: Cornell University Press, 2000.

Ovid. *Metamorphoses*. Trans. Allen Mandelbaum. New York: Harcourt Brace, 1993.

Patton, Paul, ed. *Deleuze: A Critical Reader*. London: Blackwell, 1996.

Patrick, Jonathan. 'Maupassant's *Pierre et Jean*: A Note on Mme Rosémilly.' *French Studies Bulletin* 76 (autumn 2000): 5–8.

Paulson, William. 'Pour une analyse dynamique de la variation textuelle: *Le chef-œuvre* trop *connu.' Nineteenth-Century French Studies* 19.3 (spring 1991): 404–16.

Pavel, Thomas. 'Énergie et illusion: sur les protagonistes de *Sarrasine.' French Forum* 21.3 (Sept. 1996): 301–18.

Plato. *Symposium.* Trans. Seth Benardete. Chicago: University of Chicago Press, 2001.

Plotinus. *Enneads.* Trans. Stephen Mackenna. London: Faber and Faber, 1956.

Rancière, Jacques. *Aux bords du politique.* Paris: Éditions la Fabrique, 1998.

– *La parole muette: essai sur les contradictions de la littérature.* Paris: Hachette, 1998.

– *Le partage du sensible: esthétique et politique.* Paris: Éditions la Fabrique, 2000.

– *Politique de la littérature.* Paris: Galilée, 2007.

Rose, Jacqueline. *Sexuality in the Field of Vision.* London: Verso, 1986.

Sachs, Murray. 'The Meaning of Maupassant's "Pierre et Jean."' *French Review* 34.3 (January 1961): 244–50.

Schnack, Arne. 'Surface et profondeur dans *Mademoiselle de Maupin.' Orbis Litterarum* 36 (1981): 28–36.

Schor, Naomi. *Bad Objects: Essays Popular and Unpopular.* Durham, NC: Duke University Press, 1995.

– *Breaking the Chain: Women, Theory and French Realist Fiction.* New York: Columbia University Press, 1985.

Schor, Naomi, and Elizabeth Weed, eds. *The Essential Difference.* Bloomington: Indiana University Press, 1994.

Segal, Naomi. *Narcissus and Echo: Women in the French récit.* Manchester: Manchester University Press, 1988.

Sellers, Susan, ed. *The Hélène Cixous Reader.* London: Routledge, 1994.

Serres, Michel. *Genèse.* Paris: Grasset, 1985.

– *L'hermaphrodite: Sarrasine sculpteur.* Paris: Flammarion, 1987.

Silverman, Kaja. *The Acoustic Mirror: The Female Voice in Psychoanalysis and Cinema.* Bloomington: Indiana University Press, 1988.

Sophocles. *Three Theban Plays.* Trans. Robert Fagles. New York: Penguin Books, 1984.

Spencer, Clifford. *The Art Criticism of Théophile Gautier.* Geneva: Droz, 1969.

Spinoza. *The Collected Works.* Trans. and ed. Edwin Curley. Vol. 1. Princeton, NJ: Princeton University Press, 1985.

Stivale, Charles J. *The Art of Rupture: Narrative Desire and Duplicity in the Tales of Guy de Maupassant.* Ann Arbor: University of Michigan Press, 1997.

Suleiman, Susan Rubin, ed. *The Female Body in Western Culture: Contemporary Perspectives.* Cambridge, MA: Harvard University Press, 1986.

Todorov, Tzvetan. 'Typologie du roman policier.' *Paragone Letteratura* 202 (December 1966): 3–14.

Vernier, France. 'Le corps créateur ou L'artiste contre la nature.' *Romantisme* 91 (1996): 5–17.

Vinge, Louise. *The Narcissus Theme in Western European Literature up to the Early Nineteenth Century.* Lund: Gleerups, 1967.

Vivès, Vincent. 'Le narcissisme dans la poétique de l'Art pour l'Art.' *Bulletin d'études parnassiennes et symbolistes* 23 (spring 1999): 3–19.

Waller, Margaret. *The Male Malady.* New Brunswick, NJ: Rutgers University Press, 1993.

Warhol, Robyn R., and Diane Price Herndl, eds. *Feminisms: An Anthology of Literary Theory and Criticism.* New Brunswick, NJ: Rutgers University Press, 1997.

Weil, Kari. *Androgyny and the Denial of Difference.* Charlottesville: University Press of Virginia, 1992.

Wittig, Monique. *The Straight Mind and Other Essays.* Boston: Beacon Press, 1992.

Woolf, Virginia. *Orlando: A Biography.* Ed. J.H. Stape. Oxford: Blackwell, 1998.

– *A Room of One's Own.* New York: Harcourt Brace, 1989.

Zajko, Vanda, and Miriam Leonard, eds. *Laughing with Medusa: Classical Myth and Feminist Thought.* Oxford: Oxford University Press, 2006.

Index

abstract art: and feminine materiality, 65–72; and break with specularity, 69–70

Aion, 146, 151–2, 178–9, 182, 214n29, 214–15n31

Albouy, Pierre, 158–9

androgyny, myth of, 5, 154–6, 181; androgyne, 154–9

Aristotle, 44, 72, 146

Auerbach, Eric, 50–1

Balzac, Honoré de: *Le chef-d'oeuvre inconnu*, 3, 7, 43, 50, 57–78, 132–3; *Sarrasine*, 3, 7, 50, 58–9, 100–31

Barthes, Roland : *Le plaisir du texte*, 8; *S/Z*, 32, 51–2, 208n11, 209n34

becoming, 106. *See also under* Deleuze, Gilles, and Félix Guattari

Beizer, Janet, 212n11

Belle Noiseuse, La, 61–4, 71–8, 128, 132–3

Blanchot, Maurice: and artistic subjectivity, 75–7, 82–5; and myth of Narcissus, 80–5; and Romantic aesthetic, 75–6

body: and becoming, in *Sarrasine*, 106, 112–23; and becoming, in *Le chef-d'oeuvre inconnu*, 132–3; and materi-ality, in *Sarrasine*, 101–6; and narrative, in *Sarrasine*, 109–13; and realism, 50, 101; and sexual differ-ence, 139–40; understanding of in Deleuze and Guattari, 93–7. *See also* BwO; Deleuze, Gilles, and Félix Guattari: Body without Organs

Borowitz, Helen, 104–5, 123

Bouchard, Anne, 170

Braidotti, Rosi, 184, 193n4, 205–7n33, 212–13n15

Brix, Michel, 170

Brooks, Peter, 43, 50–4, 99–100

Busst, A.J.L., 156–9

Butler, Judith, 4, 193n4, 205–7n33

BwO, 109–12, 125–8, 132. *See also under* Deleuze, Gilles, and Félix Guattari

Chambers, Ross, 207–8n8, 210n42

Chronos, 146, 151, 166, 178–82, 214n29

Cixous, Hélène, 4; critique of dialec-tics, 138–42; and Derrida, 141–2; and feminine desire, 141–2; *The Newly Born Woman*, 5

Colebrook, Claire, 205–7n33, 212–13n15, 215n33

234   Index

tween ideal and material, 106, 157–
9, 181; tradition and psychoanalysis, 85
Platonism: in *Mademoiselle de Maupin*,
170–1; Nietzschean reversal of,
171–2; in *Sarrasine*, 123
Plotinus, 44, 48–9, 55, 104–5
Poe, Edgar Allen, 37–9
politics: of literature, 6–7, 184; of
reading, 5, 6, 45; of sense, 182–4;
sexual politics, 6, 186
psychoanalysis: conception of desire,
85–91; and the feminine, 43–5; and
narrative, 40–1. *See also* subjectivity
under Oedipal
Pygmalion, 5, 7, 42–3; myth of, 53–5,
57; myth of, in *Sarrasine*, 100–1; and
Narcissus, 53–6, 58; and Narcissus,
in *Sarrasine*, 104–5

Rancière, Jacques, 195n8
realism, 4, 7, 51; and the body, 52,
101; and feminine materiality, 7, 43,
52–3, 100
representation: and desire, 88–90;
and the body, 50–2, 100–12; and
politics, 193n4; and realism, 43, 50–
2, 57; and specularity, 50, 58–9

Sartre, Jean-Paul, 51
Schor, Naomi, 159, 194n6; aesthetics
of realism, 52–3, 100, feminist narrative strategy, 8–10, 199–200n75;
reading of Irigaray, 139–40; reading
of *Pierre et Jean*, 198–9n58

scopophilia, 10, 52
sense: 148–72; aesthetics of, 181–2; as
effect, 149–50; as event, 147–9; and
language, 147–9; politics of, 182–4;
and representation, 176–9; and sexuality, in *Mademoiselle de Maupin*,
174–7, 181; and the surface, 145–7;
and time, 151–2. *See also* event
Serres, Michel, 210n51, 211n56
Showalter, Elaine, 4, 220n4
signification. *See* representation
simulacrum, 106, 146, 171–2
specularity: and art, 63–4, break with,
in art, 78–9, 97–8, 132–5; and representation, 50, 58–9; and subjectivity,
43–7
Spinoza, 92–3
Stivale, Charles, 199–200n75
Stoics, 145–9
surface: and feminism, 152–3; in
Mademoiselle de Maupin, 165–71,
180; sexuality as surface effect, 177;
simulacrum as surface effect, 177;
thought of, 136, 145–52

Todorov, Tzvetan, 14

Vinge, Louise, 48

Weil, Kari, 156–9
Wittig, Monique, 4, 205–7n33
Woolf, Virginia, 43; *Orlando*, 184–5,
191–2; *A Room of One's Own*, 183–91
writing: and difference, 143–5; as
event, 184–5